Collected Plays
of Daniel Curzon

Volume XIV

(2020-2022)

Collected Plays of Daniel Curzon (Volume XIV) © 2022

Dedicated to all the kids in Detroit who attended the plays the author put on in his boyhood – but not to the bullies who spoiled things.

For performance rights, contact the author at curzon@pacbell.net

IGNA Books

San Francisco, CA, Telephone: 415-297-9220

Collected Plays of Daniel Curzon (Vol. XIV, 2020-2022)

I. Title

Cover photographs courtesy of Daniel Curzon

ISBN 978-1-959257-00-4

Printed in the United States of America

wayne goodman books

waynegoodmanbooks@gmail.com
Instagram: @waynegoodmanbooks

Print versions at independent booksellers
Electronic versions and Audiobooks
Available online

CONTENTS

KNOTTRUMP, THE TERRIBLE

This play is not finished. You may add any ending you like.

CHARACTERS: (10)

DON KNOTTRUMP, male, 40-70, liar, amoral, narcissistic, superficially charming, President of the United States

MALARIA, his wife, lovely, foreign-born, in her forties

INVINCA, female, 20-40, his daughter, pretty, enterprising

CRIP, staff member, male, 30-50, uses crutches to help him walk

THREE OTHER MEN, various ages, to play multiple parts

THREE OTHER WOMEN, various ages, to play multiple parts

SETTING: Different rooms in a building such as the White House

LIGHTS UP

A FUND RAISER for CANDIDATE

KNOTTRUMP: Hello! (to applause from the donors) Hello! Hello! Hello! And a special hello to … me! I'm running for re-election. Can you believe it?! They say I won't win, that the first time was a fluke, but they don't know Don Knottrump, little old me! Boy, do they not know. Thank you for coming to my fund raiser – not that I need it. I'm so rich I could fund all of you! And I'd still beat you! I'm that good. Some have doubted. Some have questioned. But where are those people now? On the dust heaps behind my various resorts and hotels, that's where. I told them: don't mess with the Donald. But would they listen? No! Not them!

(Enter Lady Upperbum, British, in her 50s, vivacious.)

LADY UPPERBUM: I'm late! I'm so late! But I bring money!

KNOTTRUMP: Look who's here – it's Lady Upperbum. My biggest
donor. Welcome! Welcome! I ask you is there anybody better on
the face of this earth than Guinevere Upperbum?! Welcome,
milady. I love you and I love your pounds! Do you get it? British
pounds? (Laughs) So where's your money, lady?

(Lady Upperbum pulls a bag of money out of her large purse
and brings it to the President.)

LADY UPPERBUM: Who can resist this man He's so forthright, much
like my late husband. So uncompromising! So unsubtle! So un-
British! I love him!

KNOTTTRUMP: You hear that, everybody? She loves me. Don't tell my
wife, Malaria. Watch yourself, Guinevere. Malaria wants me all
for herself.

LADY UPPERBUM: Malaria, where are you? I'm not touching your
husband, see! (Holds herhands up.)

KNOTTRUMP: Isn't she great?! I love that woman. She can grab my
pussy anytime. If I had apussy! (Laughs)

LADY UPPERBUM: Isn't he great? Such a breath of foul air!

KNOTTRUMP: You're too kind. Mingle, everybody! Mingle! We
accept checks, credit cards,debit cards, traveler's checks, cash,
jewelry, stamps. Donate and be great! Hey, that's my new slogan.
Donate and be great!

(The President mingles with his donors, shaking hands,
clasping backs, grinning.)

LADY UPPERBUM: (to another woman) I don't know about you, but I
always feel soinvigorated when the President speaks.

WOMAN: He does brag a lot.

LADY UPPERBUM: Like the knights of old! Sir Brag-a-Lot. I just wish he'd let me kiss his toolonce.

WOMAN: What?!

LADY UPPERBUM: His scepter. He keeps it under wraps in his private chambers, I'm told.

WOMAN: I like the man, but we don't have kings here.

LADY UPPERBUM: He's going to reveal his scepter at his second inauguration. I want to kiss itso badly.

WOMAN: (not meaning it) Well, it was so nice meeting you.

LADY UPPERBUM: Don't go!

WOMAN: I'm afraid I must.

LADY UPPERBUM: Have you heard about it?

WOMAN: It?

LADY UPPERBUM: Anal penetration.

WOMAN: I beg your pardon.

LADY UPPERBUM: Anal penetration. It's the bee's knees.

WOMAN: Really? I didn't know.

LADY UPPERBUM: I just discovered it. Believe me, I did not know what I was missing.

WOMAN: Your secret is safe with me.

LADY UPPERBUM: Oh, but that's just the point. I don't want it to be a secret anymore.That's what is wrong with the world! Everybody is afraid to be discovered as a bottom. But, my word, I have never felt such power as when I finally surrendered to that urge lurking within me for god knows how many years.

WOMAN: I think your voice might be carrying across the room.

LADY UPPERBUM: Well, I hope so! For far too long people have been afraid to admit they enjoy being dominated. I am here to liberate them at last.

WOMAN: I think you're talking to the wrong person.

LADY UPPERBUM: That's exactly what I said before my first episode.

KNOTTRUMP: Hey, listen up, everybody! Hey, listen! It's your President talking!

(The crowd quiets down and listens.)

KNOTTTRUMP: I want you all to know that I just heard from my staff. Another state – as yet unnamed – is changing its abortion laws. It is going to be totally illegal in that stateby the beginning of the year. I promised it, and I delivered! And now those babies will be delivered!

(Applause from some.)

WOMAN: How wonderful!

KNOTTTRUMP: No more innocent babies murdered by those liberals! No siree! No sir! Those beautiful, beautiful babies are soon to be safe in that unnamed state. And who savedthose babies? Who?

WOMAN: You did!

(Others echo her.)

KNOTTRUMP: And yet more good news! Are you ready? … Let me cram your orifices with more good news!

CROWD VOICES: What is it?… What?… What?… Tell us!

KNOTTRUMP: Your religious freedom will no longer be undermined when you try to live whatyou believe. Your precious freedom of religion restored at last! When those trans folks try to make you bake them a wedding cake, what will you do now?

CROWD VOICES: No baking for them! ... No bake! ... No cake! Let them not eat cake!

KNOTTRUMP: This great country was founded by Benjamin Jefferson on the premise of no baking for cross-dressers! It's in the Constitution! Benjamin Jefferson explicitly cited Scriptureto prevent such atrocities. I believe it is Leviticus. Thou shall not bake unleavened bread or sweetened cookies for those who defy God's norms. I ask you what are God's norms if not the sanctity of the wedding cake? With one bride and one groom! One man and one woman!

CROWD VOICES: Yes! ... Indeed! ... Hallelujah!

KNOTTRUMP: I thought you'd like that! And who delivered this to you?

WOMAN: You did!

KNOTTRUMP: You bet your sweet behind I did. And I'm not going to stop there, believe youme! And now for some entertainment! Crip, come here! (Beckons) Where's my cripple?

(CRIP emerges from the crowd, on crutches, walking with great difficulty.)

CRIP: Here I am, our present and future. President.

KNOTTRUMP: Hey! There he be! Let's give a big hand for my cripple. (Applause) Yeah, yeah, I know I'm not supposed to use the word "cripple" anymore, but it's the best word. Enough of allthis pussyfooting around. You don't mind being called "crip," do you, Crip?

CRIP: Not that much.

KNOTTRUMP: See! Crip is a gamer! Give me the America that didn't used to pull its punchesover every little thing. We've become a nation of namby-pambies! Let's hear it out there. No more namby-pamby snowflakes. No more –

CROWD VOICES: – namby-pambies! … Snowflakes! No more!

KNOTTRUMP: Now Crip may creep you out walking the way he does. Or almost does! But he's at the heart of my Administration. Front and center. Who stopped those so-called ugly, dirtyrefugees down south? Crip did! (Applause) Who helped roll back those suffocating environ- mental protection laws that were killing the economy? Crip did!

CRIP: You're too kind, Mr. President.

KNOTTRUMP: I know I am, but what can I do?! Okay, Crip, enough about you! What about me? You didn't come here to see Crip. You came to see Yours Truly. Am I the greatest, or what?

(A trumpet blares)

(Enter INVINCA in a lovely gown. She nods to the crowd, waves.)

KNOTTTUMP: (Pointing to INVINCA) Isn't my daughter great?! Let's hear it for Invinca! (Sounds ofapplause.) Okay, enough! How about some applause for Yours Truly? (Applauds for himself.) Did yousee the crowd outside? They love me! They say I'm the most popular king since King David. Say a fewwords, Invinca. Go ahead. Go ahead.

INVINCA: Ladies and gentlemen of the court, welcome to the second coronation of my father. (Curtseysto him.) Without your support –

KING: Yeah, yeah, yeah, enough about them! What about Yours Truly?

INVINCA: Father, you're interrupting me.

KNOTTRUMP: So fucking what? Spit it out. Tell 'em what a great job I did after my first coronation. Come on, tell 'em!

INVINCA: My father lowered taxes, I believe. Or raised them?

KNOTTRUMP: One or the other. Or maybe both. But are we doing great or are we doing great?!

INVINCA: We are of course doing great. How could we not with my father at the helm of state?

KNOTTRUMP: You got it baby! Isn't she marvelous? If she weren't my daughter, I'd marry her!

INVINCA: Oh, Daddy, don't say things like that.

KNOTTRUMP: What about issuing a proclamation saying she's not my legal daughter? Isn't that possible? I can hear the wedding bells already.

INVINCA: Daddy!

KNOTTRUMP: It'll be fine. I'll have your husband killed.

(Some in the crowd applaud.)

KNOTTRUMP: I'm just kidding. Just kidding! The fund raiser is over. Go home now Go home!

BLACKOUT

SCENE 2

LIGHTS UP

The Throne Room

EMPEROR DONALD: Please! Welcome all to my next glorious reign! I am humbled that God has taken the pain to appoint me blessed, holy Emperor. True, I have worked like a cur to be here. But I

7

could not have done it without God. Thank you, Almighty, for my splendid rod! (Holds up scepter.)I can understand why He did me pick. Who better?! Just look at my wondrous, marvelous stick! (Points at his huge codpiece. All ooh and ah)

Still, I thank Him from the bottom of my heart. I have a very big one – that is, this part (Touches his heart.)At least that is what my physician telleth me! He's never seen someone with such a big one, you see. (aside) Thank you, doctor.

I had to step on a few to get where I am today. That's how this all works, no matter what they say.

And you were with me the whole "swear word" time! So whatever I did was never a crime. Hence it's you I want to especially thank. You were with me there whenever I drank the blood of a rascally, wily Minotaur. Were you not

And cheered when I bludgeoned that senator. It was you, not me, that punctured those lungs. And fractured those limbs and cut out those tongues.You all should be very proud of yourselves. For those eyeballs and such you put on those shelves at the morgue, in our temples, or in our archives. Where would greatness be if we didn't take lives?!

(Applause from the assembled.)

Now let me take this opportunityto introduce my royal family. As if you didn't know! As if they didn't glow!

Greet my wife, the Glorious Malaria. It's not Malaria – Mal*arr*ia! Is she not a creature of much beauty?!

(The wife presents herself to the crowd, who applaud.)

She doesn't look a day over… eighty, does she?

I can see you are no less than agog.
As fresh as the day I ordered her from that catalog.

WIFE: (not understanding English) What? I no deserve these compliments.

DONALD: You deserve every word, my dear! No laments!

I thank my stars that no matter what's she's heard
Fourteen years she's been here and still knows not a word!

WIFE: What can I say? I no good with languages!

(Donald gestures for her to step back. She does.)

DONALD: I could not have done it without my bride
Should I trade her in for a newer ride? (Laughs.)I jest!
She likes a man with a sense of humor.
But what if she develops a terrible tumor?!
Tumors run in her family. At least that's the rumor.
Maybe shell die and I'll have to mourn.
From some awful disease from when she did porn.
I both love her and hate her, her charms and her flaws.
If I have her killed, will that break any laws?
There she stands so sweet and supportive.
Perhaps it's enough just to have her deported.
Or banished to some magical island!
Maybe a swamp? Or maybe a highland?
Let me think upon her once more bedded.
And now made my Empress – or maybe beheaded?

PRESS: Sir! Sir!

DONALD: I don't hear you!

PRESS: I want to ask you, though I fear to –

DONALD: Enough now! I did not invite the press.

PRESS: The people need to know or they'll be in distress.

DONALD: The people are with me, from low to top.

PRESS: Without the press, your lying will not stop.

DONALD: No. What I say and what I think are true.

PRESS: You're listening just to those who flatter you.

DONALD: Not true! Let me prove it. (to crowd) How many here
approve of me?

(The crowd whistles and applauds loudly. Use sound effect.)

DONALD: What more do you need? As you can see, I am widely
beloved – as you can tell from the polls.

PRESS: These polls are from trolls whose lives you control.

DONALD: You can't even count. How many appear in this crowd?

PRESS: Right here? I'd say seven at best, though loud.

DONALD: I count a thousand. And look at that zest!
Thank you, kind masses, for you are the best!

PRESS With all due respect, sir, you're full of –

DONALD: I won the vote again and there's no doubting it.

PRESS: There are numerous doubts in all sorts of ways.

DONALD: You're a bunch of sore losers just casting a haze
On my marvelous reign, the best anywhere.

PRESS: We try to be fair.

DONALD: When I want your input, I'll ask for it.
As for your death, would you like a mask for it?
Now let me complete the intros of staff.
With no more interruptions by the chaff!

PRESS: But sir!

DONALD: (barreling ahead) Besides my wife *Malarria*, who will
always have my ear
Let me present to you my eldest child, my dear, my peer –
Now named Nepotisia, who is not only beautiful but smart.
She will guide as I rule with good in her heart.

(Gestures for daughter to step forward. She does.)

NEPOTISIA: Many thanks. Long may you rule, dearest sire.
But only because it's you who inspire
the rest of us here in this special place.
With such majesty and wisdom and grace

DONALD: Take note, one and all, that this woman here –
So delightful, so luscious, so sincere
Not only has my ear but has her father's heart,
Yes, she takes bribes but only keeps a part.
The rest she turns over to her dear old dad.
She is by far the daughter I wish I'd had.
And I do! How rare to have a thankful child
I say it proudly. For I am beguiled.

NEPOTISIA: (to courtiers) Thank you. Thanks. I'm here for you.

(The courtiers return to their places.)

PRESS: Excuse me, sir! Excuse me, please! Sir! Sir!

NEPOTISIA: Did you not hear my father's stern order?

PRESS: But it cannot be right that you take bribes
For our Constitution strictly proscribes
Emoluments to those in high places
Such action corrupts and downright disgraces
the codes of our Founders, the soul of our land.

DONALD: Hey! I'm the one now who's leading the band!
Besides, who knows what emoluments are!
It's an old -fashioned word, strange and bizarre.

NEPOTISIA: My father's so handsome, so cunning, so bright!
    Naturally people just know that he's right.
    If he weren't my father, I'd marry him.
    Oh, get over yourselves! Stop looking so grim!

DONALD: Next let me present to the court
    Two fine boys! Who count my money and also like sport!

(The two conjoined brothers step forward.)

DONALD: At their birth I was at first alarmed.
    But as they grew, inseparable, I was charmed.
    See how close they are, always together.
    They are a lesson to the world in how to tether
    For their mutual good as well as others.
    There is no sibling rivalry – just brothers!

(The two sons grab bows and arrows and start shooting into the air.)

SON #1: I shot an arrow into the air!

SON #2: And it struck not just one but a pair –

SON #1: Of humming birds, I hope! Maybe – ?

SON #2: Yes! Yes! A mother and her baby!

SON #1: Such sport! I thank my father for my skill.
    For every vicious hummingbird I kill.

DONALD: Once I was, I admit –

SON #2: Very worried about how we'd fit.

DONALD: But they turned out to be perfection.

SON #1: (to audience) Like to see our hummingbird collection?

DONALD: Let's save that for another time and place.

Our duties in this court today do run apace.

PRESS: One question for the brothers, if I may!

DONALD: Be kind in what you ask, or you will pay!

PRESS: Do you eat the hummingbirds you shoot?

SON #1: Ten hummingbirds in a pie look very cute.

SON #2: But barely make a mouthful for a man

SON #1: And we are men. Let there be no doubt about it.

PRESS: (under breath) Or you will hold your breath and pout about it?

DONALD: What's that?! Be that some slight to my sons?

SON #2: Cut off his head!

SON #1: And slice off his buns!

PRESS: My buns?!

DONALD: I will not have my family spurned!

SON #2: Every insult will be returned!

SON # 1: And your daughters pillaged and your villages burned!

DONALD: Guards! Bring out the apparatus as we planned
　　　　In case our coronation got out of hand.

　　　(Guards bring out a torture device.)

DONALD: As I've said, lo, these many a time.
　　　　Some good torture can prevent many a crime.
　　　　Give that fellow a taste of his own!
　　　　Press him to death! Let's hear him groan!

　　　(The Guards start pressing a board down on top of the Press.)

PRESS: Stop! Stop!

DONALD: So how do you like it, Press, when you're pressed?! Shall I
stop the press?!

PRESS: I'm not feeling my best. I'm feeling…

DONALD: Oppressed? Now you know how I feel.
Press on him harder! Let's hear him squeal.
Take him away! Or off to the side.

(Guards take the Press off.)

Let's finish our duties and do them with pride.
Now where are the spouses of my sons?
Are they not here, those ever-faithful ones?

SON #1: Our spouses are most certainly here!

SON #2: We never go anywhere without them quite near.

(The Sons each pull on a chain and drag in their spouses, each a
dead body attached to each separate son's wrist by a chain.)

DONALD: May I present to the court – my sons' precious wives.
They've dedicated their hearts, their love, and their lives –
How many years does this make you've been wedded?

SON #1: All told, many years, and in each of them bedded!

NEPOTISIA: Thank you, dear brothers, for your inspiration.
Just spare us the details, too much information.

SON #2: Everyone should emulate us, morals enforced.

SON #1: Married forever and never divorced!

SON #2: Faithful, stalwart, monogamous.

SON #1: Never mixing up wives, not even once.

DONALD: I know not how my dear sons do it!
But they are special boys. I always knew it.

COUNSELOR: O Emperor! May I beseech a word?

DONALD: Pray, what is that, esteemed counselor?

COUNSELOR: I beg to have but one word in your ear.

DONALD: Come, whisper what you will in my orifice.

COUNSELOR: Just some policy of state, no more than this.

> (The Emperor presents his ear to the Counselor, who whispers for some time.)

WIFE: What is he saying?

NEPOTISIA: They are just praying.

DONALD: (to Counselor) Oh, yes, that's good!

COUNSELOR: Thank you, sir. I really think you should.

DONALD: I will issue thirteen edicts by tomorrow.

COUNSELOR: I have prepared them, which you may borrow. (Takes out the edicts.)

DONALD: How prompt you are!

COUNSELOR: I hope we will not spar.

DONALD: As long as we stay on the self-same page.
That's my page, not yours to gauge.

COUNSELOR: Have I in some way offended thee?

> (The Counselor suddenly faints and falls down.)

DONALD: Oh, God!

> (Some courtiers try to revive the Counselor.)

WIFE: What's wrong?

DONALD: (to Wife) He'll be all right. He uses his faints
    to get his way when I have complaints.

WIFE: What?

DONALD: (waving the back of his hand at his wife) Shut!

    (The Wife puts a forefinger on her own lips, to mean she'll be
    quiet.)

DONALD: That's better. (about the Counselor) Wake the bitch up. But
    be gentle.
    A duplicitous he-bitch. Still, I need him for tasks fundamental.

    (The Counselor revives.)

COUNSELOR: Oh, did I faint? That damn narcolepsy!

DONALD: I'm sure if we had it, we'd give you a Pepsi!

WIFE: What's a Pepsi?

DONALD: Never mind, my deepest and dearest soul mate.
    (Aside)
    This woman from me I must amputate.
    (to the court) I am bored now! Let's end these affairs.
    Or shall we continue, if anyone dares! (Glares at them.) Away!

    (The Emperor exits in a flourish. The court clears except for
    the daughter and the counselor.)

COUNSELOR: (to the air) I had more to propose, so much more to say!

NEPOTISIA: (stopping) Then you shouldn't have fainted and fell on
    your face!

COUNSELOR: You afraid he'll listen to me, and not you, Your Grace?.

NEPOTISIA: When it comes to blood versus you, I know where I stand.

COUNSELOR: Don't be too sure of your father.

NEPOTISIA: Duplicitous, silly, wicked, a hater?

COUNSELOR: I hope you aren't saying such things of your pater!

NEPOTISIA: Don't presume too much of my father's ear.

COUNSELOR: And don't you presume on it either, my dear.

NEPOTISIA: Oh, go faint in a corner, as you are quite wont to!

COUNSELOR: I'd love to oblige. But I really don't want to.
    All I am saying is when it comes to the mighty,
    Take nothing for granted, for they can be flighty.

NEPOTISIA: My Sire loves me because I am his child.

COUNSELOR: With a love that is rare, quite spicy, not mild.

NEPOTISIA: What are you saying? Will you dare be so vicious?

COUNSELOR: Far be it from me to repeat what's delicious.

NEPOTISIA: I think you should leave now. Go have a nap!

COUNSELOR: And why don't you go and sit on his lap!?

NEPOTISIA: Refrain from telling me what I should do!

COUNSELOR: I'm sure you will always do what's best – for you!

    (Exits the Counselor.)

NEPOTISIA: Oh, pooh! (Exits.)

    (Enter Donald.)

DONALD: They all think they can con me, but not so fast.
    I am as smart as they come. I have them outclassed.
    God speaks to me nightly when I'm tucked in my bed.
    It's amazing the things that He puts in my head!
    Did you know it's a fact I'm infallibly right?
    My command of all facts is incredibly bright!

Whatever I say, though disputed by some,
Is the law of the land, and they are just dumb!
Some say self-esteem is just compensation.
In my case what's true is I'm just a sensation!
But I'm bored! And need some distraction.
I need more chaos. My one satisfaction!
Let me go find some. Wait here for some action!

(Exit Donald.)

BLACKOUT

SCENE 3

COUNSELOR'S OFFICE

COUNSELOR: At last some peace. And no more rhymes!

(Enter Counselor's husband.)

HUSBAND: There you are! I thought you and I were to have lunch.

COUNSELOR: I'm afraid I don't have time, George.

HUSBAND: You have time for the Emperor.

COUNSELOR: Well, he's my boss.

HUSBAND: Night and day, twenty-four seven?!

COUNSELOR: You knew my commitment to him when you married
me.

HUSBAND: No, I didn't! You weren't totally obsessed back then.
Didn't you used to be a woman?

COUNSELOR: The Emperor has a way of taking over your life.

HUSBAND: He's not taking over *my* life.

COUNSELOR: Sorry I haven't been available to you of late.

HUSBAND: Do you call three years "of late?"

COUNSELOR: Sex, sex, sex, that's all you ever want!

HUSBAND: No sex, no sex, no sex. That's all you ever want!

COUNSELOR: (Looking in her engagement notebook) I can give you three minutestwo weeks from next Tuesday.

HUSBAND: Gee thanks. But you'll probably just fall asleep during it.

COUNSELOR: Sorry. But I'm working for the greatest man in the world.

HUSBAND: What?! You can't be serious!

COUNSELOR: I am serious.

HUSBAND: That man is demented. You can't possibly believe a word he says.

COUNSELOR: I know you don't like him, but I do.

HUSBAND: What's happened to you?! How can you spend one minute listening to thatridiculous blow-hard, let alone working for him until you conk out?!

COUNSELOR: He's never boring.

HUSBAND: So I'm boring. Is that it?

COUNSELOR: I didn't say that.

HUSBAND: You don't have to say it. It's obvious.

COUNSELOR: I married you when nobody else would.

HUSBAND: Oh, am I supposed to thank you for that?

COUNSELOR: Yeah, maybe.

HUSBAND: You weren't exactly fighting off suitors.

COUNSELOR: I had more offers than you did.

HUSBAND: Have we really sunk to this?

COUNSELOR: Maybe you have. I've risen.

HUSBAND: You haven't risen. You think all his hot air has made you rise? Honey, you makeme worry about your sanity.

COUNSELOR: I'm getting to implement policies I have always believed in.

HUSBAND: But at what price? You lie through your teeth for that man. You demean yourselfand our children with the unrelenting bullying, bluster, and bullshit. How can you live with yourself? I just don't understand it. Truly I don't.

COUNSELOR: I put up with you for years, didn't I?

BLACKOUT

SCENE 4

EMPEROR: (entering) What other genius plans should I implement today? You won't have this brain around you forever. So shoot me... some ideas! Ah, got you there didn't I? They say I brag too much about myself. So come on you guys, come up with some suggestions.

STAFF MEMBER: What about rounding up your opponents and putting them in jail?

EMPEROR: Can I do that?

STAFF MEMBER: You can do whatever you want.

EMPEROR: Who will gather them up?

STAFF MEMBER: The Sergeant at Arms.

EMPEOR: How about a militia? I like militias. Delicious militias. How do you like the sound of that?

ANOTHER STAFF MEMBER: What about holding the next Olympics at your resort in Florida?!

EMPEROR: Can I do that?

ANOTHER STAFF MEMBER: Who's going to stop you?

EMPEROR: You're correct. They're pussies. Besides, my resort in Florida is the bestest resort inthe whole universe! We have magnificent Quonset huts with magnificent views! Fit for a sultan! Never mind a king! We have alligators in the moat around the resort, to keep the riff raff out.

ANOTHER STAFF MEMBER: Perhaps you can hire some guards to catch some trespassers andthrow them to the alligators.

EMPEROR: And we could charge our guests for the show!

ANOTHER STAFF MEMBER: We could hire the Kurds to fight the alligators. They're lookingfor jobs, right? They like to fight. So why not alligators?!

EMPEROR: I love it! Absolutely love it. And let's add some anacondas. Who will win, thealligators or the bad-ass anacondas?

ANOTHER STAFF MEMBER: Not the Kurds!

EMPEROR: Away with the Kurds! Get it? Kurds and whey?

(The assembled laugh, too hard.)

EMPEROR: Am I hilarious or what?!

(Enter Nepotisia.)

NEPOTISIA: Daddy! Daddy! I have a problem. Can you help me?

EMPEROR: What is it, punkin? Have you got a boo-boo?

NEPOSITIA: No, that was yesterday. Today I have thirteen copyrights for my purses so they canbe sold in China, and they're so complicated!

EMPEROR: I'm sort of busy right now, honey.

NEPOTISIA: Not too busy for me, surely, Daddy? What about my copyrights? (Shows papers.)

EMPEROR: Okay, let me handle it. Give them to me. (Takes them, Scribbles on them.) There, it's from the emperor, Don Knottrump. See that signature, everybody? (Shows the papers.) Now you're protected from those awful Chinese. Go forth and sell those purses!

NEPOTISIA: (gathering the papers) Oh, thank you, Daddy bear! Thank you, thank you, thank you.

EMPEROR: How about a kissy-poo for me?

NEPOTISIA: For you, Daddy, anything! (Kisses him on the cheek.)

EMPEROR: You call that a kiss?

(He takes her in his arms and gives her a long, long kiss.)

EMPEROR: See that? Now that's a kiss!

(Applause from the assembled.)

BLACKOUT

SCENE 5

CRIP'S OFFICE

(Enter Staff Member.)

STAFF MEMBER: Do you have time to speak with me, Mr. Chip?

CRIP: My name is Harrison. Mr. Harrison.

STAFF MEMBER: Sorry, I keep forgetting. I guess it's because the President, I mean the Emperor, uses the other word.

CRIP: Forget it. What's in a name? What can I do for you?

STAFF MEMBER: The Emperor wants you to sign this proclamation. (Shows it.)

CRIP: Me? Why?

STAFF MEMBER: It concerns you and your type.

CRIP: What type is that? Never mind!

STAFF MEMBER: It's about the rollback on the Disabilities Act. The Emperor thinks it's causing employers too much money to keep up on the rules. He calls them draconian.

CRIP: Well, maybe some things are. But most aren't. What exactly does the proclamation say?

STAFF MEMBER: No more handicap parking.

CRIP: Really? I use it.

STAFF MEMBER: Well, the Emperor says he sees a lot of empty parking spaces.

CRIP: And he just wants to get rid of them like that?

STAFF MEMBER: He thinks it sounds better coming from you.

CRIP: So that's why he hired me?! As if I didn't know.

STAFF MEMBER: You gonna sign it or not?

CRIP: I don't know.

STAFF MEMBER: He says you can resign.

CRIP: But –

STAFF MEMBER: It's up to you.

CRIP: I've got to stay around here so that some things are not destroyed. Here, let me sign it.

STAFF MEMBER: He'd like a note from you also.

CRIP: Exactly what kind of note?

STAFF MEMBER: Up to you. But something showing clearly whose side you're on. He suggests something like: Park and Walk for Handicap Rights.

CRIP: Are you serious?

STAFF MEMBER: Or maybe: Walk a Few Extra Steps for America!

CRIP: Oh, for God's sake. Let me write it. (He writes the suggestion.)

STAFF MEMBER: You forgot the exclamation point.

CRIP: There!

STAFF MEMBER: He has another suggestion as well.

CRIP: Which is?

STAFF MEMBER: If You Want to Ride the Bus, Get the Fuck on it by Yourself!

CRIP: I'm not putting my name to that.

STAFF MEMBER: It was just a suggestion.

CRIP: Get out of my office.

STAFF MEMBER: But –

CRIP: Get!

(The Staff Member runs off.)

BLACKOUT

SCENE 6

The Emperor's Bedroom

(Knottrump is tweeting in bed.)

(Enter his wife.)

MALARIA: Oh, God, not again! (Turns to leave.)

KNOTTRUMP: Malaria, wait! I'm almost done.

MALARIA: You're never done, Don! You are forever tweeting!

KNOTTRUMP: But my enemies must be dealt with! (Tweets on his phone.)

MELARIA: I came here, after all these months, to provide duties wifely.

KNOTTRUMP: Really? Great! I thought you had forgot where the bedroom is. I'll be with youin a jiffy.

MALARIA: Forget it. Tweet your heart up to Hell. (Turns to leave.)

KNOTTRUMP: Wait! I'll put my phone away. I promise!

MALARIA: But you won't! I keep myself all prettified, but you just keep on tweeting.

KNOTTRUMP: (tossing his phone to the side) There! The phone is gone. Come, my darling.(Holds out his arms.)

MALARIA: I don't trust you.

KNOTTRUMP: You can trust me. I'll never tweet again. Come, come, darling!

MALARIA: So much as one look at your tweet and I am out of here.

(She approaches the bed.)

KNOTTRUMP: You've got to get closer than that. (Holds out his arms.)

MALARIA: (Takes out a stop watch.) Two and one-half minutes max, as it says in our marriage contract.

KNOTTRUMP: More! Tonight I feel super horny.

MALARIA: Two and one half minutes. Starting now. (Presses the stop watch.)

KNOTRUMP: Put that damn thing away. (Grabs for the stop watch.)

MALARIA: You have your tweets. I have my stop watch. Your time is clicking.

KNOTTRUMP: You know I can't perform on a dime.

MALARIA: You used to. On a penny.

KNOTTRUMP: Well, I was younger then.

MALARIA: Tick, tick! (Holds up the stop watch.)

KNOTTRUMP: Wait! A tweet just came in. (Grabs his phone.)

MALARIA: No, no!

KNOTTRUMP: (Looking at his phone) It's from Nepotisia!

MALARIA: Don't you dare.

KNOTTRUMP: But she may be in trouble.

(The Emperor is torn between his daughter's tweet and his wife's stop watch. Finally, he chooses the tweet, looks at his phone.)

KNOTTRUMP: It *is* from my daughter.

MALARIA: What's her name today?

KNOTTRUMP: Do you mind stepping out of the room while I take this?

MALARIA: Oh, for God's sake, what is wrong with you, husband?!

KNOTTRUMP: I'll be right with you. I promise.

MALARIA: Tick, tick… bing! Your time is up. See you in a year! (Gets off the bed.)

KNOTTRUMP: It'll take just a few moments. (Grabs the phone, starts pushing keys.)

MALARIA: (running off) Happy Anniversary, my darling!

BLACKOUT

ANNOUNCED TO

CHARACTERS: (2)

MARY, a young virgin n a plain dress and head scarf, sorting lentils and olives

GABRIEL, a male archangel in a white robe with wings

MARY: (to audience) Hello. I'm Mary, a virgin. I am sitting on a three-legged stool in my parents' tiny kitchen, sorting lentils and olives into two different ceramic bowls – always busy are my hands. I am wearing one of my two dresses, the blue muslin, the one I prefer because it complements my hair and eyes. I think I have very pretty eyes, but of course I can tell no one this. They would say I am proud. Sometimes the full sleeves of my dress interfere with my sorting duties, but I simply flick them to the side and work on. (She does.) It's just another ordinary day in Nazareth.

(Suddenly, there is a rush of wind at the doorway, and a creature in a white robe appears almost floating just above the stone floor. He seemed to be almost male with large white wings. He holds his hands outstretched on either side and is about to open his mouth.)

MARY: What are you doing here?

GABRIEL: Do not fear! I bring great tidings.

MARY: I'm not interested.

GABRIEL: Really great tidings.

MARY: I said I'm not interested. (Flicks her hand at him.)

GABRIEL: You have found favor, even in this hovel.

MARY: What's that? You're gonna make my hovel sparkle?!

GABRIEL: More than you know.

MARY: I don't like being startled. You resemble our neighbor who makes sucking sounds at me whenever I go out to feed the donkey. (Demonstrates.)

GABRIEL: I am the Archangel Gabriel. I have been sent by Almighty God to announce something to you. (He smiles beatifically at her.)

MARY: Did you smile beatifically at me?

GABRIEL: I tried to.

MARY: Oh, poo! Get out! (She waves a dismissive hand at the creature and even throws an olive at his chest.)

GABRIEL: Hey!

MARY: I'm going to call my parents to send you packing.

GABRIEL: Wait! I have most holy news for you!

MARY: *Mois*t holy news? What's that?

GABRIEL: *Most* holy news.

MARY: Yay, verily, that's what all the horny chaps say!

GABRIEL: No. 'Tis true.

MARY: 'Tis not!

GABRIEL: You are a saucy virgin.

MARY: Oh, shut thy mouth. Go! I must finish the lentils.

GABRIEL: I can finish the lentils for you.

MARY: (scoffing) Yeah, right!

GABRIEL: I can. And in one fell swoop.

MARY: And what am I supposed to give in return, huh?

GABRIEL: Just to listen to my announcement.

MARY: It had better be a doozy.

GABRIEL: I'll husk the olives as well.

MARY: A lot of promises here. (She eyes the creature sideways, the
    better to decipher his honesty.)

GABRIEL: You are not very trusting, virgin.

MARY: I've learned, creature!

GABRIEL: I am losing patience. Do you want to hear what I have to say
    or not?

MARY: Spit it out and then get out. (Places both fists on her hips.)

GABRIEL: I guess I should have brought my trumpet.

MARY: Yeah, yeah, I'm waiting.

    (GABRIEL makes a poor trumpet blare sound with his lips.)

MARY: Oh, for God's sake!

GABRIEL: I'm a little rusty. I don't get to make these announcements
    that often.

MARY: I'm impressed to death.

GABRIEL: I'm going to leave!

MARY: And I'm going to heave. You want the old heave-ho? Huh?
    (Puts her fingers to her mouth to signal that she is about to puke
    on him.)

GABRIEL: Maybe I have the wrong virgin. Let me check the address again.

(He ducks outside to check the address near the door.)

(Mary hurries to the door to shut it. But the creature scurries back in before she can.)

GABRIEL: There's no address outside.

MARY: It's B.C., buster. What do you expect?

GABRIEL: All right, this is your last chance to hear the message from Almighty God.

MARY: I'm going to call my father. And my mother. Believe me, you don't want to mess with my mother.

GABRIEL: Here I go! (Makes as if to leave.)

MARY: Go on.

GABREL: I'm leaving. No big news for you, virgin.

MARY: Bye bye, bird-boy.

GABRIEL: You're going to be the mother of God! *Gotcha!*

MARY: What?!

GABRIEL: I have been commanded by Almighty God to come here and announce to you that you are soon to be great with child. And that child is the son of God!

MARY: You're shitting me.

GABRIEL: Would God Almighty shit you?

MARY: I wouldn't put anything past Him. Have you read His book?

GABRIEL: It's an offer you can't refuse.

MARY: I'm going to be an unwed mother?!

GABRIEL: You'll have your boyfriend as cover.

MARY: The news will get out, believe me, in this burg.

GABRIEL: We promise to zap any wagging tongues.

MARY: They can be vicious.

GABRIEL: They'll be dead before they can say "illegitimate." Deal?

MARY: Why me?

GABRIEL: Why not?

MARY: So you just show up here and announce that I'm pregnant, without so much as a by your leave?

GABRIEL: We thought you'd be pleased.

MARY: You couldn't at least ask me first? "Hey, Mary, do you want to be the mother of God?"

GABRIEL: Jesus Christ! You don't seem to be the least bit grateful that you have been chosen for this special honor.

MARY: It's my body! And I control it!

GABRIEL: But you'll be carrying the savior of the world! All sins will be forgiven through your son! What's not to like?

MARY: What if I have an abortion instead?

GABRIEL: You wouldn't!

MARY: It's my choice, not God's.

GABRIEL: Woman, you dare not defy God's will!

MARY: Creature, don't tell me how to live my life!

GABRIEL: But you have already been, finally, touched by God.

MARY: I didn't even have sex! Even once!

GABRIEL: It will be a miraculous birth. People will venerate you for millennia.

MARY: No, they won't. And what about my mother?!

GABRIEL: But I tell you they will! It is written.

MARY: It's still early. It can be unwritten.

GABRIEL: I told God you were a bad choice!

MARY: He should have listened to you.

GABRIEL: God listens only to Himself.

MARY: Well, tell Him he picked the wrong womb, okay? I can visit the apothecary down the lane before the day is out.

GABRIEL: No! Please! No! Humankind is counting on you!

MARY: Next time you want a baby mama *ask*, asshole!

(She pushes the archangel out and slams the door behind him.)

BLACKOUT

THE BAD SON

An ill father and his son try to escape Afghanistan

CHARACTERS: (4)

FATHER, in his forties, unable to walk on his own, traditional Afghan clothing, one heel bandaged

SON, in his twenties, more modern clothing

SOLDIER #1, with gun

SOLDIER #2, with gun

SETTING: a room in a poor house in Afghanistan, modern day

FATHER: (sitting on several cushions) Hurry, Yariel! They won't wait for us!

SON: (entering with two suitcases) I'm going as fast as I can, Father!

FATHER: If we miss the plane, we will die!

SON: If you had hurried earlier, we wouldn't be in this predicament.

FATHER: I had to say my prayers.

SON: Yes, but they could wait.

FATHER: Prayers before are better than prayers after!

SON: (under his breath) Or never.

FATHER: What did you say?

SON: Never mind.

FATHER: I hope it wasn't more of your blasphemy.

SON: Is there anything else that you want to pack in your suitcase? I
don't think there is any more room, but –

FATHER: Your mother's wedding ring. Blessings be upon her head. I
have it. (Pats pocket.)

SON: Let me have it.

(The Father finds the ring and hands it to Son. Turning away,
the Son puts it into the secret compartment of his suitcase.)

SON: She would have been packed two days ago.

FATHER: Yes, she was a saint. I, on the other hand, am a hopeless
sinner.

SON: You are not hopeless, Father.

FATHER: But I *am* a sinner? Is that what you mean?

SON: I have also packed some coins in a secret pocket in my suitcase.
Though they are almost worthless.

FATHER: Did you get banknotes?

SON: I tried. The bank was closed.

FATHER: Still, well done for trying! … You have a secret compartment?

SON: Did you sign your visa papers – in all three places?

FATHER: I think so. In my suitcase.

SON: (exasperated) Father!

FATHER: It is all too much for me! I don't think I can make it.

SON: I packed fresh bandages for your heel. You will make it. Also the
medications.

FATHER: They smell nasty. I smell nasty.

SON: No, you don't.

FATHER: I should not have looked away from my diabetes. Another sin!

SON: We will win out in the end. We will make the plane. And when we are safe, we will get your neuropathy cured.

FATHER: (beckoning for help, trying to stand up) You won't abandon me, will you, Yariel? Please tell me that you won't.

SON: (helping his father to stand) I will do my best.

FATHER: (standing on one leg) Oh, do better than that!

SON: Father!

FATHER: We must not forget to smile in the face of adversity.

SON: That too can come later, not before.

FATHER: I wonder if you should change the bandage on my heel before we leave.

SON: Really?

FATHER: Never mind. So I get sepsis, so it is as God wills.

SON: I'll change the bandage if you truly want me to. But it takes almost an hour.

FATHER: No, only forty-five minutes if you don't dawdle.

SON: Please say we can do it later.

FATHER: Perhaps you are right. On the plane, there may be a doctor or a real nurse.

SON: Or even an entire hospital on the plane. Of course, only if God is willing.

FATHER: Do not say prayers if you don't mean them.

SON: Let us not quarrel, Father. Not now.

FATHER: If you would listen, we would not quarrel.

SON: Our ride should be here any minute.

FATHER: I'm not sure we can count on your cousin.

SON: He said he'd be here at eight. And he'll call first.

FATHER: Why don't you call him? Call him. He forgets things.

SON: If you insist. (Takes out a cell phone.) I think his number is saved.
     (Shakes the cell phone.)

FATHER: What's wrong?

SON: I guess I turned it off, to save power. (Attempts to turn on the cell
     phone.)

FATHER: Is it broken?

SON: Wait! It's coming.

     (They both look at the cell phone.)

SON: The battery's dead.

FATHER: Damn it!

SON: I tried to charge it last night. But there was no electricity.

FATHER: They said there would be electricity soon.

SON: Another promise!

FATHER: Shhh. Someone will hear.

SON: They only hear what they want to hear.

FATHER: Why don't you check outside. Crazy Karim may be waiting in
     his truck. Do you have the money he wants?

SON: It's in my suitcase. The second payment.

FATHER: Good. Perhaps he did call, but your cell phone did not work. As I have said many times, they are useless.

SON: They are not always useless, Father. Sometimes they are invaluable.

FATHER: Yes, without value.

SON: (putting his phone into a pocket) I will check for Karim. (The Son helps his Father to his cushions.) Will you be all right on your own for one minute? I will wait outside until I see him.

FATHER: I will be fine.

SON: Do you need to go to the bathroom first?

FATHER: No. Go!

SON: I will be right outside if you need me. (He exits.)

(The Father immediately manages with difficulty to get up on one foot. He hops toward the suitcases. He unzips several pockets, looking for the secret pocket. He sees some clothing but does not remove it.)

FATHER: (finding the secret pocket) Ah!

(He checks to make sure the Son can't see him.)

Secret pocket, my ass!

(He pulls out a folded printed paper. There is a reproduced photo on the paper, but the audience can't see it.)

FATHER: (unfolding the paper) Oh, my God!

(He tries to return the paper to the secret pocket but fumbles.)

(Re-enter the Son.)

SON: What are you doing, Father?

FATHER: What are you doing?!

SON: Don't touch my belongings.

FATHER: Why would I touch such a thing, if I had known what was there?!

SON: Put it back, please.

FATHER: We are not taking that on the plane!

SON: It is personal.

FATHER: It is pornographic!

SON: Why did you have to be such a snoop?!

FATHER: Why did you have to have as picture of another man's genitals in your luggage?"

SON: You make it sound funny, Father.

FATHER: It is not funny in the least. It is obscene. Why do you have it? Why do you have it?

SON: A friend asked me to carry it for him?

FATHER: Don't be smart with me! Do you think I don't know what you do with it? Do you think I don't hear you in the night with it? I just thought it was a picture of a woman!

SON: Maybe it is a woman.

FATHER: You are not a good son. You blaspheme. You rub yourself as you look at this. (Throws the photo onto the floor.)

SON: We can tear it up.

FATHER: You cannot even make up a fake reason why you have this thing!?

SON: It's ... it's ... art.

FATHER: You fuck! Art, my ass!

SON: Karim may be outside waiting. (Starts to exit.)

FATHER: Forget the plane! We are going to settle this before we get on any plane.

SON: May I be so crass as to remind you, Father, that you need me to help you stand up, to help you with your bandages and medications. You cannot let that picture interfere with your health.

FATHER: I know that!

SON: Then we will discuss it later. Or never.

FATHER: But the penis is engorged! How can you? How can you?!

SON: Because I do not have the real thing in my bed, Father? Maybe when we get somewhere else besides this godforsaken country I will have!

FATHER: Over my dead body.

SON: Don't be melodramatic.

FATHER: No! Don't you salivate over cocks! (covering his face with his hands) My son, my son! Oh, my God!

SON: Oh, for God's sake. Nobody's asking you to look at the picture!

FATHER: This is what comes of you going to Chicago for that year. I should never have let you go.

SON: I shouldn't have come back.

FATHER: No, you shouldn't have.

SON: I seem to remember hearing you beg on the phone for me to come home and help you. That was me, right? That was you?!

FATHER: I wouldn't have asked if I'd known what you've become.

SON: I came home because I thought I owed it to you.

FATHER: I thought it was because you loved me.

SON: I do love you. But you do not make it easy.

FATHER: Your mother indulged you too much.

SON: No she didn't. She was almost as harsh as you.

FATHER: I am sure that she thanks you from Heaven.

SON: (to Heaven) Peace, Mother!

(Knock at the door.)

FATHER: Who is that?

SON: Karim, I would guess.

FATHER: Don't let him in! He'll steal something.

SON: Don't alienate him. He's our only ride, crazy or not!

FATHER: That we should have to rely on such a fool!

SON: *Shhh.* He'll hear you.

(There is another knock on the door.)

SON: Coming!

FATHER: Don't let him in!

SON: He can help with the suitcases!

FATHER: I can help with them!

(The Father attempts to move a suitcase, but he can't do it. He tries the other suitcase, again to no avail.)

SON: Don't! You will injure your back.

FATHER: We must lock up the house as we leave.

SON: I doubt that it's going to matter if we lock up.

FATHER: To keep Karim from coming in here, taking things. God knows what else you have in your room. (Gestures off.)

SON: What did you do with my picture?

FATHER: (looking around) I don't know.

(There is another knock on the door.)

SON: (calling) Karim? We are coming!

FATHER: (calling) In a minute, Karim!

(Both the Father and the Son look for the pornographic photo. They even open both suitcases.)

SON: I can't find it. What did you do with it?

FATHER: You must have hidden it away again!

SON: I did not. It's here somewhere.

(There is another knock on the door.)

SON: Karim, stop knocking! We are coming!

FATHER: They will find it when we go through customs. They will not let us through.

SON: (finding the photo under a suitcase) Here it is!

FATHER: Tear it up.

SON: They will, if they find it, see what it is by putting the pieces together. The Taliban.

FATHER: Then let us burn it! (Grabs the photo from the Son.)

SON: Do you have any matches?

FATHER: No.

SON: Why not? You smoke!

FATHER: I thought I would give up smoking finally!

SON: How can we get rid of it?

FATHER: (bitterly) Why don't you eat it?!

SON: Father, you are cruel.

FATHER: No, I am 'amusing.' Like my son.

SON: Give me the photo.

(The Father hands it to the Son.)

SON: (reluctantly) I will swallow it.

FATHER: No!

SON: Yes.

(The Son tears off a piece of the photo with his teeth, tries to chew, but then spits it out.)

FATHER: I will throw it into the privy, where it belongs.

SON: It will still be there, if somebody really wants to find it. I told you to get a flush toilet!

FATHER: That I should my life come down to this – hiding homosexual pornography in my toilet!

BLACKOUT

(Lights up slowly. Two days later.)

SON: (to Father, who is sitting on his cushions with prayer beads) Thank God the electricity is back on.

FATHER: Yes, I know.

SON: My cell phone is charged again.

FATHER: I know. God is merciful. (He fingers his prayer beads.)

SON: Isn't He, though. Do you want me to make you some food?

FATHER: No.

SON: I don't mind.

FATHER: No.

SON: I see that you have your *subha.*

(The Father does not acknowledge this comment.)

SON: I'm sorry we didn't make the plane.

FATHER: God wasn't willing.

SON: I'm sorry Karim did not wait for us.

FATHER: He will burn in Hell.

SON: We should not have paid him upfront.

FATHER: Don't rely on the crazy.

SON: He can't help it.

FATHER: Or on your only son.

SON: Or on your only father.

FATHER: You will burn in Hell too.

SON: We'll see.

FATHER: We will!

SON: We can try for another plane.

FATHER: No need to.

SON: We should try.

FATHER: My life is over. No need to.

SON: Don't say that.

FATHER: I already said it.

SON: A new life awaits us. I'm sure of it.

FATHER: I'm sure of it as well.

>   (There is a hard knock on the door.)

SON: Is that possibly Karim?

FATHER: (deliberately not answering)

SON: Could it be?

>   (There is another hard knock.)

>   (The Son hurries to the offstage door.)

>   (He backs into the main room. Two armed Taliban soldiers
>   enter. They are carrying Kalashikov-74 rifles.)

SOLDIER #1: Yariel Navid?

SOLDIER #2: Taliban!

SOLDIER #1: Come with us!

SON: Why? Why?

SOLDIER #2: You know why.

> (They seize him.)

SON: (turning toward his father) Father! Help me! Save me!

SOLDIER #2: Do not call for your father. It is your father who told us about you and your ways!

SON: Father!

> (The Father looks away from his son.)

> (The two soldiers drag the Son offstage.)

> (The Father won't look at them, fingering his prayer beads until they hurt his hands.)

BLACKOUT

BODY LANGUAGE

CHARACTERS: (4)

MALE CHRIS, a man of any age, 35-70

FEMALE CHRIS, a woman of any age, 35-70 (They should be close in age to each other.)

MALE FRIEND, about the same age as MALE CHRIS

FEMALE FRIEND, about the same age as FEMALE CHRIS

(It can also be cast with both leads men.)

SETTING: Upstage there should be a closet with a door that opens and that can be locked with a key.

PLAYING TIME: About 45 minutes

SCENE 1

> (LIGHTS UP on male-female couple embracing in their living room.)

MALE CHRIS: (removing himself from the other person's arms) Whoa! I think that's enough for now.

FEMALE CHRIS: Really?

MALE CHRIS: You never know where it might lead.

FEMALE CHRIS: (not pleased) All right, if you say so.

MALE CHRIS: Don't take it personally.

FEMALE CHRIS: How am I supposed to take it then? Generically?

MALE CHRIS: (changing the subject) Where's Pookie?

FEMALE CHRIS: I don't know. She was on the cat thing the last time I saw her.

MALE CHRIS: I think she's sick.

FEMALE CHRIS: She's faking it, to get some attention.

MALE CHRIS: She's never sick.

FEMALE CHRIS: Maybe she's dying.

MALE CHRIS: Hey! Don't say that!

FEMALE CHRIS: My saying it or not saying it won't make it happen. Or not happen.

MALE CHRIS: (calling) Pookie! Are you okay?

FEMALE CHRIS: (pretending to be the cat) "I'm dying! I'm dying! I'm dying!"

MALE CHRIS: No, you're not.

FEMALE CHRIS: (as the cat) "I'm going to die right in the middle of your bed!"

MALE CHRIS: You do and I'll kill you!

FEMALE CHRIS: (coming over to MALE CHRIS, very close, waits)

MALE CHRIS: What are you doing?!

FEMALE CHRIS: Am I doing something?

MALE CHRIS: You're hovering.

FEMALE CHRIS: I can remember when you loved me hovering.

MALE CHRIS: (changing the subject) Pookie! Get up! Do you want some yum yums? (Starts to leave.)

FEMALE CHRIS: (following him, very closely) Yeah, let's feed Pookie some yum yums together.

MALE CHRIS: Why don't you stay here?

FEMALE CHRIS: Why don't I come with you?

MALE CHRIS: Maybe I want a little personal space?

FEMALE CHRIS: I can't even get a hug?

MALE CHRIS: You're making me uncomfortable.

FEMALE CHRIS: (insincerely) Sorry!

MALE CHRIS: You're not very good at reading body language, are you?

FEMALE CHRIS: Wow! I guess not.

MALE CHRIS: I'm going to check on Pookie. (Starts to exit.)

FEMALE CHRIS: (Rushes after him and encircles him from behind.) Got ya!

MALE CHRIS: (removing his arms) Oh, for Christ's sake, Chris, stop it!

FEMALE CHRIS: I just want a hug!

MALE CHRIS: Can't you take a hint?!

FEMALE CHRIS: Do you want a divorce?

MALE CHRIS: No!

FEMALE CHRIS: You don't want sex. You don't want a hug. What do you want?

MALE CHRIS: How about a pause? Would a pause be too much to ask?

FEMALE CHRIS: Are you going gay on me?

MALE CHRIS: Oh, for God's sake! What a cliché! No, I'm not!

FEMALE CHRIS: You might as well be.

MALE CHRIS: Why are you insisting that we talk about this?

FEMALE CHRIS: *Because!*

MALE CHRIS: Well, I don't want to talk about it. Not now, not ever.

FEMALE CHRIS: Cat got your tongue?

MALE CHRIS: Because whatever it is I can't put it into words, all nice and laid out on a plate.

FEMALE CHRIS: Like a yum yum?

MALE CHRIS: Yeah, like a yum yum.

FEMALE CHRIS: You think I want to live like this?

MALE CHRIS: I don't know. Do you?

FEMALE CHRIS: Absolutely not. No. …No. … Never. In case it's not clear enough, that's a no.

BLACKOUT

SCENE 2

MALE CHRIS: (on cell phone) Hi! Can you come over? I need someone to talk to.

MALE FRIEND: Sure. (Enters immediately.) What do you want to talk about?

MALE CHRIS: (putting the phone down) What took you so long?

MALE FRIEND: I had to sign some mortgage papers.

MALE CHRIS: Really?

MALE FRIEND: My life goes on even without you. What do you want to talk about?

MALE CHRIS: My love life. Make that my lack of a love life.

MALE FRIEND: I'm leaving now. (Turns to exit.)

MALE CHRIS: Hey! … Please.

MALE FRIEND: Is there anything more boring than other people's love lives?

MALE CHRIS: Their mortgage papers?

MALE FRIEND: You got me. But I didn't call you to discuss *them*, did I?

MALE CHRIS: Let's discuss them then. Did you get a decent rate?

MALE FRIEND: Three point four.

MALE CHRIS: Really? Is that good?

MALE FRIEND: In today's market, yeah.

MALE CHRIS: Adjustable or fixed?

MALE FRIEND: I like my mortgages like my dogs?

MALE CHRIS: (Throws his hands up, not comprehending.)

MALE FRIEND: Fixed!

MALE CHRIS: How much is your property worth?

MALE FRIEND: You're right! Let's discuss your love life.

MALE CHRIS: You're sure?

MALE FRIEND: No, but what are friends for if not to bore them with your troubles?

MALE CHRIS: Thanks. I think. It's Chris.

MALE FRIEND: Yeah?

MALE CHRIS: She won't leave me alone. Always touching and hugging and –

MALE FRIEND: And this is bad?

MALE CHRIS: Very bad.

MALE FRIEND: She's attractive.

MALE CHRIS: So I understand. I just don't want to have sex with her anymore.

MALE FRIEND: You've given up sex? What else is there?

MALE CHRIS: Just with Chris.

MALE FRIEND: So you want a divorce?

MALE CHRIS: Not really. I just don't want to touch the woman any longer.

MALE FRIEND: What do you want me to do about it? Have sex with her?

MALE CHRIS: No!

MALE FRIEND: I don't mind, if it will help a buddy out.

MALE CHRIS: Are you going to take this seriously or not?

MALE FRIEND: I'm taking it seriously, as seriously as it needs to be taken. So separate. Don't live together anymore.

MALE CHRIS: I would, but I don't want to be lonely.

MALE FRIEND: Lots of married people stop having sex. I've heard.

MALE CHRIS: Yes, but that's mutual. Chris doesn't want to stop.

MALE FRIEND: And you've told him this?

MALE CHRIS: By body language.

MALE FRIEND: You slap his hands away?

MALE CHRIS: Not quite. I don't want to hurt his feelings.

MALE FRIEND: What do you do then? Paint me a picture.

MALE CHRIS: I - I deflect. (Demonstrates avoiding hands.)

MALE FRIEND: And he still keeps coming back?

MALE CHRIS: Yes.

MALE FRIEND: What does he think you mean by running away from him?

MALE CHRIS: I'm not sure. Maybe that I'm not feeling well. Or it's a phase.

MALE FRIEND: Are you sick? Is it a phase?

MALE CHRIS: I don't believe so. I think it's permanent. Do you have any suggestions?

MALE FRIEND: (thinks) No.

MALE CHRIS: No?

MALE FRIEND: No. Okay, I've got to go. See ya! (Exits.)

MALE CHRIS: That's it?

BLACKOUT

SCENE 3

(Enter FEMALE CHRIS.)

FEMALE CHRIS: (calling) Chris?

MALE CHRIS: (offstage) Yeah?

FEMALE CHRIS: Can I see you for a minute?

MALE CHRIS: I'm busy.

FEMALE CHRIS: What are you doing?

MALE CHRIS: It's personal!

FEMALE CHRIS: Are you in the shower?

MALE CHRIS: I am!

FEMALE CHRIS: With the bathroom door open?

MALE CHRIS: Sorry! It gets too hot in here. (Closes the bathroom door, more muffled) How's that?

FEMALE CHRIS: Are you masturbating in the shower?

MALE CHRIS: (Pause.) What's it to you?

FEMALE CHRIS: You'd rather masturbate alone than have sex with me?

MALE CHRIS: (Pause.) I don't know what to say to that.

FEMALE CHRIS: I don't get you.

MALE CHRIS: It's complicated.

FEMALE CHRIS: It's selfish.

MALE CHRIS: Why can't we just *not* talk about it?

FEMALE CHRIS: You're hurting my feelings!

MALE CHRIS: Can't you ever just leave something alone?

FEMALE CHRIS: It's also adultery.

MALE CHRIS: *What?!*

FEMALE CHRIS: You're being unfaithful to me.

MALE CHRIS: You don't own my sperm!

FEMALE CHRIS: Yes, I do.

MALE CHRIS: No, you don't.

FEMALE CHRIS: You made a vow.

MALE CHRIS: Oh, for God's sake!

FEMALE CHRIS: So stop right now!

MALE CHRIS: I will not! I'm being faithful – to myself.

FEMALE CHRIS: I'm going to come in there!

MALE CHRIS: A moment or two for myself, please!

FEMALE CHRIS: No. Till death do us part!

MALE CHRIS: Is that a threat?

FEMALE CHRIS: Maybe. Have you stopped?

MALE CHRIS: I'm not telling you!

FEMALE CHRIS: I'm coming in there!

MALE CHRIS: With what, a gun?

FEMALE CHRIS: Don't tempt me. I just want a hug.

MALE CHRIS: Nobody wants a hug that much.

FEMALE CHRIS: Just one hug, and then I'll leave.

MALE CHRIS: I don't believe you.

FEMALE CHRIS: This is so embarrassing. Why do I have to beg you?

MALE CHRIS: Don't beg me! ... You've made me lose my erection.

FEMALE CHRIS: Good!

BLACKOUT

SCENE 4

(Enter FEMALE FRIEND to FEMALE CHRIS.)

FEMALE FRIEND: I heard you need a shoulder to cry on.

FEMALE CHRIS: (vacuuming furiously) Thanks but no thanks.

FEMALE FRIEND: Are you sure? You never vacuum. Something must
be wrong.

FEMALE CHRIS: What do you mean?! I love to vacuum! (Vacuums
even harder.)

FEMALE FRIEND: Chris, is it Chris?

FEMALE CHRIS: Who?

FEMALE FRIEND: Your husband.

FEMALE CHRIS: I don't have a husband.

FEMALE FRIEND: There hasn't been enough time for a divorce.

FEMALE CHRIS: Divorces start long before they start! And you can
quote me!

FEMALE FRIEND: Are you going to divorce him?

FEMALE CHRIS: (abandoning the vacuum cleaner) Oh, I'm so unhappy! (Runs to FEMALE FRIEND.) I need a hug! (They hug.) (Pulls back from the hug.) But I don't want to hug somebody who doesn't want to hug me.

FEMALE FRIEND: (hugs FEMALE CHRIS) 'Course you don't.

FEMALE CHRIS: Do I smell bad?

FEMALE FRIEND: Of course you don't! (Sniffs her.) Maybe a little day-old perfume.

FEMALE CHRIS: Really?

FEMALE FRIEND: No, no, no. I was kidding.

FEMALE CHRIS: I don't want kidding right now.

FEMALE FRIEND: Of course you don't! (Hugs her again.) There!

FEMALE CHRIS: Are you a lesbian?

FEMALE FRIEND: This is my reward for comforting you?

FEMALE CHRIS: Are you part of the Gay Agenda?

FEMALE FRIEND: I am the Gay Agenda. And I've been waiting to pounce on your agenda for years.

FEMALE CHRIS: Now I know you're kidding? … Aren't you?

FEMALE FRIEND: I must say you think very highly of yourself.

FEMALE CHRIS: It's Chris's fault. He's made me feel undesirable, and I …

FEMALE FRIEND: Took it out on me.

FEMALE CHRIS: There's nothing wrong with being a lesbian.

FEMALE FRIEND: I know that.

FEMALE CHRIS: As long as you're a nice lesbian.

FEMALE FRIEND: I think you don't even have to be a nice one anymore, and it's still okay.

FEMALE CHRIS: Really? I haven't been keeping up.

FEMALE FRIEND: Anyway, I'm not a lesbian, and I'm sorry I came over. So I'd better be – (Starts to leave.)

FEMALE CHRIS: Wait! Don't go. I need your non-lesbian advice on Chris.

FEMALE FRIEND: Is he a lesbian?

FEMALE CHRIS: I don't think so.

FEMALE FRIEND: Is he thinking of turning lesbian?

FEMALE CHRIS: If he were turning into a lesbian, he'd probably want to touch me, a woman, not run away from me. Unless I'm not his type, even as a lesbian.

FEMALE FRIEND: Lesbians have types?

FEMALE CHRIS: I suppose they do. Doesn't everybody?

FEMALE FRIEND: Let's get off this topic, what do you say?

FEMALE CHRIS: I could ask Chris if he's turning into a lesbian.

FEMALE FRIEND: Would he tell you?

FEMALE CHRIS: Of course that would mean he'd have to change sex first and then change into a lesbian, wouldn't it?

FEMALE FRIEND: Beats me.

FEMALE CHRIS: Why is life so complicated?

FEMALE FRIEND: It's not. Do you want me to speak to Chris?

FEMALE CHRIS: You'd speak to Chris?

FEMALE FRIEND: No. But do you want me to?

FEMALE CHRIS: I don't know what you'd say.

FEMALE FRIEND: I'd come right to the point and ask: "Why don't you want to touch her anymore?"

FEMALE CHRIS: You wouldn't! You wouldn't have the nerve.

FEMALE FRIEND: Yes, I would.

FEMALE CHRIS: He'd accuse you of butting in.

FEMALE FRIEND: I'd say you asked me to.

FEMALE CHRIS: You can't do that!

FEMALE FRIEND: Do you want my help or not?

FEMALE CHRIS: You'd ask him point blank why he is being so standoffish?!

FEMALE FRIEND: What do you think he'll say?

FEMALE CHRIS: I don't know. I don't think I want to know.

FEMALE FRIEND: I don't think I can help you.

FEMALE CHRIS: Sure you can.

FEMALE FRIEND: I'm leaving.

FEMALE CHRIS: (loudly) No!

FEMALE FRIEND: (loudly) Yes!

(FEMALE FRIEND exits.)

FEMALE CHRIS: Friends, my ass!

BLACKOUT

SCENE 5

(Enter MALE CHRIS to FEMALE CHRIS, who is sorting laundry.)

MALE CHRIS: (low key) Hi.

FEMALE CHRIS: (low key) Hi.

MALE CHRIS: How's your day been?

FEMALE CHRIS: So so.

MALE CHRIS: Mine too. I almost got fired.

FEMALE CHRIS: (no reaction)

MALE CHRIS: I filed some wrong paperwork.

FEMALE CHRIS: (holding up a pair of shorts) Do you want these? They're ripped.

MALE CHRIS: You don't care that I was almost fired?

FEMALE CHRIS: (about the shorts) Do you want these or not?

MALE CHRIS: I don't know.

(FEMALE CHRIS throws the shorts on the floor.)

MALE CHRIS: Hey!

FEMALE CHRIS: They're dirty already.

MALE CHRIS: Are you talking to your friends about us?

FEMALE CHRIS: (after thinking it over) No. Are you?

MALE CHRIS: (after thinking it over) No.

BOTH: (together) Good!

FEMALE CHRIS: I never talk about my dirty laundry with others.

MALE CHRIS: I could say that you used to tell your mother that I had a crooked dick. But I won't.

FEMALE CHRIS: You used to tell your mother that I had a loose pussy.

MALE CHRIS: I did not!

FEMALE CHRIS: Ah, but you did.

MALE CHRIS: I seriously doubt that you and my mother discussed your pussy. Ever!

FEMALE CHRIS: How little you know women.

MALE CHRIS: And how little you know men.

FEMALE CHRIS: Men are from Mars. They're Martians.

MALE CHRIS: And women are from Venus. Venus Fly-Traps.

FEMALE CHRIS: (making a sound) Buzz, buzz!

MALE CHRIS: I'm sorry if I have hurt your feelings in some way.

FEMALE CHRIS: Feelings? Who has feelings?

MALE CHRIS: I'm trying to apologize.

FEMALE CHRIS: Is that what this is? It's hard to tell.

MALE CHRIS: I just want there to be peace between us.

FEMALE CHRIS: But why? The other is so much more exciting.

MALE CHRIS: I don't like the tension.

FEMALE CHRIS: There's always tension between men and women.

MALE CHRIS: There doesn't have to be.

FEMALE CHRIS: Apparently there does.

MALE CHRIS: Do you want a divorce?

FEMALE CHRIS: Um, not today. I guess.

MALE CHRIS: Tomorrow?

FEMALE CHRIS: Who knows.

MALE CHRIS: Want to take a lover, Lady Chatterley?

FEMALE CHRIS: Thanks.

MALE CHRIS: I mean …

FEMALE CHRIS: I know what you mean. You want to take a lover. But no thanks.

MALE CHRIS: I think men get restless.

FEMALE CHRIS: And women don't?!

MALE CHRIS: Don't start lecturing, please!

FEMALE CHRIS: Perhaps you need a lecture.

MALE CHRIS: I can lecture too, you know.

FEMALE CHRIS: Go ahead.

MALE CHRIS: Believe me I can. I just didn't do it before.

FEMALE CHRIS: Wonderful you. How restrained.

MALE CHRIS: I didn't because I wanted sex from you.

FEMALE CHRIS: And now that you don't want it, you can say what's been bottled up. Is that it?

MALE CHRIS: Pretty much.

FEMALE CHRIS: That doesn't say very much about your inherent honesty.

MALE CHRIS: No, but it does about my sex drive.

FEMALE CHRIS: What makes you think I want your precious body so much? Trust me, it's not that great!

MALE CHRIS: I know it's not that great.

FEMALE CHRIS: A little affection doesn't have to lead to you thrusting and grunting like a rabid monkey.

MALE CHRIS: It doesn't?

FEMALE CHRIS: Lord knows, it doesn't take that long. You'd think you'd hardly miss the time!

MALE CHRIS: Finished with the insults?

FEMALE CHRIS: I've just started. Got any for me?

MALE CHRIS: Be careful what you wish for.

FEMALE CHRIS: I can handle it. Get it off your chest. Let's clear the air around here. (Swipes at the air.)

MALE CHRIS: It might poison the air.

FEMALE CHRIS: Let's see, shall we?

MALE CHRIS: I'm not trying to insult you.

FEMALE CHRIS: That's funny. You've managed to do so amazingly well without even trying.

BLACKOUT

SCENE 6

   (Enter FEMALE FRIEND to MALE CHRIS.)

FEMALE FRIEND: You called?

MALE CHRIS: (exercising) I was about to.

FEMALE FRIEND: I got right on it.

MALE CHRIS: Did Chris ask you to talk to me?

FEMALE FRIEND: No. Yes. Sort of. It was my idea.

MALE CHRIS: I think it's past the talking stage.

FEMALE FRIEND: You're never past the talking stage.

MALE CHRIS: How much did he tell you?

FEMALE FRIEND: Just that you're having intimacy issues.

MALE CHRIS: Intimacy issues?! Like a rash?

FEMALE FRIEND: I'd like to help.

MALE CHRIS: Jesus! How intrusive! Is nothing off-limits?

FEMALE FRIEND: Chris wants to save your marriage. And so do I.

MALE CHRIS: Well, you can't.

FEMALE FRIEND: He can't figure out what she's done wrong.

MALE CHRIS: He's done nothing wrong. There is no wrong here. It's
    just over.

FEMALE FRIEND: And yet you don't want a divorce?

MALE CHRIS: Divorces are expensive.

FEMALE FRIEND: She'll give you a clean break and ask for nothing.

MALE CHRIS: I don't believe it.

FEMALE: Your money and her money can be separated.

MALE CHRIS: That'll be a first!

FEMALE FRIEND: Chris has always kept her money separate from
    yours.

MALE CHRIS: Is that what she tells you? It's not true. She has mooched and leeched off me for years.

FEMALE FRIEND: Mooched and leeched? My, that sounds like a loving husband!

MALE CHRIS: I've never bought into this dynamic that the man is supposed to pay.

FEMALE FRIEND: Why? Too stingy?

MALE CHRIS: I don't like being taken advantage of. It's also like I'm paying for sex. I don't like being a John to a prostitute!

FEMALE FRIEND: Wow! Is that how you see it? Most people don't.

MALE CHRIS: Most people are blind to their own victimization. I don't care that most men are brainwashed into giving diamond rings and flowers and houses and cars in order to secure a regular supply of vaginal, oral, or anal.

FEMALE FRIEND: Well, women put up with a lot that don't want in order to be married! A lot!

MALE CHRIS: You're making my point for me. Give me presents and I'll give you a body part! It's disgusting!

FEMALE FRIEND: You're reducing it to –

MALE CHRIS: I'm reducing it to what it is! Well, I'm fed up with participating in the system.

FEMALE FRIEND: Chris doesn't ask for things from you.

MALE CHRIS: Of course she does. Every time we go out to dinner she expects me to pay.

FEMALE FRIEND: Well, the man pays.

MALE CHRIS: Well, this man doesn't want to. And never did want to.

FEMALE FRIEND: So you want Chris to pay for your dinners?

MALE CHRIS: I want her to pay for her own dinners, not always smiling and being coy and flirtatious when it comes time to pay the bill.

FEMALE FRIEND: Everybody does it. Why does it bother you so much?

MALE CHRIS: Because it makes me feel like I can't get a date, a kiss, a cuddle, or an orgasm unless I pay for it!

FEMALE FRIEND: Well, women don't make as much as men.

MALE CHRIS: Please! Even when they make more than men, they want men to pay! I dated a lot more women than you ever did. So don't tell me what women do and don't do and want and don't want!

FEMALE FRIEND: You never should have married, Chris or anybody else.

MALE CHRIS: No, the institution of marriage should be different!

FEMALE FRIEND: I somehow doubt that's going to happen.

MALE CHRIS: Change has to start somewhere.

FEMALE FRIEND: And this is what's behind it all?

MALE CHRIS: It isn't just one thing.

FEMALE FRIEND: So when you wife tries to hug you, you view it as some kind of "financial" overture? Have I got that right?

MALE CHRIS: Don't go telling Chris all this!

FEMALE FRIEND: Why not? How else are things going to get better?

MALE CHRIS: Things aren't going to get better. She is what she is, and I'm no longer what I was. So things are not going to get "better."

FEMALE FRIEND: Then maybe "bitter" if not "better"?

MALE CHRIS: I think you've got it.

BLACKOUT

SCENE 7

(Lights up halfway.)

MALE CHRIS: (in bed by himself) … Are you awake?

FEMALE CHRIS: (in separate bed) … No.

MALE CHRIS: Do you want to talk or go to sleep?

FEMALE CHRIS: I am asleep.

MALE CHRIS: … Okay.

FEMALE CHRIS: What do you want to talk about?

MALE CHRIS: Never mind. I just thought you might want to talk.

FEMALE CHRIS: You're so thoughtful.

MALE CHRIS: (very flat) That's me.

FEMALE CHRIS: So smug.

MALE CHRIS: Boo!

FEMALE CHRIS: Boo?

MALE CHRIS: I'm scaring the ghosts out of our bedroom.

FEMALE CHRIS: Is that what you think is in our bedroom?

MALE CHRIS: Maybe we should have separate bedrooms.

FEMALE CHRIS: Good idea. You snore like a buzz saw anyway.

MALE CHRIS: So do you.

FEMALE CHRIS: I do not.

MALE CHRIS: Whatever.

FEMALE CHRIS: You also fart.

MALE CHRIS: I'm sorry.

FEMALE CHRIS: Do I fart?

MALE CHRIS: …No.

FEMALE CHRIS: You sure?

MALE CHRIS: I'm sure.

FEMALE CHRIS: You're quite the catch.

MALE CHRIS: (Doesn't reply.)

FEMALE CHRIS: A snoring, farting Romeo.

MALE CHRIS: (Doesn't reply.)

FEMALE CHRIS: But I made my bed. How does the rest of it go?

MALE CHRIS: Now you must lie in it.

FEMALE CHRIS: And you in yours.

MALE CHRIS: (Doesn't answer.)

FEMALE CHRIS: Do you love me at all? Is there anything left?

MALE CHRIS: Yes.

FEMALE CHRIS: Lucky me. I guess I'll have a bedtime snack, on those crumbs.

MALE CHRIS: Actually there is a lot of love left.

FEMALE CHRIS: Really?

MALE CHRIS: Of course.

FEMALE CHRIS: Of course? Now I know everything: you're lying in your bed, and you're *lying* in your bed.

SLOW FADE

SCENE 8

(Lights up, both CHRISES fully dressed.)

FEMALE CHRIS: Did you sleep well?

MALE CHRIS: Well enough. You?

FEMALE CHRIS: I slept like a baby.

MALE CHRIS: Good for you.

FEMALE CHRIS: I cried all night.

MALE CHRIS: I'm sorry. …You did not!

(There is the sound of some critter scratching at a door slightly offstage.)

FEMALE CHRIS: What's that noise?

MALE CHRIS: Is it Pookie? (calling) Pookie?

FEMALE CHRIS: It doesn't sound like her.

MALE CHRIS: That's the cat door, right?

(Another scratching sound is heard.)

FEMALE CHRIS: I assume so.

MALE CHRIS: It's raccoons.

FEMALE CHRIS: I thought that was over, they were gone.

MALE CHRIS: They remember.

FEMALE CHRIS: You shouldn't have left cat food out.

MALE CHRIS: That was a year ago.

FEMALE CHRIS: They remember.

MALE CHRIS: What are we going to do about it?

FEMALE CHRIS: They don't usually come in the daytime.

MALE CHRIS: Do you have the soaker gun?

FEMALE CHRIS: I thought you had it.

MALE CHRIS: I think I know where it is. (Hurries off, away from the scratching noise.)

FEMALE CHRIS: (calling) Make sure it's cold water, not hot!

MALE CHRIS: (calling) Maybe it I use hot, they'll stay away this time!

FEMALE CHRIS: (calling) Don't scald the raccoon! They were four of them last time, with two babies!

MALE CHRIS: (calling) I promise not to scald the babies. Just the adults.

FEMALE CHRIS: (calling) You can't scald the parents! Who will look after the babies?!

MALE CHRIS: (re-entering with a soaker gun) So sensitive!

FEMALE CHRIS: What are you doing?

MALE CHRIS: I'm getting some water for this gun. It evaporated.

FEMALE CHRIS: Put some soap in the water.

MALE CHRIS: I'm on it! No scalding, just soap in their eyes!

FEMALE CHRIS: Hurry up! They're going to get away!

(There is another sound of scratching offstage.)

MALE CHRIS: They're bold.

(Sound of attempted forced entrance against the cat door.)

MALE CHRIS: Jesus!

FEMALE CHRIS: Wait! (Runs offstage the same way he did earlier.)

MALE CHRIS: Are you going to help me with this or not?

FEMALE CHRIS: (calling) I'm getting something! … I'm looking!

MALE CHRIS: (calling) I'm going to the cat door!

FEMALE CHRIS: (calling) Wait for me!

MALE CHRIS: (calling) They're going to get away!

FEMALE CHRIS: (re-entering with a flag folded around a stick) I found it!

MALE CHRIS: What's that?

FEMALE CHRIS: (unfurling the flag) A flag. (Waves it about.) To scare away the raccoons!

MALE CHRIS: Do you want them to laugh at you?

FEMALE CHRIS: They won't be laughing when I shake this at their babies! (Waves and shakes the flag.)

(Another sound of forced entrance at the cat door.)

MALE CHRIS: (Hurries offstage toward the sound.) (offstage) Its face is halfway through the cat door!

FEMALE CHRIS: (calling) Shoot it with the soaker!

MALE CHRIS: (calling) I don't have any water in it yet!

FEMALE CHRIS: (calling) Oh, for God's sake, shoot it. Shoot it!

MALE CHRIS: (calling) The plug is stuck! I don't think I can get any
water into it!

FEMALE CHRIS: (calling) Shoot it!

(He slowly re-enters with soaker at his side.)

MALE CHRIS: Are we still talking about the raccoons?

(Another harder sound of a raccoon at the cat door.)

BLACKOUT

SCENE 9

(Lights up on FEMALE FRIEND, who is using a toothpick
assiduously.)

MALE CHRIS: (entering) Can we talk?

FEMALE FRIEND: Don't you knock?

MALE CHRIS: I did. You didn't answer.

FEMALE FRIEND: Maybe that's for a reason.

MALE CHRIS: Continue with what you were doing.

FEMALE FRIEND: I intend to. (Picks at teeth.)

MALE CHRIS: It's about me and Chris.

FEMALE FRIEND: When isn't it?

MALE CHRIS: There's a lot of anger there.

FEMALE FRIEND: I'm not taking sides. Just give Chris what she wants.

MALE CHRIS: You're no help!

FEMALE FRIEND: Do I still have that piece of kale in my teeth? (Shows teeth.)

MALE CHRIS: I don't think so.

FEMALE FRIEND: I can still feel it.

MALE CHRIS: You're fine.

FEMALE FRIEND: No, I'm not. I have kale stuck in my teeth. I don't feel comfortable trying to remove it with you watching me.

MALE CHRIS: Yeah, it is pretty gross.

FEMALE FRIEND: Well, you're the one who barged in! Not me!

MALE CHRIS: What if I turn my back? (Turns his back.) Like this.

FEMALE FRIEND: You can still hear me picking.

MALE CHRIS: Try me.

FEMALE FRIEND: (Uses the toothpick.) How's that?

MALE CHRIS: I can barely hear it.

FEMALE FRIEND: What do you want me to say?

MALE CHRIS: Tell me how to save my relationship with Chris, without sex.

FEMALE FRIEND: Maybe it's not possible.

MALE CHRIS: You think so?

FEMALE FRIEND: Close your eyes and think of England.

MALE CHRIS: When I close my eyes, I think of her doing stuff that completely turns me off.

FEMALE FRIEND: Such as?

MALE CHRIS: The way she drives – she's dangerous. The way she can be so passive with her mother. It drives me crazy! The way she wants me to stop the raccoons from getting in and then won't let me actually stop them once and for all.

FEMALE FRIEND: Sounds like you're making up excuses.

MALE CHRIS: No, I'm not! I have built up a ton of bad memories and can't get them out of my head.

FEMALE FRIEND: Maybe you should see a therapist.

MALE CHRIS: I thought you were my therapist.

FEMALE FRIEND: I'm afraid I'm nobody's therapist.

MALE CHRIS: The way she tickles Pookie's butt. It's obscene!

FEMALE FRIEND: What?!

MALE CHRIS: It's thing after thing after thing. Sometimes it's the very thing I used to love about her. And now I can't stand that very thing! Does that make any sense?

BLACKOUT

SCENE 10

(MALE CHRIS is sitting on a sofa, reading a book.)

(Enter FEMALE CHRIS, agitated.)

FEMALE CHRIS: What are you doing?

MALE CHRIS: (gestures to the book) What does it look like?

FEMALE CHRIS: I had a terrible day at work today.

MALE CHRIS: Change jobs.

FEMALE CHRIS: I want sex. To calm my nerves.

MALE CHRIS: (about the book) Have you read this?

FEMALE CHRIS: I want sex. Now.

MALE CHRIS: What is that supposed to mean?

FEMALE CHRIS: What?!

MALE CHRIS: I can never figure out what women want.

FEMALE CHRIS: You're not funny.

MALE CHRIS: Did I say I was funny?

FEMALE CHRIS: I want you to do me.

MALE CHRIS: Sounds like a trap to me. Are you Vice Squad?

FEMALE CHRIS: My boss wants me.

MALE CHRIS: Well, good for him! Is he the one with the piercing?

FEMALE CHRIS: Yes. In his eyebrow.

MALE CHRIS: You hate piercings.

FEMALE CHRIS: Yes.

MALE CHRIS: (about the book) This is really good. It's about snakes.

FEMALE CHRIS: I hate snakes.

MALE CHRIS: Or maybe it's about leprechauns.

FEMALE CHRIS: I hate leprechauns.

MALE CHRIS: You're hard to please.

FEMALE CHRIS: Can a woman rape a man?

MALE CHRIS: Now we're getting heavy.

FEMALE CHRIS: No, maybe we're getting somewhere.

MALE CHRIS: Call me old-fashioned, but I don't think that's a good idea.

FEMALE CHRIS: I wonder what it feels like to rape a man.

MALE CHRIS: God, it must have really been a rotten day at work.

FEMALE CHRIS: Make him scream as you thrust a dildo or something into him.

MALE CHRIS: (laughing) A dildo?

FEMALE CHRIS: A sharp dildo, with serrated edges.

MALE CHRIS: You've thought too much about this.

FEMALE CHRIS: Until he shits himself. And weeps.

MALE CHRIS: Is that from a poem?

FEMALE CHRIS: Yeah, the one I'm writing.

MALE CHRIS: Lyrical or narrative?

FEMALE CHRIS: I haven't decided yet.

MALE CHRIS: Can't wait to read it.

FEMALE CHRIS: You'll be the first to read it. And the last.

MALE CHRIS: You're scaring me.

FEMALE CHRIS: I want sex.

MALE CHRIS: I don't want sex.

BLACKOUT

SCENE 11

(Lights up on MALE CHRIS, brushing his teeth. It does not have to be realistic.)

(Enter FEMALE CHRIS, carrying a jar.)

FEMALE CHRIS: Can you open this? (Shows him the jar.)

MALE CHRIS: You can't?

FEMALE CHRIS: Evidently not.

MALE CHRIS: There's a new can opener in the top drawer. It has a hook for jars.

FEMALE CHRIS: I tried it. It didn't work.

MALE CHRIS: Did you bang on the top with a heavy spoon and then twist with a dish towel?

FEMALE CHRIS: Can't you just open it?

MALE CHRIS: Here, let me see it.

(He hands the jar over. MALE CHRIS tries to open it but can't.)

MALE CHRIS: (straining) Can't do it. (Hands the jar back.)

FEMALE CHRIS: You didn't try very hard.

MALE CHRIS: You didn't try very hard either.

FEMALE CHRIS: How do you know?

MALE CHRIS: Maybe the jar just doesn't want to open.

FEMALE CHRIS: But I want a pickle.

MALE CHRIS: You want a … ? (Shows frustration with her.)

FEMALE CHRIS: Why do you have to make everything about *you*?!

MALE CHRIS: About me? Oh, God! Here, give it to me! (Reaches for the jar.)

FEMALE CHRIS: Don't break it.

MALE CHRIS: Perhaps that's the only way to get it open.

FEMALE CHRIS: I could get a hammer.

MALE CHRIS: You could. But let me try again. (He tries to twist the lid off, can't.)

FEMALE CHRIS: A real man could get it off.

MALE CHRIS: A strong woman could get it off even faster.

FEMALE CHRIS: It's about upper body strength.

MALE CHRIS: Oh, I thought it was because of sexism.

FEMALE CHRIS: Give it to me. (Gestures for the jar.) I'm sorry I asked.

MALE CHRIS: So am I.

FEMALE CHRIS: Give it to me!

MALE CHRIS: Why do men always have to do the shit work?

FEMALE CHRIS: Because they get all the perks!

MALE CHRIS: No, they don't. Not anymore. But they sure get the shit work.

FEMALE CHRIS: It's getting impossible to be around you anymore.

MALE CHRIS: And yet you stay!

FEMALE CHRIS: (about to cry) You're mean.

MALE CHRIS: Now you're going to cry! No, *you're* mean! You cry or threaten to cry and I do the shit work. How equal is that?!

FEMALE CHRIS: I do shit work!

MALE CHRIS: Only when you can't get out of it. (imitating her) "Oh, Chris, can't you carry the groceries up from the car? Please!"

FEMALE CHRIS: I only do it because I know you like to carry the groceries up from the car!

MALE CHRIS: Bull! (imitating her) "Oh, Chris, can't you lift my seventeen bags into the trunk of the car? Pretty please!"

FEMALE CHRIS: Seventeen bags won't fit into the trunk of the car! So I'd never ask.

MALE CHRIS: (imitating her) "Oh, Chris, can you re-program my DVR for the thousandth time? I must have touched something!"

FEMALE CHRIS: (shouting) A marriage is supposed to be a partnership! A partnership!

MALE CHRIS: (shouting) Exactly my point!

BLACKOUT

(Sound of a glass jar crashing in the dark.)

SCENE 12

(Lights up on both CHRISES at a table in a restaurant, opposite each other. There is a candle.)

MALE CHRIS: (looking around) This is nice.

FEMALE CHRIS: It is. Very romantic.

MALE CHRIS: Good choice.

FEMALE CHRIS: (looking over the menu) I'm feeling vegetarian.

MALE CHRIS: (looking over his menu) Good choice.

FEMALE CHRIS: I'm paying.

MALE CHRIS: No need to.

FEMALE CHRIS: I'm paying.

MALE CHRIS: Good choice.

FEMALE CHRIS: Stop saying that.

MALE CHRIS: Bad choice?

FEMALE CHRIS: I can't seem to win.

MALE CHRIS: I know the feeling.

FEMALE CHRIS: (about the menu) They have quesadillas.

MALE CHRIS: Interesting choice.

FEMALE CHRIS: Do you know that they tax tampons?

MALE CHRIS: I beg your pardon?

FEMALE CHRIS: Because they're for women.

MALE CHRIS: They tax men's things!

FEMALE CHRIS: No, they don't.

MALE CHRIS: Yes, they do.

FEMALE CHRIS: It's part of the War on Women.

MALE CHRIS: That's quite a slogan.

FEMALE CHRIS: You don't think there's a War on Women?

MALE CHRIS: As a matter of fact, no.

FEMALE CHRIS: You used to call yourself a feminist, back when we
    first got together.

MALE CHRIS: I've grown.

FEMALE CHRIS: Grown? So now you're back to being a sexist pig?

MALE CHRIS: Let's just say I'm an *ex*-feminist.

FEMALE CHRIS: (makes scoffing sound)

MALE CHRIS: I am.

FEMALE CHRIS: Since when?!

MALE CHRIS: Let's have a pleasant evening.

FEMALE CHRIS: Since when?

MALE CHRIS: Since feminism went from an A-plus idea to a C-minus one.

FEMALE CHRIS: What?!

MALE CHRIS: You asked.

FEMALE CHRIS: We haven't even begun the fight yet!

MALE CHRIS: Down with those tampon taxes!

FEMALE CHRIS: You think that's a C-minus idea?

MALE CHRIS: Dump those tampons in Boston Harbor!

FEMALE CHRIS: Not funny.

MALE CHRIS: Of course not. Only men and their body parts are funny.

FEMALE CHRIS: You want to make fun of women's body parts?

MALE CHRIS: Every social movement eventually goes to the C-minus version of itself. Or lower. Full of half-truths and great big pieties.

FEMALE CHRIS: You have a problem with strong women.

MALE CHRIS: No. ... But I don't want to fuck them.

FEMALE CHRIS: Nice!

MALE CHRIS: It may not be nice, but it's what I think. Shall we order?

BLACKOUT

SCENE 13

(Lights up on MALE CHRIS crouching far upstage right.)

(Enter FEMALE CHRIS, not sure where he is.)

FEMALE CHRIS: I know you're in here somewhere.

MALE CHRIS: (Puts his hand over his mouth.)

FEMALE CHRIS: I want a baby. … Did you hear me? I want a baby!

MALE CHRIS: (after a pause) Buy one.

FEMALE CHRIS: (seeing him) You owe me a baby.

MALE CHRIS: (sarcastically) Yeah, just what we need.

FEMALE CHRIS: You thinking I'm joking?

MALE CHRIS: Probably not.

FEMALE CHRIS: Did you hear me? I want a baby.

MALE CHRIS: (emerging from hiding) Okay, I'll buy you a baby.

FEMALE CHRIS: Or we could adopt!

MALE CHRIS: Even worse idea.

FEMALE CHRIS: It would bring us together.

MALE CHRIS: Or tear us even more apart.

FEMALE CHRIS: I saw this brochure. All those big, sad eyes.

MALE CHRIS: Do you not know the statistics on adopted children?

FEMALE CHRIS: We could get one from Moldova.

MALE CHRIS: No.

FEMALE CHRIS: It would be so grateful.

MALE CHRIS: They always turn out to be horrible. They slash their new family to death.

FEMALE CHRIS: We'd save a life.

MALE CHRIS: And then eat that family.

FEMALE CHRIS: Bring some love into this relationship.

MALE CHRIS: Then feed their bones to the raccoons.

FEMALE CHRIS: Do good for once.

MALE CHRIS: No good deed goes unpunished.

FEMALE CHRIS: Why are you always so negative?

MALE CHRIS: Then blacken their reputations as parents. Posthumously.

FEMALE CHRIS: Thank god, I don't listen to you.

MALE CHRIS: Say we tried to sodomize them in their cribs.

FEMALE CHRIS: You probably would try to sodomize them in their cribs!

MALE CHRIS: Then we agree after all? We shouldn't adopt.

FEMALE CHRIS: It was just an idea.

MALE CHRIS: So was Auschwitz.

FEMALE CHRIS: I think we are reaching a crescendo in this marriage.

MALE CHRIS: With a happy ending?

BLACKOUT

SCENE 14

> (Lights up on FEMALE CHRIS sitting in a chair, which represents a car, facing the audience.)

> (Lights up a cigarette or a joint or perhaps just opens a package of gum and begins to chew.)

> (Stares over the heads of the audience.)

> (Mimes turning on the car's radio. Music.)

> (Continues to stare at something in the distance.)

> (Enter MALE CHRIS, comes up to the car, taps on the window.)

FEMALE CHRIS: (not startled) You startled me.

MALE CHRIS: What are you doing out here in the car?

FEMALE CHRIS: Hanging out.

MALE CHRIS: It's five A.M.

FEMALE CHRIS: So?

MALE CHRIS: What are you doing?!

FEMALE CHRIS: What do you care?

MALE CHRIS: You're on the street. It's not safe.

FEMALE CHRIS: I'm fine. I'm listening to the radio.

MALE CHRIS: You can't listen in the house?

FEMALE CHRIS: It's peaceful out here. So calm.

MALE CHRIS: You're acting weird.

FEMALE CHRIS: Go back to sleep.

MALE CHRIS: I worry about you.

FEMALE CHRIS: Yeah.

MALE CHRIS: I do.

FEMALE CHRIS: I'm fine!

MALE CHRIS: I saw you staring at something.

FEMALE CHRIS: You going to call the police?

MALE CHRIS: Should I?

FEMALE CHRIS: I'm meditating.

MALE CHRIS: You were staring. Are you stalking somebody?

FEMALE CHRIS: Don't worry, it wasn't you.

MALE CHRIS: What is it you see? (He looks where she was staring.)

FEMALE CHRIS: Do you really want to know?

MALE CHRIS: I do.

FEMALE CHRIS: Our neighbor likes to undress for me.

MALE CHRIS: What?!

FEMALE CHRIS: Three doors down – Mr. Chow.

MALE CHRIS: That's hilarious.

FEMALE CHRIS: He loves to strip. I love to watch.

MALE CHRIS: You're not serious. Are you?

FEMALE CHRIS: He dances for me too.

MALE CHRIS: Mr. Chow? He must be seventy.

FEMALE CHRIS: He's still very limber.

MALE CHRIS: Does he know it's you?

FEMALE CHRIS: Of course he knows it's me. It's just for me.

MALE CHRIS: What about his wife?

FEMALE CHRIS: It's after she goes to bed. And after you go to bed.

MALE CHRIS: And what else goes on after I go to bed?

FEMALE CHRIS: He does his special moves.

MALE CHRIS: I think that's illegal. Pornography.

FEMALE CHRIS: Oh, he doesn't do anything dirty. Just graceful.

MALE CHRIS: Oh, that's tai chi!

FEMALE CHRIS: How would you know what it is?!

MALE CHRIS: (imitating tai chi) He's not dancing for you! He's doing his exercises!

FEMALE CHRIS: I guess it's all in the eye of the beholder.

MALE CHRIS: You're going to get arrested as a Peeping Tom!

FEMALE CHRIS: He leaves his shade up. He mouths things at me.

MALE CHRIS: He mouths things? What things?

FEMALE CHRIS: Wonderful, intimate things. Just for me.

MALE CHRIS: Are you sure you don't need an eye exam?

FEMALE CHRIS: Leave it to you to ruin a beautiful experience.

MALE CHRIS: Come back inside. Okay?

FEMALE CHRIS: Why go back in there, when I can have the loveliness of the night out here?

BLACKOUT

SCENE 15

(Lights up on FEMALE CHRIS in garden with gardening shears.)

(Enter FEMALE FRIEND.)

FEMALE FRIEND: There you are! I looked all over the house.

FEMALE CHRIS: You have to tend to your garden sometimes.

FEMALE FRIEND: (looking around) Your garden looks great! I don't think I've ever been out here before.

FEMALE CHRIS: It's overgrown. Those trumpet plants have gotten out of hand. (She snips at some invisible plants.)

FEMALE FRIEND: I thought I'd check to see how you are. You and Chris.

FEMALE CHRIS: We're magical.

FEMALE FRIEND: Magical?

FEMALE CHRIS: We haven't spoken in a week.

FEMALE FRIEND: That's not good.

FEMALE CHRIS: Better than screaming at each other.

FEMALE FRIEND: Well, there is that.

FEMALE CHRIS: (a bit loopy) Mary, Mary, quite contrary, how does your garden grow? (Snips at invisible plants.)

FEMALE FRIEND: Are you all right, Chris?

FEMALE CHRIS: Don't I seem all right?

FEMALE FRIEND: Frankly, no.

FEMALE CHRIS: I'm fine. I finally know what I am going to do about Chris and me.

FEMALE FRIEND: Do you want to tell me?

FEMALE CHRIS: I don't think it's a happy ending.

FEMALE FRIEND: So you're going ahead with a divorce.

FEMALE CHRIS: Something like that.

FEMALE FRIEND: Has he finally agreed? Or you've agreed?

FEMALE CHRIS: Something like that.

FEMALE FRIEND: Where is he? I didn't see him.

FEMALE CHRIS: In the shower. Did you look in there?

FEMALE FRIEND: No.

FEMALE CHRIS: He likes showers, long showers. I tell him he's wasting water. I haven't watered these plants out here for ages, and yet they grow and grow. Why is that?

FEMALE FRIEND: (concerned about her friend) I don't know. They're hardy? It's good to be hardy, in this life.

FEMALE CHRIS: God, you're boring!

FEMALE FRIEND: What?!

FEMALE CHRIS: Every word out of your mouth is boring as hell.

FEMALE FRIEND: Hey, I'm just trying to help.

FEMALE CHRIS: I get it. You're trying to numb my pain by making me so bored I can't feel anything.

FEMALE FRIEND: Chris!

FEMALE CHRIS: So thanks. It's working.

FEMALE FRIEND: Maybe I should come back some other time.

FEMALE CHRIS: Maybe you should.

FEMALE FRIEND: Are you okay?

FEMALE CHRIS: I'm at peace. Didn't you say you were leaving?

FEMALE FRIEND: Okay, if that's what you want. I hope you feel better. … I'll call you.

FEMALE CHRIS: Don't bother. Goodbye! (She snips at more invisible plants) I won't be here much longer.

FEMALE FRIEND: You won't be –

FEMALE CHRIS: Didn't we say goodbye?

FEMALE FRIEND: (unnerved) I guess we did. (She hesitates, but then exits.)

FEMALE CHRIS: (not looking at the other woman) Good.

BLACKOUT

SCENE 16

   (Lights up on FEMALE CHRIS entering, still carrying the
   garden shears. Places the shears on a table.)

FEMALE CHRIS: (shouting) Honey, are you still home?

MALE CHRIS: (calling, offstage) Still here! Was somebody here?

FEMALE CHRIS: (calling) Just Bridget.

MALE CHRIS: (calling, offstage) I thought I heard somebody.

FEMALE CHRIS: (quietly) But you couldn't be bothered to check.

MALE CHRIS: (calling, offstage) What did she want?

FEMALE CHRIS: (calling) Oh, nothing.

MALE CHRIS: (calling, offstage) Well, she must have wanted
      something!

FEMALE CHRIS: (calling) It doesn't matter. (quietly) Nothing matters.
      (calling) Are you about done?

MALE CHRIS: (calling) Just about!

FEMALE CHRIS: (quietly) Just about.

> (FEMALE CHRIS takes a key out of a pocket and examines
> it.)

FEMALE CHRIS: Key. (Places the key back into a pocket.)

> (FEMALE CHRIS walks over to the closet door and opens it.)

FEMALE CHRIS: Closet door. (Leaves it open.)

> (FEMALE CHRIS gets a bottle of red wine that she has
> already de-corked.)

FEMALE CHRIS: Red wine.

> (She gets two wine glasses and puts them on the table. Takes a
> powder out of a pocket, opens it, and pours it into one of the
> wine glasses.)

FEMALE CHRIS: Powder.

(FEMALE CHRIS pours wine into both glasses. Looks at each.)

(Thinks of something. Goes away and comes back with a spoon.)

FEMALE CHRIS: Spoon.

(Stirs the powder in the glass. Looks at it.)

FEMALE CHRIS: How delicious.

MALE CHRIS: (calling) I'm finished!

FEMALE CHRIS: (quietly) He's finished.

MALE CHRIS: (calling) Let me dry off!

FEMALE CHRIS: (calling) Would you like some wine?

MALE CHRIS: (calling) So early?

FEMALE CHRIS: (calling) Oh, have some. It's already open.

MALE CHRIS: (calling) Oh, okay. I'm easy.

FEMALE CHRIS: (quietly) He's easy.

(Gets up and takes the garden shears from the table and hides them just offstage. She does not hurry.)

(MALE CHRIS enters with a towel around his waist, with another rubbing, drying his hair.)

MALE CHRIS: What a perfect shower.

FEMALE CHRIS: (flatly) Was it? I'm happy for you.

MALE CHRIS: Where's that wine?

FEMALE CHRIS: It's right here, freshly poured.

MALE CHRIS: Didn't you let it breathe?

FEMALE CHRIS: I did. I stirred it.

(MALE CHRIS comes to the table and takes the glass of wine
that FEMALE CHRIS points to.)

MALE CHRIS: This one?

FEMALE CHRIS: That one.

(MALE CHRIS takes a sip of his wine.)

MALE CHRIS: It tastes funny.

FEMALE CHRIS: That's because it's expensive.

MALE CHRIS: Really? (Takes another sip) A bit yucky.

FEMALE CHRIS: It'll taste much better by the time you get to the end.

MALE CHRIS: You think?

FEMALE CHRIS: Trust me.

MALE CHRIS: All right. Here goes nothing. (He drains the wine glass.)
Ah!

FEMALE CHRIS: (flatly) Ah. … Another?

MALE CHRIS: Sure. I was going to take a nap anyway.

(FEMALE CHRIS pours him a second glass of wine.)

MALE CHRIS: (reacting to the first glass) Wow! That's strong!

FEMALE CHRIS: Did it go right to your head?

MALE CHRIS: It did! What's it called?

FEMALE CHRIS: Beddy bye.

MALE CHRIS: Beddy bye? (He looks at the label.) It says Generic
Wine.

FEMALE CHRIS: That's to disguise how expensive it is. It's only for the cognoscenti.

MALE CHRIS: You're shitting me.

FEMALE CHRIS: Is that what I'm doing?

MALE CHRIS: You're acting sort of funny.

FEMALE CHRIS: Am I? How about you? How are you feeling? Funny?

MALE CHRIS: I'm (Gets groggy) I'm a little woozy.

FEMALE CHRIS: (in a mocking child's voice) Him a little woozy.

MALE CHRIS: I think I need to sit down for a minute. (Staggers)

FEMALE CHRIS: Him needs to sit down for a minute.

MALE CHRIS: Why are you talking like that?

FEMALE CHRIS: I'm talking perfectly normal. It must be the wine.

MALE CHRIS: Maybe you're right. Did you put something in the wine?

FEMALE CHRIS: … Yes. Do you feel it breathe?

MALE CHRIS: I think I'm going to pass out. (He gets up from the table.)

FEMALE CHRIS: Here, let me help you. (She gets up as well, starts to guide him.)

MALE CHRIS: Where are we going?

FEMALE CHRIS: Over here. (She guides him toward the closet.)

MALE CHRIS: Hey, the closet door is open.

FEMALE CHRIS: Is it? Well, let's close it.

(Guides him closer to the closet.)

MALE CHRIS: I think I'm going to fall.

FEMALE CHRIS: Hang on to the closet door. I'll get something.

> (He clutches the closet door. FEMALE CHRIS goes offstage
> and returns with the garden shears behind her back.)

MALE CHRIS: What have you got? Are you going to help me or not?
(He can barely stand.)

FEMALE CHRIS: Sure, honey, let me assist you.

> (Comes over and pushes him into the closet, then goes in
> herself with the garden shears in both hands.)

MALE CHRIS: What are you doing? Chris? Oh, my God, you wouldn't!

> (There is the sound of the shears snipping.)

FEMALE CHRIS: Oh, but I would!

> (We hear a scream from MALE CHRIS.)

> (FEMALE CHRIS comes out of the closet without the shears.
> She is holding something in her hand.)

> (Slams the closet door shut, takes the key from her pocket, and
> locks the door, returns the key to the pocket.)

MALE CHRIS: (inside the locked closet) Oh, my God! Oh, my God!

> (FEMALE CHRIS sits at the table, waits, then takes a sip of
> the wine without sleeping powder in it. She is still holding
> something in her hand.)

MALE CHRIS: I'm bleeding! Chris! Oh, my God! I'm bleeding to death!

FEMALE CHRIS: (quietly) Don't worry. You'll nod off soon enough.
(Takes another sip of wine.)

MALE CHRIS: Chris! Chris! Let me out! I'm going to die! My penis! My penis!

(FEMALE CHRIS throws the thing in her hand across the stage.)

FEMALE CHRIS: Who the hell cares about your goddamned penis!

(Takes another sip of wine.)

BLACKOUT

QUEEN LEAR,
a Comedy

CHARACTERS:

QUEEN LEAR, Queen of Britain, over forty

GONORRHEA, Queen Lear's eldest daughter

REAGAN, Lear's middle daughter

DUKE of ALBANY, husband of Gonorrhea

DUKE of CORNWALL, husband of Reagan

EARL of KENT

EARL of WORCHESTERSHIRE

EDGAR, son of Worchestershire, later Poor Tommy

EDMUND, a bastard

OSWALD, Gonorrhea's servant

FOOL, elfish youngster, non-binary

ASSORTED OTHERS, as needed

Plus CORDELIA, Queen Lear's youngest daughter

I.1   Enter Kent, Earl of Worchestershire, and Edmund

KENT: Is not this your son, my lord?

EARL of W: He is my bastard.

EDMUND: I am his bastard.

KENT: I cannot wish the fault undone, the issue of it being so handsome.

EARL of W: That sounds very homoerotic. Are you one of those?

KENT: Are you a homophobe?

EARL of W: A what?!

KENT: It's 500 A.D. What else can I expect!?

EARL of W: Are you coming on to my son?

KENT: I can notice that your son is handsome without coming on to him.
Jesus!

EDMUND: My services to your lordship.

KENT: Thanks, but I'm not gay.

EDMUND: I'm not gay either. Just flexible.

EARL of W: I didn't hear that! … The Queen is coming.

Sound of a coronet. Enter Lear, Cornwall, Albany, Gonorrhea,
Reagan, Cordelia.

LEAR: Attend the lords of France and Burgundy over there,
Worchestershire. (*says all the syllables*).

EARL of W: It's pronounced Woo, sire.

LEAR: Woo? Oh, whatever!

EARL of W: I shall attend them over there, my liege.

Exeunt Earl of W. and Edmund.

LEAR: Meanwhile, give me the map there. Know that we have divided
in three our queendom and 'tis our fast intent to shake all cares
and business from our age, conferring them on younger strengths,
while we unburdened crawl toward death.

REAGAN: Don't say that, Mummy!

GONORRHEA: No, don't! We love you so, Mummy!

LEAR: Tell me, my daughters, since we will divest us both of rule, interest of territory, cares of state, and common sense, which of you shall say doth love us most?

CORDELIA: (*correcting*) More. Between the two of them. More.

LEAR: Cordelia, you are always so precise.

CORDELIA: I try.

LEAR: So that we our largest bounty (among you *three*, please note) may extend, pray tell. Hint, hint. Gonorrhea, our eldest born, with such a lovely name, speak first.

GONORRHEA: Ma'am, I love you more than words can wield the matter, deeper than eyesight, bigger than a breadbox, beyond infinity, no less than life, as much as child e'er loved or mother found, so much I love thee!

LEAR: Well, that's a start.

CORDELIA: What bullshit.

GONORRHEA: Shut your mouth, she-bitch.

LEAR: And what says our second daughter, our dearest Reagan?

REAGAN: In my heart, I find that my sister, dearest Gonorrhea, names my very deed of love. Only she comes too short. My love for our mother is so profound that I don't care what you leave me in your will. In fact, I promise to die before you do and leave you everything I own!

LEAR: Well said!

CORDELIA: I like my mother some days. Other times, she's a monster. What more can I say?

LEAR: Reagan, to thee and thine remain this ample third of our fair kingdom!

REAGAN: Thanks, Mummy.

LEAR: Cordelia, my favorite, what can you say to draw a third more opulent than your sisters?

CORDELIA: Nothing.

LEAR: Nothing?

CORDELIA: Nothing.

LEAR: Nothing will come of nothing. Speak again.

CORDELIA: I love your majesty according to my bond. But you're being silly and foolish to make us praise you like we're Donald Trump's cabinet.

LEAR: Like who?

CORDELIA: Somebody in the future, who's worse than you.

LEAR: 'Silly' and 'foolish' are not the words of a grateful offspring,

CORDELIA: Making us bray in court how much we love you is not the wisdom of a monarch.

LEAR: So young and so untender.

CORDELIA: So young and true.

LEAR: Let it be so1 Thy truth shall be thy dower! Here I disclaim all my parental care and as a stranger to my heart hold thee from this forever!

KENT: My queen –

LEAR: Peace, Kent! Come not between the dragon and her wrath!

KENT: But Your Majesty –

LEAR: Majesty is right! Call Burgundy, Cornwall, and Albany. With my two remaining loving daughters' dowers digest the third. Let pride, which she thinks plainness, marry Cordelia!

CORDELIA: I don't need to marry. I can be a scribe or a milkmaid.

LEAR: Or a prostitute!

CORDELIA: Like you, Mummy? You sold yourself to the highest bidder.

LEAR: I did what any smart woman does.

CORDELIA: Well, I won't! I will sleep alone and need no royal battering ram to make me happy.

LEAR: Hence and be gone, my daughter no more!

KENT: Royal Majesty, whom I have honored as my Queen –

LEAR: Yes, blindly, blindly, blindly, like all my subjects,

KENT: Not this time!

LEAR: (*striking him*) O vassal! Stop thy mealy mouth.

KENT: No, I must tell thee when thou dost evil.

LEAR: To come betwixt our sentence and our power, take thy reward. Five days we do allot thee for provision to shield thee from disasters of the world and on the sixth turn thy hated back upon our queendom. If on the tenth day following thy banished trunk be found in our dominion, that moment is thy death!

KENT: Are you sure this is not yet another rash and impetuous act?

LEAR: If you're so wise, why won't you born a King? Huh?!

KENT: I was not born a King perhaps because I did not have ancestors who were willing to kiss ass and kill rivals to achieve such so-called greatness! (*to Cordelia*) The gods to their dear shelter take thee, maid. (*to Gonorrhea and Reagan*) And your large, well-rehearsed speeches may you future deeds approve, that good effects may spring from words of loove. [sic] Excuse my rhyme. It's circa 500 A.D.

LEAR: Your rhyme's a crime! At any time. But not mine!

KENT: Thus Kent – that is I – bids you all adieu.

LEAR: Speak Old English! Not Old French!

KENT: He'll shape his course in a country new. I'm off to Florida. Fuck you!

(*The others gasp as one.*)

Flourish, Enter Earl of Worchestershire with France and Burgundy.

EARL of W: 'Tis I, the Earl –

LEAR: – of Worchestershire. (*mangling the pronunciation*)

EARL of W: Precisely, Your Majesty.

LEAR: I know that! (*to France*) Will you with those infirmities she has take my wretch of a daughter for your wife?

FRANCE: I thought she was to pick her husband from three boxes, of lead, silver, and gold.

LEAR: We don't have time for such judicious choices as that. Will you accept Cordelia, the scorpion, or nay?

FRANCE: I must say nay. No dowry, you say?

CORDELIA: Please make known, Mother, that it is no vicious blot, murder, or foulness, no unchaste action or dishonoured step that hath deprived me of your grace and favour.

LEAR: Better thou hadst not been born than not to have pleased me better.

CORDELIA: A bit harsh, my Queen and mother. All I did was refuse to puke forth my guts in praise of you.

LEAR: Why else have children, unless, of course to till the soil or tend to our arthritis?!

CORDELIA: I do not need a mother who thinks such plans. Nor husband neither.

FRANCE: Fairest Cordelia, thee and thy virtues here I seize upon. I take up what has been cast away. More have I to say!

CORDELIA: No more, I pray! Too many words and words and words today.

FRANCE: But I can fashion them into blank verse, if I may.

CORDELIA: (*sweetly*) No more words. Especially no rhymes! Blank means no rhyme.

FRANCE: (*whispering*) My dearest, if I take thee to wed, may I at least, from time to time, perchance expect a little head?

CORDELIA: A little head? My head is little. … We'll see.

FRANCE: Then I am thine! Come, my fair Cordelia.

Exeunt France and Cordelia

GONORRHEA: (*to Reagan*) Sister, I think our mother will want to house with you.

REAGAN: And soon with you, sister dear.

GONORRHEA: You see how full of changes her old age is. She has always loved our little sister most and yet with what poor judgment hath now cast her off appears too grossly.

REAGAN: 'Tis the infirmity of her age. Yet she hath ever but slenderly known herself. We need a Place for Mom.

GONORRHEA: There is a place I know that she will hate.

REAGAN: She can't expect us to look after her just because she left us a fortune.

GONORRHEA: Indeed. My castle needs a new flying buttress. And the drafts are horrendous!

REAGAN: Mine too!

GONORRHEA: We must do something. We must look after ourselves. It's circa 500 A.D.!

Exeunt

I.2   Enter Edmund

EDMUND: Always be wary when a bastard enters alone. He's probably not happy. Wherefore should I stand in the plague of custom and permit others to deprive me for that I am some twelve or fourteen moonshines lag of a brother. Why bastard? Wherefore base/? When my dimensions are as impressive as a god's. (*Touches his crotch*) And my shape as true as honest madam's issue. Why brand they us with 'bastardy." Says who?! Just because I came not from a dull, stale, tired, legitimate bed?! Well then, legitimate Edgar, precious Edgar, I must have your land. If this letter speed and my evil invention thrive, I grow, I prosper! If only my stupid father would come by.

Enter Earl of Worchestershire

EARL of W: Edmund, how now? What news?

EDMUND: So please your lordship none. (*Ostentatiously hides the letter.*)

EARL of W: Why so earnestly seek you to put up that letter there?

EDMUND: I know no news, my lord.

EARL of W: Know no news? What paper were you reading?

EDMUND: What letter? I know no letter.

EARL of W: No, no, you do! Or perhaps I am wrong?

EDMUND: I beseech you, sir, pardon me. It is merely a letter from my brother that I have not all o'er read, and for so much as I have perused, I find it not fit for your o'erlooking. No, no!

EARL of W: Yes, yes. Give me that letter, boy.

EDMUND: No, not so, sire. I think you will hate it.

EARL of W: As I am Earl of Worchestershire, let me see it. Let me see it!

EDMUND: I'm sure my brother wrote it simply to test my virtue. (*Waves the letter.*)

EARL of W: (*grabbing and reading the letter*) "Our father is a tyrant and we should off him." What does this mean?

EDMUND: I know not, dearest father.

EARL of W: (*reading more*) "If our father would sleep until we waked him, you, Edmund, should enjoy his revenue forever." I smell a conspiracy here! My son Edgar wrote this? When came you to this? Who brought it?

EDMUND: There's the cunning of it, my lord. I found it thrown in at the casement of my closet.

EARL of W: You are in the closet?

EDMUND: My reading and writing room.

EARL of W: Oh. You know the character here to be your brother's?

EDMUND: It is his hand, my lord, but I hope his heart is not in the contents.

EARL of W: As I am an Earl, the writing is his! What more proof do I need?! Hath he never sounded you before on such?

EDMUND: Never, my lord. But I have heard him oft maintain it to be fit that, sons at perfect age and foolish fathers declined, the father should become the ward to the son, and the son thus manage the family revenue, no matter what the father wants.

EARL of W: O villain, villain! His very opinion in this letter!

EDMUND: You think so?

EARL of W: Unnatural, detested, brutish villain! Go, Edmund, seek him. I will apprehend him. Where be he?

EDMUND: He be not far. Only be most careful not to injure thyself with a false charge.

EARL of W: But it's all written there!

EDMUND: If your honour judge it meet, I will place you where you shall hear us confer of this and by the proof auricular shall you wisely have your satisfaction of his dastardly intent. In the future, they will call it the Internet.

EARL of W: He cannot be such a monster, surely.

EDMUND: Of course not. Don't call me Shirley.

EARL of W: I'll call you anything I want to!

EDMUND: Just not Shirley. Honored sire.

EARL of W: How about Gwyneth? Can I call you Gwyneth? Ha, ha!

EDMUND: As it pleases you. I will seek Edgar presently and convey the business as I shall find means, and acquaint you withal.

EARL of W: These late eclipses in the sun and moon portend no good to us. Love cools, joints creak, friendships fall off, brothers divide, girls take boys' names. Discord, bond cracked 'twixt son and father I don't mean to complain. But machinations, hollowness, treachery, monkeypox, Woe, O woe! And the true-hearted Kent banished. His offence, honesty, 'tis strange. WOE!

EDMUND: (*to the audience*) This is the excellent foppery of the world, that when we are sick in fortune – often the surfeit of our own behaviour – we make guilty of our disasters the sun, the moon, the stars, as if we are villains of necessity, knaves, thieves, assholes, by a divine thrusting-on, or our ancestors who were mistreated and we can never escape from that. Take some responsibility for yourself. And here ends the author's message. (*Enter Edgar.*). Pat, he comes! My cue is villainous melancholy, with a sigh like Tom of Bedlam. (*Big sigh.*) O these eclipses do portend these divisions. (*Sings*) Fly me to the moon!

EDGAR: How now, my brother Edmund! What serious contemplation are you in?

EDMUND: I am thinking, brother, of a prediction I read the other day.

EDGAR: Don't read bad stuff and it won't happen.

EDMUND: Of what should follow these eclipses.

EDGAR: I fear pregnant snakes under my bed, cows with seven udders!

EDMUND: Yes, and unnaturalness between the child and the parent.

EDGAR: You don't mean the "I" word?!

EDMUND: Nay. Not that. Dissolution of ancient amities, divisions in state, maledictions against king and nobles, banishment of friends, dissipations of cohorts, nuptial breaches –

EDGAR: So many, brother! You are, unlike I, glib of tongue.

EDMUND: When saw you our father last?

EDGAR: The night gone by, as you would say. Last night.

EDMUND: Spake you with him?

EDGAR: I spaked for two hours. He, like you, is verbose of tongue. He read my astronomical chart. I have a great future!

EDMUND: Parted you on good terms? Found you no displeasure in him toward you?

EDGAR: None at all. Why would he?

EDMUND: Art thou sure?

EDGAR: Some villain hath done me wrong!

EDMUND: That is my fear. Villains abound in circa 500 A.D. and forward too. Beware our father's rage. Retire with me to my lodging.

EDGAR: But I'm too young to retire.

EDMUND (*aside to audience*) My brother's none too bright. (*to Edgar*) I mean, I will bring you to hear my lord speak of you. If you go abroad, go armed.

EDGAR: I'm staying home. I'm not planning to go abroad. Armed, you say?

EDMUND: Yay, open carry! I am no honest man, if there be any good meaning toward you. Pray you, away!

EDGAR: Shall I hear from you anon?

EDMUND: You shall, as I am your non-resentful, loving brother.

Exit Edgar

A credulous father and a brother noble, and a bit stupid both, woe to their offspring, But not to me! I take after my mother. My practices ride easy. Before long, if not by birth, let me have lands by wit! I shall win by being a total shit!

I.3   Enter Gonorrhea and Oswald, her servant

GONORRHEA: Did my mother strike my gentleman for chiding of the Queen's Fool?

OSWALD: Ay, madam.

GONORRHEA: By day and night she wrongs me every hour. She commits one gross crime or other that sets us all at odds. I'll not endure it! When she returns from hunting baby foxes, I will not speak with her. Say I am sick with a plague of some dreadful kind. And you shall do well if you come slack of your former services to the Queen. The fault of it I'll answer.

OSWALD: She's coming, madam. I hear her. (*Loud offstage noise.*)

GONORRHEA: Put on what negligence you please. If she distastes it, let her let her stay with my sister, whose mind and mine I know in that are one not to be overruled by an idle old woman, that would manage those authorities that she hath given away! Now, by my life, old, demented fools are babes again and must be beaten as all the philosophers instruct. Remember, Oswald, what I have said.

OSWALD: Indeed, Madam Gonorrhea.

GONORRHEA: I'll text my sister to hold my very course.

OSWALD: I don't believe we have texts yet, Madam.

GONORRHEA: Why doesn't someone invent a text?! So that I can keep my silly old mother in check?!

I.4   Enter Kent in disguise, a bad one

KENT: Now banished Kent, in disguise, if thou canst serve where thou dost stand condemned, so may it come to pass thy royal mistress, whom thou lovest, despite my banishment, shall find thee full of labours. Such do I signal to the world my virtue! (*Crosses himself.*)

Horns within. Enter Lear with an Attendant.

LEAR: Let me not stay a jot for dinner! Go, get it ready. I want that fox for an appetizer!

Attendant exits

LEAR: What art thou? You look like Kent in disguise.

KENT: A mere peasant, ma'am. (*Keeps trying to improve his disguise throughout the scene.*)

LEAR: What wouldst thou have with us?

KENT: I do profess to be no less than I seem to serve her truly that will put me in trust.

LEAR: Yeah, yeah, so you say! Thou dost mightily resemble my late friend and counselor Kent.

KENT: As I am an honest peasant, I deny being Kent! I just request service, with a reasonable salary and no beatings.

LEAR: Who wouldst thou serve?

KENT: You.

LEAR: Dost thou know me, fellow?

KENT: No, ma'am, but you have that in your countenance which I would call royal.

LEAR: What's that?

KENT: (*after thinking*) A strong, strong woman who is very strong.

LEAR: I like this man. Go on.

KENT: Your strength is so boundless I cannot name it all. (*aside*) I know how to butter.

LEAR: I like this man indeed. What services canst thou do?

KENT: I can flatter with the best of them. And do it night and day.

LEAR: How old art thou?

KENT: Twenty-eight.

LEAR: You lie, sir! But then don't we all, when it comes to age and bloodlines. Follow me, fellow, you can serve me. Dinner. Dinner! Where's my knave, my Fool? Somebody get me my Fool! How can we have dinner without a Fool?!

Enter Attendant

LEAR: Where's that mongrel daughter of mine?

ATTENDANT: My lady, your daughter is not well.

LEAR: Gonorrhea is not well? What's wrong with her?

ATTENDANT: To my judgment, your highness is not being entertained with the ceremonious affection as you were wont.

LEAR: Ha! Sayest thou so?

ATTENDANT: I beseech your pardon, my lady, if I be mistaken, for my duty cannot be silent when I think your highness wronged.

LEAR: Aye, I have perceived a most faint neglect of late. Not a single kiss upon my ass since Tuesday last! I will look further into it. And where's my Fool? I have not seen him this two days.

ATTENDANT: Since my young lady's going into France, the Fool hath much pined away.

LEAR: No more of that! I have noted it well. Go you and tell my eldest daughter I would speak with her, plague or no plague.

ATTENDANT: Yes, my lady.

Exit Attendant

Enter Oswald

LEAR: O, you, sir, you! Come you hither. Who am I, sir?

OSWALD: My lady's ancient mother.

LEAR: My lady's ancient mother! You whoreson dog! You slave! You cur! Is a cur a dog? You are a double dog! And a skunk besides.

OSWALD: I am none of these, my lady, I beseech your pardon. Especially I am no skunk!

LEAR: Do you bandy words with me, you rascal? (*She strikes Oswald.*)

OSWALD: I'll not be stricken, my lady.

KENT: Nor tripped neither. You base … base football player? (*Trips him.*)

OSWALD: What?! Football player? Why that?

KENT: It's in the text. If you can read, slave!

LEAR: I thank thee, the man who resembles Kent but is not. Thou servest me by tripping for me, and I will love thee for it.

KENT: (*to Oswald*) Come, slave, arise, away! I'll teach you class difference. Away! Away! (*Pushes Oswald out.*) Vile nobody!

LEAR: Now, my friend, I thank thee. Even a strong, strong woman, can always use a good kicker. (*Gives him a coin.*)

Enter the Fool

FOOL: Your Fool is here. Am I a boy or a girl? I won't tell.

LEAR: I love that you are non-binary. How now, my pretty knave! How dost thee?

FOOL: I take a feather on a stick. (*Demonstrates.*)

LEAR: Yes, and?

FOOL: That is how I *dust*! (*Dusts with the invisible feather.*)

LEAR: Most witty! I have my Fool again!

FOOL: I'll be here until noon, if not all week!

LEAR: Not your best wit. But 'twill do!

FOOL: (*under his breath*) Screw you, Your Majesty.

LEAR: Have you heard what my daughters have done to me?

FOOL: Here, take my Fool's cap.

LEAR: Why, my boy? My girl?

FOOL: For giving them all your estate. Only a fool – small f – would do that. Take it!

LEAR: Take heed, sirrah, the whip!

FOOL: You frighten me not. I'll fetch your daughters to beat you. Is it funny yet?

LEAR: A pestilent gall is this to me. But I need to hear it.

FOOL: Sirrah, I'll teach thee a speech.

LEAR: Do.

FOOL: Mark it, nuncle. Leave thy drink and thy stud and fall in the mud!

LEAR: This is nothing, Fool.

FOOL: That's what you gave me for it? Can you make no use of nothing, nuncle head?

(*Holds out hand for money.*)

LEAR: Why no, sir, nothing can be made out of nothing.

FOOL: That sounds familiar. No?

LEAR: A bitter Fool!

FOOL: Dost thou know the difference, my girl, between a bitter Fool and a sweet one"

LEAR: No, smartass, teach me.

FOOL: The Queen who gave away her throne
Can always gnaw upon a bone!
The Queen who is her own Fool
Shall never lack a mouth to drool.

LEAR: Dost call me a real fool, Fool?

FOOL: All thy other titles that you were born with you have given away!
Hey, nonny, nonny!

LEAR: I'll hey nonny, nonny you!

KENT: This is not altogether fool, my lady.

LEAR: Oh, shut up!

KENT: Yes, Majesty.

FOOL: Nuncle, I'm still waiting for my crown. (*Hand out.*) Like you!

LEAR: Well, you can wait till you die, which from the looks of you, is not too far off!

FOOL: I shall sing a rhyme about it.

LEAR: When were you wont to be so full of rhymes, sirrah?

FOOL: Ever since thou madest thy daughters thy mothers, as when thou gavest them the rod and puttest down thine own breeches to spank. La, la, la.

LEAR: Listen, boyish girl, or girlish boy, I'll have you whipped on your non-binary ass!

FOOL: I marvel what kin thou and thy daughters are. They will have me whipped for speaking true. You'll have me whipped for lying. And sometimes I whip myself, just for the hell of it. What's a poor Fool to do? Here comes your mother, Queen!

Enter Gonorrhea

LEAR: How now, Gonorrhea! Thou art of late too much in the frown.

FOOL: Thou wast a pretty thing when thou hadst no need to care for her frowning. Yet, forsooth, I will hold my tongue. (*Hold his tongue with his fingers.*)

GONORRHEA: Not only, sir, this your all-licensed fool but others of your insolent retinue do hourly carp and quarrel –

FOOL: And puke! (*Places fingers on his tongue again.*) Oops, milady will take away my license!

GONORRHEA: I'll clobber thee, you'd better watch!

LEAR: Touch not my Fool!

FOOL: (*grabbing his crotch*) Grab not her Fool!

GONORRHEA: You filthy wanton!

FOOL: Double negative! No, no!

LEAR: You said you were my loving daughter.

GONORRHEA: I said so when thou wert worth the loving.

FOOL: Whoop, jug, I love thee!

LEAR: Shush. Who is it that can tell me who I am? Am I not Queen Lear?!

FOOL: Queen Lear's shadow. Oops! (*Places fingers on his tongue.*)

GONORRHEA: You make my house more like a tavern or a brothel, so low do you go.

FOOL: What's a brothel? Who can tell me what's a brothel?!

GONORRHEA: When I get finished with you, you'll be working in a brothel!

FOOL: A Fool in a brothel! I won't be the first. I love it! I love it! I'll be here till noon!

GONORRHEA: We'll see what you love when you're sucking six dicks at once!

FOOL: Who's counting? Hey, nonny nonny! (*sings*) Six dicks a-licking!

LEAR: Saddle my horses. Call my train together!

FOOL: Choo choo!

LEAR: (*to Gonorrhea*) Degenerate, unnatural daughter! *American*! Yet have I left a true daughter, Reagan.

GONORRHEA: You strike my people and your disordered rabble make servants of their betters.

Enter Albany, husband of Gonorrhea

LEAR: O, sir, are you come at last! Prepare my horsies – horses. I will leave your monster wife.

ALBANY: Pray, ma'am, be patient.

LEAR: I am being patient! O Lear, Lear, Lear! Beat at this gate that let thy folly in. (*Strikes her own head.*)

FOOL: That's not good for your head. It's too light!

LEAR: Go, go, my people.

Exeunt Kent and Attendant

GONORRHEA: Yet more people!?

LEAR: Hush!

ALBANY: Your Majesty, I am as guiltless as I am ignorant of what hath moved you.

LEAR: It may be so, my lord. (*Kneels.*) Hear, Nature, hear! Dear goddess, hear! Suspend thy purpose if thou didst intend to make this creature fruitful. Into her womb convey sterility. Dry up in her the organs of increase. And from her body never spring a babe to honour her. If she must teem, create her child of spleen that it may live and be a thwart, disnatured torment to her. Amen!

FOOL: Hey, the Fool's here! Who's up for a good time?

LEAR: Let it stamp wrinkles in her brow of youth with torrents of tears that fret channels in her cheeks, turn all her mother's pains to laughter and contempt that she may feel how sharper than a serpent's tooth it is to have a child named Gonorrhea!

FOOL: A bit harsh, nuncle.

LEAR: Away! Away!

Exit Lear

ALBANY: Good gods, whence comes this?!

GONORRHEA: Never afflict yourself to know more of it. Let her disposition have that scope as dotage give it. I told you we needed a Place for Mom!

Enter Lear

LEAR: (*to Gonorrhea*) I am ashamed that thou hast the power to shake my womanhood thus, that these hot tears which break from me perforce should make thee worth them. Blasts and fogs upon thee. These old eyes of mine will I pluck out if I have to see you again. But I have another daughter – what's her name …

GONORRHEA: Reagan.

LEAR: Reagan! When she shall hear of this of thee, with her nails she'll flay thy wolfish visage!

Exit Lear

GONORRHEA: Did you hear that?

ALBANY: How could I not?

GONORRHEA: What, Oswald, ho! (*to Fool*) You, thing, after your mistress!

FOOL: Nuncle Lear, nuncle Lear. Tarry! Take the Fool with thee. … But first, a rhyme!

> I feel a whipping coming on!
> I do not want one – my back upon.
> Should I stay here, with Gonorrhea?
> Or should I flee to North Korea?
> O hell, either way is hell to me!
> I wish it wasn't circa 500 A.D.!

Exit Fool

GONORRHEA: Good riddance to the little rat. Oswald, I say! Where are you?

ALBANY: I like not these turmoils.

GONORRHEA: Safer than to trust too far. I know my mother's heart. I have writ my sister –

ALBANY: Reagan?

GONORRHEA: Reagan, yes. Not Cordelia. Keep up! I told her not to comfort our mother. But to back me in all this. (*Enter Oswald*) Oswald at last!

OSWALD: Ay, madam.

GONORRHEA: Take this missive and away to horse. Inform my sister Reagan. Inform her full and add such reasons of your own why she must not soothe our mother, the former Queen of Britain.

OSWALD: My best I shall do, gracious lady.

GONORRHEA: Oh, do better than that!

　　Exeunt

I.5　　Enter Lear, Kent, the Fool, and Attendants.

LEAR: (*to Kent*) Take you this letter to the Earl of Worchestershire. He will assist me.

KENT: I will not sleep, my lady, until I have delivered your letter.

FOOL: If a man's brains were in his heels, were he not in danger of kibes?

LEAR: What the fuck does that mean?

FOOL: The hell if I know!

LEAR: Ha, ha, ha!

FOOL: Shalt thou see thy other daughter, who you think will use you kindly. To me, she's as like the other as a sister is. So I can tell what I can tell.

LEAR: What canst tell?

FOOL: Whoop, jug, I love thee!

LEAR: Tell me!

FOOL: Canst thou tell me why one's nose sits in the middle of one's face?

LEAR: No.

FOOL: Why, to keep one's eyes on either side of one's face, so that a person can smell out or smell into. Or –

LEAR: Enough word play! I did her wrong.

FOOL: Canst tell me how an oyster makes his shell?

LEAR: No.

FOOL: Nor I neither. But I can tell why a snail has a house on its back.

LEAR: Why?

FOOL: Why, to put her head in, not to give it away to her daughters.

LEAR: I will forget my royal nature. So kind a mother – Be my horsies – horses ready?

FOOL: Thy asses are gone about them.

LEAR: How many asses does it take to round up horsies?

FOOL: Thou wouldst make a good fool, madam.

LEAR: To take back my gifts to them! Monster ingratitude!

FOOL: If you were my fool, nuncle, I'd have thee beaten for being old before thy time.

LEAR: How's that?

FOOL: Thou shouldst not have been old till thou hadst been wise.

LEAR: O let me not be mad, not mad, sweet heaven! Keep me in temper!

FOOL: Too late! Too late!

LEAR: Are my horsies – horses – ready?

ATTENDANT: Ready, my lady.

Exeunt all but the Fool

FOOL: (*to audience*) I suppose you expect yet more wit? And some you can even understand? (*Clears his throat*)

How do you expect this play to end, I ask?
Will it turn sour, with bloodied eye sockets and such rot?
I'd rather that it didn't. And to make it so is my task.
But I am but a lowly Fool and can only do so much to steer this plot.
Humor will take you just so far.
People laugh. But then dismissive are!

Exit the Fool

II.1   Enter Edmund and Servant by opposite doors

EDMUND: Save thee, sirrah.

SERVANT: And you, sir.

EDMUND: *Que sera*, sirrah?

SERVANT: I know not Spanish, sir.

EDMUND: What news of my father, the Earl?

SERVANT: I have been with your father and given him notice that the Duke of Cornwall and his lovely wife Reagan will be here with him tonight. You have heard this?

EDMUND: Not I.

SERVANT: There are rumors of war.

EDMUND: From whom?

SERVANT: Somebody.

EDMUND: No doubt.

SERVANT: Fare you well, sir!

Exit Servant

EDMUND: A war. Good news! I will see how I can profit from this war! The Duke of Cornwall will be here tonight. This weaves itself perforce into my business to unseat my brother – you remember Edgar. Silly Edgar. I now must act! (*Calls*) Brother, a word! Descend! Brother, I say!

Enter Edgar

Have you not spoken against the Duke of Cornwall. Or against Albany?

EDGAR: Not a word. I am sure of it.

EDMUND: I hear our father coming. Pardon me, in cunning I must draw my sword upon you. Draw!

EDGAR: What do you want me to draw with? I have no pencil!

EDMUND: Draw your sword! Seem to defend yourself! (*Aloud*) Yield! Come before my father! Torches, torches! (*to Edgar*) Flee, brother, flee!

Exit Edgar

Some blood drawn on me would beget opinion of my fierce endeavor. I have seen drunkards do more than this in sport. (*Edmund wounds himself in the arm.*) Stop, stop! Father, father!

Enter Earl of W. and servants with torches

EARL of W: Now, Edmund, where's the villain who attacked you?

EDMUND: Here stood he in the dark, his sword out, mumbling of wicked charms.

EARL of W: Not charms! Oh, my God! But where is he now?

EDMUND: Look, sir, I bleed. Edgar did it.

EARL of W: What more proof do we need of his villainy?!

EDMUND: Flee this way, sir! Avoid him!

EARL of W: Pursue him, Edmund. Go after him!

EDMUND: He tried to persuade me to murder your lordship, but I did tell him the revenging gods did all their thunder bend against parricides. Seeing how I stood opposed to his unnatural purpose, with his sword he charged home my body, lashed mine arm. After which he suddenly fled. His name is Edgar! (*spelling it*) E-d-g –

EARL of W: Let him flee far. Not in this land shall he remain uncaught. And once found, dispatched, as I am an Earl!

EDMUND: Yes, dispatch him before he can defend himself with lies and more lies.

EARL of W: The noble Duke of Cornhole, my master comes tonight –

EDMUND: I think you mean Cornwall.

EARL of W: What did I say?

EDMUND: Cornhole. Don't call him that.

EARL of W: He is my patron what'er his name. By his authority I will proclaim Edgar a murderous coward who shall be brought to the stake.

EDMUND: When I dissuaded him from his foul intent, and found him adamant, I threatened to discover him like the good son I am. He replied, 'Thou unpossessing bastard, dost thou think, if I would stand against thee, anyone would believe you? No, I should deny it all and I would be believed.'

EARL of W: O strange and hardened villain! Would he deny his very letter?! I curse the day I begot him! Even though he was legitimate and you weren't.

(Trumpets within)

I hear trumpets within! Hark, the Duke's trumpets within!

EDMUND: (*aside*) One day I will have trumpets.

EARL of W: Loyal and natural boy, I hear thee, when I want to. You shall one day have trumpets.

EDMUND: Most kind father. (*Bows*)

Enter Cornwall, Reagan, and Attendants

CORNWALL: How now, my noble friend, I have heard strange news of thy son Edgar.

REAGAN: If it be true, all vengeance comes too short. How dost my lord?

EARL of W: O madam, my old heart is cracked, it's cracked.

REAGAN: Did your Edgar seek your life?

EARL of W: O lady, lady, I shame myself to name it.

REAGAN: Was he not companion to those riotous knights who tended upon my mother?

EDMUND: Yes, madam, he was of that consort.

REAGAN: I have this present evening heard so from my sister. Our mother keeps ignominious company. If they come to sojourn at my house, I won't be there.

CORNWALL: Nor I, assure thee Reagan. Edmund, I hear that you have shown your father kind offices.

EDMUND: It was nothing much, mere offering of my life. After all, I'm just a bastard.

EARL of W: My dear Edmund did receive this hurt you see. (*Points to wound.*)

CORNWALL: Is Edgar pursued?

EARL of W: Aye, my good lord.

CORNWALL: If he be taken, he shall never more be feared of doing harm. As for you, Edmund, whose virtue and obedience doth so much commend themselves, you shall be ours. Natures of such deep trust we shall much need.

EDMUND: I shall serve you, sir, as I do my father. (*Bows.*)

CORNWALL: I think you know not why we came to visit you.

EARL of W: I had hoped you would call first.

CORNWALL: My phone was not working.

EARL of W: I understand. Phones don't work very well in circa 500 A.D.

REAGAN: I told my husband not to rely on new-fangled crap like phones! But he would not hear. Earl, we wish to impose upon your hospitality for some days until we sort out how best to deal with my mother, who is the former Queen of Britain, as you may recall.

EDMUND: Milady, have you tried a Place for Mom?

REAGAN: We'll see her put somewhere, you can count on that!

EDMUND: (*Aside to Reagan*) And perhaps even a Place for Dad, in my case?

REAGAN: (*Aside*) We'll talk anon.

EARL of W: I'm not going into a home!

Exeunt

II.2   Enter Kent and Oswald from opposite sides

OSWALD: Good dawning to thee, friend. Art of this house?

KENT: Aye.

OSWALD: Where may we set our horses?

KENT: In the mire.

OSWALD: Prithee, if thou lovest me, tell me.

KENT: I love thee not. Prithee.

OSWALD: Why then, I care not for thee.

KENT: I care not if you care not for me. Prithee!

OSWALD: Why dost thou use me thus? I know thee not.

KENT: Fellow, I know thee.

OSWALD: Oh?

KENT: You serve the lady Gonorrhea. A base, proud, shallow, beggarly, finical rogue! And a skanky skunk!

OSWALD: And you look like Kent in disguise! A bad one!

KENT: Draw, you skunky rogue! (*Brandishes a sword*)

OSWALD: Help, ho! Murder! Help!

KENT: Strike, you slave! (*Oswald attempts to escape.*) Stand and fight!

Enter Edmund, Cornwall, Reagan, the Earl of W. and servants.

EDMUND: How now, brown cow, what's what?! Tut! Tut! I am Edmund the Bastard!

KENT: Tut! Tut! Up your butt! Come, come, young master. Draw, you rascal!

EARL of W: Weapons upon the public byways and highways? It's come to this in this day and age?! Oh, 'tis my misfortune to live in circa 500 A.D.!

CORNWALL: Keep peace, upon your lives. He dies that strikes again.

KENT: Thou shalt not tamper with my right to bear arms! Read the Second Amendment of the Magna Carta, you elite creeps! (*Blesses himself.*)

(*All kneel in deference to the mention of the Magna Carta.*)

ALL: The Magna Carta!

CORNWALL: What is the problem here? Speak.

OSWALD: I am scarce in breath, my lord.

KENT: And that breath is bad! Scoundrel! Ruffian! Poop sniffer!

OSWALD: Poop sniffer?! I am no poop sniffer! Never have I sniffed poop!

CORNWALL: (*to Kent*) You are a strange, yet familiar, fellow. You epithets blow the mind.

KENT: He be of the house of Gonorrhea, and thus an enemy of my lady, Queen Lear.

CORNWALL: Boy, when you take sides, you do so with gusto.

KENT: 'Tis easy when it is the likes of this 'prithee' fellow! Rogue! Dog! Gonorrhea lover!

CORNWALL: Enough!

KENT: Yet he is an unbolted, one-suited, phlegm-coughing pip!

CORNWALL: I know not what these things are! Know you no ordinary vocabulary?

KENT: I do, sir, but anger hath a privilege to insult anew!

CORNWALL: Methinks thou art some relative of Kent, who is banished now from court.

KENT: Nay, sir. Not so. (*Tries to disguise himself more.*)

CORNWALL: I will hear no more base terms. This is Britain! Even if it is circa 500 A.D.

KENT: That such a slave as this should wear a sword! A plague upon your epileptic visage!

OSWALD: Careful now. I cannot help my epilepsy.

KENT: I'll help you cure it – by death!

EARL of W: This is some fellow who having been praised for bluntness doth affect a saucy roughness. He cannot flatter, he! These kind of knaves I know, which in this plainness harbor more craft more corrupter ends than twenty easy flatterers.

OSWALD: Yay, yay, you say!

CORNWALL (*to Oswald*) What was the offence you gave him, other than being of the house of Gonorrhea?

OSWALD: I never gave him any. He thinks he will score points with the Queen, Her Majesty.

KENT: The Queen! The former Queen of Britain?!

ALL: (*kneeling*) The Queen!

(*All rise.*)

CORNWALL: Fetch forth the stocks! You stubborn knave, we'll teach you –

KENT: I am too old to learn. Call not your stocks for me.

CORNWALL: But they are good stocks! You'll make a fortune. (*Laughs*)

KENT: I fear some scam in these stocks.

CORNWALL: All right, you had your chance. (*calling*) Bring in those other stocks, the ones with holes! (*Enter servant with wooden stocks*) There shall he sit till he learns respect and temperance.

REAGAN: Be not too lenient, husband. At least a year in the stocks!

KENT: A year?! I'll stay another year as long as my Queen needs me!

REAGAN: You'll be dead by noon by thirst.

KENT: I will still find spit to lather up your face, madam!

CORNWALL: Are you mad, fellow? Fuck not with my wife! She'll have your eyes.

EARL of W: Let me speak in this. Let me beseech your grace not to do so. His fault is much, and the Queen, his mistress, will check him for it. Do not lower thyself to stock this churl. Any more than you would stock a barn with rotten corn. If I may jest. The Queen would take it ill. She is the former Queen of all Britain, you know.

CORNWALL: You may not jest in my presence, especially with so poor a jest. And as for the Queen, there is only so much more we'll take from her.

REAGAN: My sister may receive much more worse to have her gentleman here, her Oswald, abused and assaulted for following her affairs. Put in his legs! (*Kent is put in the stocks.*) Come, my lord away! For his devotion he shall pay!

Exeunt all but Earl of W. and Kent

EARL of W: I am sorry for thee, friend. 'Tis the Duke's pleasure, egged on by his wife, both whose disposition all the world well knows will not be stopped.

KENT: A curse upon them both.

EARL of W: But I'll entreat for thee.

KENT: Pray do not, sir. I have watched and traveled hard. Some time I will sleep out, the rest of the time I'll whistle.

EARL of W: Do not. 'Twill be taken ill.

KENT: 'Twill give me a thrill!

Earl of W. shakes his head and exits.

KENT: Somehow I have received a letter even though I be in the stocks! I will peruse this letter, which I am sure is from Cordelia, who hath most fortunately been informed of my fate here. How swift is the post in circa 500 A.D. that I should receive her letter! (*Tries to get the letter in front of his eyes, but he can't*). All weary am I with heavy eyes. So I must sleep before I read. Fortune, good night! I sleep! (*He falls asleep immediately.*)

II.3   Enter Edgar

EDGAR: I heard myself proclaimed, and by the happy hollow of a tree I
        escaped, for now. I will preserve myself and take the basest,
        poorest shape that ever penury brought to man. My face I'll grime
        with filth, twist my hair in knots and, nearly naked, outface the
        winds and persecutions of the sky. Like the beggars on the
        streets, I will shout and prance and will, of course, be invisible to
        every eye. No one will recognize me one whit when I become
        Poor Tommy. (*Screams*) I'm Poor Tommy! Edgar, I nothing am!

        Exit Edgar

II.4   Kent is still in the stocks asleep.

        Enter Lear, the Fool, and a Gentleman.

LEAR: I have heard naught from my daughters. Why do children never
      write?!

KENT: (*waking up*) Hail to thee, noble mistress!

LEAR: Ha! It is that man who resembles Kent. How lucky that we
      stumbled upon him. It is good that Britain is a small country.

FOOL: Ha, ha! In the stocks! What witty remark can I make about that?
      He wears cruel but lovely garters?

LEAR: What's he that hath so much thy place mistook to set thee here,
      sir?

KENT: Your son and daughter.

LEAR: No. Not the Duke and Duchess of Cornwall!

KENT: Yes.

LEAR, No, I say.

KENT: I say yea.

FOOL: (*singing*) You say nay! And I say yea! Let's call the whole thing off!

KENT: Your Fool is merry.

FOOL: Call me fool. But don't call me Mary! *Boing*!

LEAR: Fool, shut up, for five seconds. (*The Fool zips his mouth shut in pantomime.*) By Jupiter, I swear no! They durst not do this. They could not, would not do such violent outrage upon my man. I am the Queen of all Britain!

KENT: My Queen, when I was at their home, I did commend your highness's letters to them. But before I could speak more, from Gonorrhea did Oswald deliver other letters –

LEAR: So many letters! It's hard to keep them straight, even for a Queen!

KENT: Those other letters they read, ignoring yours, and taking to horse commanded me to follow and attend the leisure of their answer to you, and gave me cold looks. I drew my sword, of course, at that other messenger—

LEAR: Did my daughter Reagan read my messages or not?!

KENT: I know not.

FOOL: Hey, nonny, nonny! He who hath daughters—

LEAR: Shut up, Fool!

FOOL: But you pay me to be annoying.

LEAR: Not that annoying!

FOOL: Just doing my job!

LEAR: (*to Kent*) Where is this daughter, whichever one she be?

KENT: With the Earl, within.

LEAR: Follow me not. Stay here.

KENT: I am in the stocks, sir. I cannot follow.

Exit Lear.

GENTLEMAN: Are you sure you made no more offence than what you spoke of?

KENT: None.

GENTLEMAN: You look like Kent, who was banished by the Queen.

KENT: I am none, sir. Mind your own small business. Why comes the Queen with such a small number?

FOOL: Hadst thou been set in the stocks for that question, thou didst well deserve it.

KENT: Why?

FOOL: You are too rash to learn anything.

KENT: Where learned you this, Fool?

FOOL: Not in the stocks, fool.

Enter Lear and Earl of W.

LEAR: They deny to speak with me!? They say they are sick! They are weary! They have travelled all the night!? May the gods screw them!

EARL of W: My dear lady, you know the fiery quality of the Duke of Cornwall and his Reagan.

Both are unmovable and fixed.

LEAR: Vengeance, plague, death, confusion on them! I will speak with Cornwall and his Reagan! Or I am not Queen Lear!

EARL of W: Well, my good lady, I have informed them so.

LEAR: Informed them? Dost thou understand me, man?

EARL of W: Aye, my good lady.

LEAR: Good lady, my ass! The Queen would speak with Cornwall, the
dear mother would with her daughter —what's her name – speak.

EARL of W: Reagan, I think. I would have all well betwixt you.

Exit Earl of W.

LEAR: O my heart, my rising heart! But down!

FOOL: Down wantons, down! I am Queen of all Britain! Hey, nonny,
nonny! Rule, Britannia!

Enter Cornwall, Reagan. Earl of W. and servants

LEAR: At last! Good morrow to you both.

CORNWALL: Hail to your grace.

REAGAN: I am glad to see your highness.

LEAR: That's news to me. If I were a King, you wouldst not make me
wait!

REAGAN: Yes, we would. Let's free your man. (*She and Cornwall free
Kent from the stocks.*)

LEAR: Beloved Reagan, your elder sister has laid a vulture on my breast.
(*Touches her heart.*)

REAGAN: I hear such scuttlebutt, but believe it not. Not Gonorrhea.

LEAR: What?!

REAGAN: I cannot think my sister wouldst fail her obligation. If,
madam, perchance she has restrained the unseemly riots of your

followers, this on such ground and to such wholesome end as clears her from all blame.

LEAR: My curses on her.

REAGAN: O Mother, you are old. You should be ruled and led by some discretion that discerns your state better than yourself.

LEAR: You art not putting me in a Place for Mom! Never!

REAGAN: I pray you that to our sister you make return and say you have wronged her.

LEAR: Ask her forgiveness? Do you mark how this becomes a Queen?! (*Kneels.*) 'Dear daughter, dearest, Gonorrhea, I confess that I am old. On my knees I beg that you will vouchsafe me clothing, bed, and food. Kick me, daughter! Kick!'

REAGAN: These are unsightly tricks, but stir not my heart. Return you to my sister.

LEAR: Never, Reagan. All the stored vengeance of heaven fall on her ungrateful head! Strike her young bones with leprosy!

CORNWALL: Fie, madam, fie! Such excess!

LEAR: You nimble lightnings dart your blinding flames into her scornful eyes! Infect her beauty! You fen-sucked fogs fall and blister her!

REAGAN: So will you wish on me as well when the rash mood is on.

LEAR: No, Reagan, thou shalt never have my curse. Her eyes are fierce, but thine do comfort and do not burn. Thou better knowest the offices of nature, the bond of childhood, the dues of gratitude, nor hast thou forgot the half of the queendom wherein I thee endowed.

REAGAN: It took you long enough!

LEAR: What trumpet's that?

REAGAN: I hear no trumpet. (*Trumpet sounds.*) Ah, 'tis my sister's trumpet! This approves her letter that she would soon be here. Both letter and trumpet confirm!

LEAR: Another letter! And yet none to me!

Enter Oswald

REAGAN: Did your lady come?

OSWALD: I know not. You'll have to ask her. It was good for me! Oh, you meant is she come here?

LEAR: This man is he whose easy-borrowed pride dwells in the fickle grace of her he follows.

CORNWALL: Is Gonorrhea here or not?

Enter Gonorrhea

LEAR: O heavens! Gonorrhea is here! Art thou not ashamed to look upon this beard, if I had one?

GONORRHEA: (*to Reagan*) O sister! (*They embrace.*)

LEAR: O Reagan, do you embrace this viper?

REGAN: I do! And yet again I embrace my Gonorrhea! (*They embrace again.*)

GONORRHEA: How do I offend? All is not offence that dotage terms so.

LEAR: O my sides! They will burst! How came my man, who resembles my former servant Kent, to be in the stocks?! It was no accident! He did not fall into the stocks!

CORNWALL: I set him there, madam, but his own disorders deserved no less.

LEAR: Did you!? Did you!? Do you not know that to put my man in the stocks is tantamount to putting me, the divinely appointed Queen of all Britain, in the stocks?!

REAGAN: Oh, mother, being weak, be so. Return and sojourn with my sister here, dismissing half your train. Choo, Choo, as your Fool would say. Then later come to me, if you must.

LEAR: Return to her? No, rather I abjure all roofs and choose to wage against the enmity of the air, to be the comrade of the wolf and the rat-eating owl! Return with Gonorrhea? Persuade me rather to be slave to this detested skunky-crotch groom! (*Points to Oswald.*)

OSWALD: Hey! I can hear you!

GONORRHEA: At your choice, ma'am.

LEAR: I prithee, daughter, or so you say, do not make me mad. I will trouble thee no more. Farewell. We'll no more meet, no more see one another.

GONORRHEA: Good! Farewell!

LEAR: But yet thou art my flesh, my blood. Or is it a disease that's in my flesh?

GONORRHEA: O Jesus!

LEAR: But I'll not chide thee more.

GONORRHEA: I'll bet.

LEAR: Let shame come when it will. I can be patient. I can stay with my Reagan. I and my hundred knights.

REAGAN: Not altogether so. I looked not for you yet, nor am provided for your welcome. Give ear to my sister. And do not make demands that cannot be met!

LEAR: Is this well-spoken?

REAGAN: I dare avouch it, ma'am. Why not fifty followers? What should you need of more? Yea, why so many? How in one house should so many people under two commands hold amity? 'Tis hard, almost impossible.

GONORRHEA: Why might not you, madam, receive attendance from those that Reagan calls servants, or from mine?

REAGAN: I now do spy a danger. I entreat you to bring but five and twenty. To no more will I give place or notice. The rest can rest on the streets or in the gutters.

LEAR: I gave you all –

REAGAN: But you gave it, Mother!

LEAR: You said five and twenty.

REAGAN: I misspoke. Zero is a more charming number.

LEAR: Wicked creatures yet do look well-favoured when others show care more wicked. Not being the very worst stands in some rank of praise. (*to Gonorrhea*) I'll go with thee. Your fifty doth double twenty-five.

GONORRHEA: What need you them, or ten, or five?

REAGAN: Or even one?

LEAR: O reason not the need! Our basest beggars are in the poorest thing superfluous. Allow not nature more than nature needs. You heavens, give me the patience I need. You see me here, you gods, a poor, old lady, as full of grief as age, wretched in both.

REAGAN Oh, here we go again! Enough!

LEAR: And let not women's weapons, water drops, stain my woman's cheeks.

GONORRHEA: We won't!

LEAR: No, you unnatural hags, I will have such revenges on you both
that all the world – I will do such things –

REAGAN: We're waiting!

LEAR: What they are yet I know not, but they shall be the terrors of the
earth.

GONORRHEA: Boo hoo.

LEAR: You think I'll weep. Nay, I'll not weep. This heart shall break
into a hundred flaws before I'll weep. O Fool, I shall go mad!

FOOL: Whoop, jug, I love thee!

LEAR: Come, watch me go mad!

Exeunt Lear, the Fool, Kent, Earl of W. and a Gentleman

CORNWALL: What a drama Queen! Let us withdraw. There will be a
storm.

REAGAN: My house is small. That old woman and her people cannot be
well bestowed.

GONORRHEA: It's her own fault that she has put herself from rest.

REAGAN: If she just didn't play the Self-Pity Card so much! I will take
her, but not one follower.

GONORRHEA: So am I purposed. Where is my lord of Worchestershire?

CORNWALL: He followed the old woman. But look, he is returned!

Enter the Earl of W.

EARL of W: The Queen is in high rage.

REAGAN: What a surprise!

EARL of W: She calls for a horse. But I know not whither she intends to go.

CORNWALL: 'Tis best to give her way, is it not?

GONORRHEA: Entreat her by no means to stay.

EARL of W: Alack, night comes on and bleak winds do sorely ruffle. No one should be outdoors this night. You might get wet.

REAGAN: O sir, our injuries are too oft self-imposed. Shut up your doors. The raging Queen is attended by a desperate train –

GONORRHEA: Choo choo!

CORNWALL: Shut up your doors, who will, 'tis a wild and tragic night. My Reagan counsels well. Come out of the storm.

REAGAN: Here we all go! Choo, choo!

   Exeunt

III.1   The storm rages. Enter Kent and a gentleman from opposite sides.

KENT: Who's there, besides foul weather?

GENTLEMAN: One minded like this weather.

KENT: I know you. Where's the Queen?

GENTLEMAN: Contending with the fretful elements. Tears at her white hair.

KENT: I get the picture.

GENTLEMAN: Unhomed she runs, unbonneted, distraught.

KENT: Enough detail!

GENLEMAN: Oh, but sir, there is so much more to say.

KENT: Not another syllable!

GENTLEMAN: Even the lion and the belly-pinched wolf keep their fur dry –

KENT: Good grief, man! Just tell me who is with the Queen?

GENTLEMAN: None but the Fool, who will not cease his cruel jests.

KENT: I hear that the King of France marches toward this divided country to stifle these rebellious dukes who may well do hateful harm against the proud, sad Queen.

GENTLEMAN: Is this for true, or merely hapless hope?

KENT: I hope it is not hapless hope, nor rootless rumor –

GENTLEMAN: Nor fruitless fiction nor flimsy whimsy –

KENT: Exactly!

GENTLEMAN: I will further talk with them, man who resembles Kent.

KENT: No, do not. If you would have confirmation of who I be, despite my outward cover, open this purse –

GENTLEMAN: You carry a purse?!

KENT: Not a purse purse! A purse from circa 500 A.D. (*Shows a sack purse.*) See what it contains. If you happen to see Cordelia, the Queen's forgotten daughter, show her this ring in this purse and she will tell you who that fellow is that yet you do not know for sure.

GENTLEMAN: You?

KENT: *Shhh*! No more! Fie on this storm! I will go seek the Queen.

GENTLEMAN: Wait! Have you no more to say?

KENT: When we have found the Queen – in which you go that way, I go this – he who lights upon her first yells to the other.

GENTLEMAN: Like this? (*yells*) Queen! O Queen!

KENT: 'Twill do. Anon!

The two exit in opposite directions.

III.2   Storm. Enter Lear and the Fool. The Queen's hair is blown into an absolute mess.

LEAR: Blow winds and crack your cheeks!

FOOL: But not these, my sweet butt cheeks! Please not those!

LEAR: You cataracts and hurricanoes, spout till you have drenched our steeples, drowned the cocks!

FOOL: Only spare my cock!

LEAR: Singe my white, somewhat colored, hair!

FOOL: O nuncle head, in, ask for thy daughters' blessing. Here's a night that pities neither wise men nor fools.

LEAR: Rumble thy bellyful, sky! Spit! Spout! Spoot!

FOOL: Spoot?

LEAR: I tax not you, elements, with unkindness. I never gave you queendoms, called you children. Let fall your horrible pleasure. Here I stand, your slave, a poor, infirm, weak, and despised – but still strong – old woman! O, ho! My hair! My hair!

FOOL: Shall I sing you a rhyme or a lullaby?

LEAR: No.

FOOL Without a lullaby I will die!

LEAR: If you must.

FOOL: Thank ye, Majesty. (*Clears throat*)

> There once was a Queen in old Britain
> Who by her daughters was bitten.
> She thought by her screaming
> To overcome scheming.
> But she wound up alone and be-shitten!

LEAR: You are my joy, boy. (*Hugs him*) Or my girl pearl?

FOOL: Are you my mother?

LEAR: Hush!

FOO9L: Is that a yes? Is Kent my father? Is Edmund? Is anybody?

LEAR: Hush, darling.

FOOL: Is that a no?

LEAR: So many, many questions.

FOOL: May a poor Fool make one request?

LEAR: And what is that?

FOOL: Kill Claudio.

LEAR: Who's Claudio?

FOOL: Oops! That must be another play. I'm forgetting my lines.

LEAR: No one will notice.

FOOL: A demented Queen and her dying, forgetful Fool. How tragic!

(*They strike a tragic pose together.*)

Enter Kent

KENT: There you are, my Queen! How fortunate I should stumble upon thy whereabouts.

FOOL: Father, is that you?

KENT: (*ignoring him*) My cod-piece is soaked!

FOOL: Is that a riddle?

KENT: How about this weather, huh?!

FOOL: Is *that* a riddle?

LEAR: I am a woman more sinned against than sinning!

KENT: Your Grace, nearby is a hovel. Some friendship will it lend you against the tempest. Repose you there while I return to the castle and force them to render you courtesy.

LEAR: You expect me to stay in a hovel?! My wits begin to turn. The art of our necessities is strange and can make vile things precious. Come, to your hovel, poor fool. I have one part in my heart that's sorry yet for thee.

FOOL: I feel a song coming on. (*Clears throat, then belts out*) "Everything's coming up roses! For you and for me!'

LEAR: I hope so, boy. (*to Kent*) Come, bring us to this hovel.

Exeunt Lear and Kent

FOOL I'll speak a prophecy ere I go:

> There will come a time when there will be no crime.
> There will be an age when everyone will be a sage.
> In just about a minute
> This whole world and all the people in it
> Will live in peace and joy.
> And I will be the perfect boy. Or girl.
> No pain, nor sorrow, no scams – tomorrow!

Every man will be a king.
And every person will have everything.
Oh, just put your mind to it
And we can surely do it.
Oh, do not be so cynical!
Here we are, at life's pinnacle!
If life is not a romance novel.
Hey, at least you have a filthy hovel!

Fool exits

INTERMISSION

III.3   Enter Earl of W. and Edmund, with lights

EARL of W: Alack, alack, Edmund, when I desired their leave that I
        might pity the Queen, they took from me the use of mine own
        house, charged me on pain of perpetual displeasure neither to
        speak of her, entreat for her, or any other way sustain her.

EDMUND: Most savage and unnatural. Of course, it is circa 500 A.D.

EARL of W: Go to. Say you nothing! I have received a letter this night.
        'Tis dangerous to be spoken, so I have locked the letter in my
        closet. These injuries the Queen now bears will be avenged. Go
        you and talk with the Duke. If he ask for me, tell him I am ill and
        gone to bed. If I die for it, the Queen must be relieved. There are
        strange things afoot, Edmund. Pray you, be careful.

        Exit the Earl of W.

EDMUND: This shall the Duke of Cornwall instantly know, and of that
        letter too. This seems a fair deserving and must secure me what
        my father loses – no less than all. The younger rises when the old
        doth fall!

        Exit Edmund

III.4   Enter Lear, Kent, and the Fool to a sign that says MOTEL 6

KENT: Here is the place, my lady. Pray, enter. It is not much, but the
tyranny of the open night is worse.

(*Storm rages.*)

LEAR: Let me alone.

KENT: Good lady, you must enter here.

LEAR: Wilt break my heart. A Motel 6?!

KENT: I had rather break mine own. Yet, Your Majesty, please enter.

LEAR: O Reagan, Gonorrhea, and … What's Her Name?

KENT: Cordelia.

LEAR: Cordelia. Your old, kind mother, whose frank heart gave all! O,
that way madness lies. Let me shun that. No more of that!

KENT: Yeah, shun that.

LEAR: You go in first to this motel. (*to the Fool*) Or you, boy, go first,
like a canary in a coal mine.

FOOL: Nay!

LEAR: I'll pray and then I'll sleep. And maybe fix my hair!

Exit the Fool

LEAR: Poor, naked wretches, wherever you be, let me editorialize a
while. Have we, have I taken too little care of you? O, audience,
expose thyselves to feel what wretches feel! And not just here, or
at Les Miz. Buy a ticket for that unhoused wretch outside the
theater and let him sit on your lap at the matinee! Share your
cookie in the intermission! (*looking off*) What is that creature over
there?

EDGAR: (*as Poor Tommy within*) It is I, Poor Tommy!

> Enter the Fool.

FOOL Come not in here, Majesty. For here is a spirit, a goblin. Help! Help!

KENT: Give me thy hand. What spirit is it?

FOOL: He says his name is Poor Tommy.

EDGAR: Poor Tommy has a poor tummy!

KENT: Perhaps I should not go in!

> Enter Edgar

EDGAR Away! The foul fiend follows me. Fie, fie, foul fiend!

FOOL: Fuck that foul fiend, says the Fool!

LEAR: Didst thou give all to thy daughters? And so thou hast come to this?

EDGAR: The foul fiend hath led Poor Tommy through fire, whirlpool, and quagmire.

LEAR: What about ratsbane in your porridge?

EDGAR: Yea, that too!

LEAR: What about sour milk from a cranky elk?

EDGAR: Gallons!

LEAR: Couldst thou save nothing at all?

FOOL: He did reserve a nasty blanket, else we had been shamed.

EDGAR: Do you like my blanket? (*Shows off his blanket*)

FOOL: (*dirty*) Hey, nonny, nonny!

LEAR: Now all the plagues in the air light on his daughters!

KENT: He hath no daughters, madam.

LEAR: Death, traitor! Nothing could have subdued his faculties to such a state but his selfish daughters. Those pelican daughters!

KENT: Pelican daughters?

EDGAR: (*Makes bird noises.*)

FOOL: This night will turn us all to fools and madmen. With bad hair!

EDGAR: Obey thy parents, even when they're wrong. Wear clothes even when they don't fit. Poor Tommy's a-cold. And my tummy's upset.

LEAR: Listen to this man!

EDGAR: I have been a serving man and did the deed of darkness with my mistress. I have made oaths and broke them in the face of heaven. Do not go out naked in a storm. Stay out of brothels except on Sundays or if there is a discount. Don't trust your brother, especially if he's a bastard.

LEAR: Is this man no more than this? Consider him well.

KENT: He looks like Edgar, the Earl's boy.

LEAR: Unaccommodated man is no more than this, a poor, bare, forked animal –

FOOL: Fucked animal.

LEAR: Forked. Off, off, you lendings! Come, unbutton here. (*Tears off her clothes.*)

FOOL: (*singing*) Button up your overcoat, when the wind is free. Take good care of yourself. You belong to me. Eat an apple every day.

Get to bed by three. Take good care of thyself. Thou belongst to me! Look, here comes a walking fire.

Enter the Earl of W. with a torch.

EDGAR: This is the foul fiend! Aroint thee, witch, aroint thee!

EARL of W: Edgar?

EDGAR: Nay! Never!

KENT: How fares your grace? Is it your grace?

EARL of W: It is I – the earl of Woo!

LEAR: What's he? Woo who?

KENT: I know not. It may be the Earl.

FOOL: He who, he who? And boo hoo hoo on such a night as this.

EARL of W: Your names!

EDGAR: I'm Poor Tommy, who swallows the odd cockroach, the green muck on the standing pool. Who is whipped from here to Worchestershire.

FOOL: Whipped? (*Enjoys the idea*)

EDGAR: My disguise is working!

EARL of W: Edgar?

KENT: I am a counselor to the Queen.

EARL of W: Kent?

KENT: Nay! Never!

LEAR: And I am the Queen of Romania!

ALL: Your Majesty!

151

(All genuflect.)

LEAR: Who do I have to screw to get a decent night's lodging around here?!

EARL of W: Go in with me. I have ventured to come to seek you out and bring you where both fire and food be ready.

LEAR: First let me talk with this philosopher. *(to Edgar)* What is the cause of thunder?

KENT: Good madam, take his offer. Go into the house.

EDGAR: Thunder is the indigestion of the gods!

LEAR: I thought so! What is your study in this life?

EDGAR: How to prevent the fiend and to kill vermin.

>   *(Scratches at a flea.)*

LEAR: Excellent! Let me ask one word in private.

>   *(Lear and Edgar talk apart.)*

KENT: Importune her once more, my lord, to go with you. Her wits begin to fester. And her hair, my God!! Her unholy hair!

EARL of W: Who can blame her? Her daughters seek her death. Ah, that good man Kent said it would be thus, poor banished man.

KENT: I wonder what happened to him. A goodly fellow.

EARL of W: Most likely dead in some bog.

KENT: I always liked him.

EARL of W: Thou sayest the Queen grows mad. I'll tell thee, friend, I am almost mad myself. I had a son, a bastard not only in name but in character. Yet I loved him. And yet he sought my life. True to tell thee, the grief of it hath crazed my precarious wits.

LEAR: I'll go in! But this philosopher, his company I demand.

FOOL: Please no more mad people!

EDGAR: Poor Tommy's a-cold.

FOOL: The poor Fool is a-colder! My wits! My wits! My hair! My hair!

EARL of W: (*to Edgar*) In fellow, there, into the hovel. Keep thee warm.

KENT: This way, madam.

LEAR: I will keep with my philosopher.

KENT: Let him come in. Go along with us, sirrah

LEAR: Come, good Armenian.

EDGAR: Who?

EARL of W: No words, no words! Hush!

EDGAR: Thank the gods, nobody recognizes me!

    Exeunt

    Enter Cornwall and Edmund

CORNWALL: I will have my revenge ere I depart his house.

EDMUND: On my father? How, my lord?

CORNWALL I am not surprised that Edgar turned on him.

EDMUND: How ill-saddled am I with a bad brother and a bad father! Here is the letter that I spoke of. O heavens, that this treason were not, or not I the detector of it!

CORNWALL: Alas, poor you. Go with me to my Duchess. Also known as the Duchess of Cornwall.

EDMUND: If the matter of this letter be certain, you have mighty business in hand.

CORNWALL: True or false, it hath made thee Earl of Worchestershire. (*mangles the name*)

EDMUND: Easy for you to say, my lord. I fear it will not be that easy.

CORNWALL: Seek out where thy father is, that he may be ready for apprehension.

EDMUND: (*Aside*) If I find my father comforting the Queen, it will stuff this Duke's suspicion more fully. (*Aloud*) I will persevere in my course of loyalty to you, though the conflict be sore between that and my blood.

CORNWALL: I will lay trust upon thee, Edmund, and thou shalt find a dearer father in my love.

Exeunt

Enter Kent and Earl of W.

EARL of W: Here is better than in the open air. Take it thankfully. I will piece out the comfort with what addition I can. I will not be long from you. Have I mentioned that you remind me of someone?

KENT: My genes are replicated by many in this area, sir.

EARL of W: Perhaps that is it.

Exit Earl of W.

Enter Lear, Edgar, and the Fool

FOOL: (*to audience*) Enter Lear, Edgar, and the Fool! Lucky you!

EDGAR: (*to audience*) Beware the foul fiend! (*Scratches at fleas.*)

FOOL: (*to Lear*) Tell me, auntie, whether a madman be a gentleman or a yokel?

LEAR: A Queen, a Queen!

FOOL: Yes, I fear some queens are less than queenly.

EDGAR: Will somebody please scratch my back?

FOOL: I'll scratch thy back.

EDGAR: (*Points*) Here! Give a good one!

FOOL: I will scratch like a bitch!

EDGAR: No, gently, gently. Do not hurt my fleas.

FOOL: Gently then. (*Edgar presents his back*) He's mad who trusts in the tameness of a Fool. (*He scratches Edgar's back with his Fool's scepter.*)

How's that? No more foil fiend?

EDGAR: Divine. Don't stop.

FOOL: How's this? (*Scratches Edgar's butt*) Good?

EDGAR: Too good. I fear it is a sin.

FOOL: I scratch my own backside sometimes.

EDGAR: TMI.

FOOL: We Fools get very tired of always entertaining everybody else. By the way!

LEAR: (*to Edgar*) Come, sir, sit here, most learned justice. (*to the Fool*) And thou, sapient sir, sit here. We shall have a trial!

KENT: Madam, how do you? Will you lay down and rest?

LEAR: (*correcting*) Lie down. I will not! I'll see the trial first. Bring in the evidence! (*to Edgar*) Thou robed man of justice, take thy place. (*to the Fool*) And thou, his fellow of equity, bench by his side. (*to Kent*) You are on the commission. Sit your banished butt as well.

KENT: I know naught of any banished butt, but for you I will sit.

EDGAR: Let us deal justly.

FOOL: I fear some commentary about injustice is to descend upon us.

LEAR: Arrange Gonorrhea first! She mistreated the poor Queen, her mother.

FOOL: Come hither, mistress. Is your name Gonorrhea?

LEAR: She cannot deny it.

(*Somebody pushes a stool so it is the focus of the trial.*)

FOOL: (*singing*) I just met a girl, Gonorrhea! Gonorrhea!

EDGAR: She's taken the form of a stool! So many disguises!

LEAR: She is lower than a stool! A stool has more pity!

KENT: Peace, madam! It is not your daughter.

LEAR: It is! (*Kicks another stool into focus.*) And here is Reagan! Prime in bitchery! (*Kent moves the two stools.*)

LEAR: They are escaping! Stop them! Stop them!

EDGAR: (*aside*) My tears begin to take the Queen's part so much they may mar my counterfeiting,

LEAR: (*aside*) Do my eyes deceive me? Is this not Edgar, the very son of Worchestershire?!

EDGAR: The Queen suspects me, I can tell! More make-up., it must be! (*Applies more dirt to his face.*)

LEAR: See those invisible dogs over there?

EDGAR Nay!

LEAR: They bark at me. (*Barks*)

EDGAR: Poor Tommy will throw his head at them. (*Pretends to throw his head*) Avaunt, you curs!

LEAR: Avaunt! Avaunt! No dogs allowed! No dogs allowed! Nor rats.

EDGAR: Gibberish, gibberish, and more gibberish on thee!

LEAR: When I am back in power, you, sir, shall be of my knights. But I do not like your fashions. They must be altered!

KENT: Good Queen, the trial is over, so come and rest awhile.

LEAR: So it shall be. We'll go to supper in the morning.

FOOL: And I'll go to bed at noon. (*Exits, then returns.*) That means because I'm sick and I'm not coming back in this play. I'm probably going to die. Got it? Die! … Bye.

Exit the Fool.

Enter the EARL of W.

EARL of W: Come hither, friend. Where is the Queen, my sovereign?

KENT: There, sir, but trouble her not. Her wits are gone.

EARL of W: Have you tried a Place for Mom?

KENT: Not yet.

EARL of W: Are you sure that's the Queen? Is she in disguise? Her hair!

KENT: Who knows?!

EARL of W: 'Tis not a good age when so many are in disguise!

(*Kent re-arranges his disguise.*)

KENT: The times, sir, it is the times.

EARL of W: Good friend, I prithee take the Queen in thy arms I have heard of a plot of death upon her. There is a litter ready. Lay her in it. And drive to Dover, where thou shalt find both welcome and protection.

KENT: Drive? In a car? It's circa 500 A.D.

EARL of W: Get there how you will, sir. Bother me not with details. Take up thy mistress and depart. If you shouldst dally half an hour, her life with thine and all that offer to defend her stand in assured loss. Take up, take up, and follow me that will to some means of transportation give them conduct.

KENT: Come, those who can bear the Queen!

Re-enter the Fool

FOOL: I can almost bear her! Whoop, jug, I love thee!

EARL of W: Come, come away!

Exeunt Kent, Earl of W, and the Fool bearing off the Queen

EDGAR: How light and portable my pain seems now. Now that Poor Tommy, a monarchist to the core, hast seen his Queen treated thus. And what more will hap this night! It makes me want to scream. (*Screams, then exits.*)

Enter Cornwall, Reagan, Gonorrhea, Edmund, and servants.

CORNWALL: (*to Gonorrhea*) Post speedily to my lord your husband, show him this letter. The army of France has landed, including your youngest sister, named … ?

GONORRHEA: I don't remember. Perhaps my other sister, Reagan, remembers?

REAGAN: She's been gone so long I don't remember.

EDMUND: It's Cordelia.

GONORRHEA: Oh, yes. Well, what about her?

CORNWALL: Before she gets here, seek out the traitor Worchestershire, who has harboured the Queen.

Exeunt some servants

REAGAN: Lock him up! Lock him up!

GONORRHEA: Pluck out his eyes!

REAGAN: Or worse!

EDMUND: What's worse than that!?

CORNWALL: Leave him to my displeasure. Edmund, the revenges we are bound to take upon your traitorous father are not fit for your beholding. Stay here. Let all posts and email betwixt us be swift and well punctuated. Farewell to all here. And soon we say farewell to the Earl of Woo too!

REAGAN: Soon the Earl of Woe!

EDMUND: (*to audience*) And *I* become the Earl of Worchestershire!

Enter Oswald

CORNWALL: How now? Where's the Queen?

OSWALD: My lord of Woo hath conveyed her hence. Some six and thirty of her knights met her at a gate and are now gone with her to Dover, where they boast to have well- armed friends.

CORNWALL: Get horses for your mistress.

Exit Oswald

GONORRHEA: I'm going to Dover?

CORNWALL: Indeed!

GONORRHEA: How do I get there?

CORNWALL: Your servants will know the way. Edmund, go with
Gonorrhea!

Exeunt Gonorrhea and Edmund

CORNWALL: Somebody get the Earl! Pinion him like a thief and bring
him before us. Exeunt several servants! (*Exeunt those servants.*)
We next shall do a curtsy to our wrath, which men may blame but
not control.

Enter the Earl of W., brought in by servants.

REAGAN: 'Tis he, the traitor!

CORNWALL: Bind fast his fat old arms.

EARL of W: What means your grace? Good my friends, consider you are
my guests. Do me no foul play.

CORNWALL: Bind him, I say!

SERVANT: I hate this job! (*Servants tie Earl's hands.*)

REAGAN: Hard, hard! O filthy Queen-ass kisser!

EARL of W: Unmerciful lady as you are, I'm none.

REAGAN: I've seen you kiss my mother's ass a thousand times! And in a
thousand ways!

CORNWALL: To this chair bind him! Villain, thou shalt find –

REAGAN: Let me pluck his beard! (*She does.*) What a poor beard to
pluck!

EARL of W: By all the gods, 'tis most ignobly done to pluck me by the
beard.

REAGAN: You ain't seen nothing yet! And soon you will see nothing at
all!

EARL of W: Naughty lady, the hairs which thou dost ravish from my chin will quicken and accuse thee. I am your host!

CORNWALL: Come, sir, what letters had you late from the King of France and what's her name.

EARL of W: Cordelia?

CORNWALL: Yes, Cordelia!

REAGAN: Answer! We know the truth!

CORNWALL: What confederacy have you with the traitors invading Britain?

REAGAN: To whose coddling hands you have sent the lunatic Queen. Speak!

EARL of W: Any letters I received I could not read, so poor was the handwriting.

CORNWALL: Cunning.

REAGAN: And false.

CORNWALL: Where hast thou sent the Queen?

EARL of W: To Dover.

REAGAN: Wherefore to Dover? Wast thou not charged at peril –

CORNWALL: Wherefore to Dover? Let him answer that.

EARL of W: I am tied at the stake, but I must stand the course and speak not.

REAGAN: Wherefore to Dover, bitch?

EARL of W: Because I would not see thy cruel nails pluck out her poor old eyes, nor thy fierce sister in her anointed flesh stick boarish fangs.

CORNWALL: See it shalt thou never. Fellows, hold the chair. Upon these eyes of thine I'll set my foot.

EARL of W: Give me some help! O, cruel! O, ye gods, no!

REAGAN: Even for me, the eyes do seem a bit much.

CORNWALL: You're right, my dove. I have another idea. Bare his chest!

(*The servants bare the chest of the Earl.*)

EARL of W: What's what?!

CORNWALL: Here's what! (*He twists a nipple of the Earl.*) A twist of his tit will give him a fit!

EARL: Not my tit! Not one bit!

REAGAN: Excellent substitute, my lord and husband. Now do both!

CORNWALL: You think?

REAGAN: Both at once!

(*Cornwall twists the Earls nipples with glee.*)

CORNWALL: Take that, evil traitor!

EARL of W: No more! No more, I pray!

SERVANT: Hold your hands, my lord! I have served you ever since I was a child, through no consent of mine, but better service have I never done you than now to bid you hold.

REAGAN: How now, you talking dog!

SERVANT: Lay not another hand upon his nipples!

CORNWALL: Not only upon his nipples but upon my sword too! (*Draws his sword.*)

SERVANT: Do not make me stab thee, sir.

CORNWALL: Villain! (*Lunges at him.*)

SERVANT: (*drawing his sword*) Come then, fat ass, and see how you do against the lower class!

(*Wounds Cornwall.*)

REAGAN: Give me a sword. A peasant stand up thus! No way!

(*She takes a sword and runs the servant through from behind.*)

SERVANT: O, I am slain! My lord, may your aching nipples bear witness to the evil here.

(*He dies.*)

CORNWALL: (*to the Earl*) How do your tits feel now, old man? Do you want more?!

EARL of W: Some decency. Are you incapable of the merest decency?!

CORNWALL: I think you enjoyed it!

EARL of W: You are wrong, sir, so wrong. Most wrong. Where's my son Edmund? Edmund, enkindle all the sparks of nature to avenge this horrid act!

REAGAN: Oh, treacherous villain! Thou call'st on him that hates thee. It was he that made clear thy treasons to us.

EARL of W: O my follies! Then Edgar, my other son, was abused. I am but an old fool, with twisted tits. (*Hangs his head.*)

REAGAN: Go thrust him out at gates and let him ache his way to Dover.

EARL of W: (*touching his nipples*) O ye gods, my nipples!

Exit servant with the Earl

IV.1   Enter Edgar

EDGAR: To be the lowest and most dejected thing of fortune stands still
in some little hope. Welcome then thou unsubstantial air that I
embrace!

Enter the Earl of W.

EARL of W: I think I am near Dover now. (*A man passes nearby*) Excuse
me, person unknown to me. Are we close to Dover? Or must I
trudge on?

MAN: You are very near to the cliffs of Dover.

EARL of W: Good. I thank thee.

EDGAR: How fortunate! There is my father!

EARL of W: O my poor nipples. How they ache with every step.

EDGAR: What tortures have they done to him?!

MAN: (*to the Earl*) I do know you, I see now. You are the Earl of
Worchestershire.

EARL of W: Good friend, be gone. Lest others hurt you.

MAN: (*clutching his nipples*) Nay, not that! But I will not abandon you.

EARL of W: Though these tits give me fits, I will to the cliffs! A poor
triple rhyme, but mine own. O dear son Edgar, if only you were
here! Unlucky victim of thy foolish father's wrath!

MAN: How now! Who's that? (*Points at Edgar.*) Is that Edgar?

EDGAR: O gods, I am discovered!

MAN: Or is it poor, mad Tommy?

EARL of W: Is he by any chance a beggar man?

MAN: Madman and beggar too.

EARL of W: He has some reason left, else he could not beg.

MAN: We must find hope even if it is tiny and lives under a rock.

EARL of W: Nay! As flies to mean little boys are we to the gods –

MAN: They make us their favourite pets?

EARL of W: They kill us for their sport!

MAN: I think there is a plan for each of us. A plan we may not see.

EARL of W: Oh, shut up! Go, go, let me end myself and these tits!

EDGAR: How should this be? Should I speak to my father or not?

EARL of W: If only my good son were here to speak to me!

EDGAR: Bless thee, master!

EARL of W: I will ask this madman to lead me to the cliffs.

MAN: But, sir, he is mad!

EARL of W: I know, but what great theatre when the mad lead the tit-injured! Oh, ouch! Be gone, person!

MAN: I can only do so much. I will be gone, come what will. (*Exits.*)

EARL of W: (*to Edgar*) Sirrah! Come hither!

EDGAR: I cannot continue in this way.

EARL of W: Come hither, fellow!

EDGAR: And yet I must. What, pray tell, can I do for you?

EARL of W: Mad fellow, dost thou knowest the way to the cliffs of Dover?

EDGAR: (*to audience*) Should I lead my own father to the cliffs of death?

EARL of W: O these nips cannot be borne another moment!

EDGAR: Shall I end his suffering?

EARL of W: Here, take this purse. That I am wretched makes thee the happier. Dost thou know the way to Dover or not?

EDGAR: I have a bad sense of direction.

EARL of W: There is a cliff whose high and bending head looks fearfully in the confined deep. Bring me but to the very brim of it and I'll repair the misery thou dost bear with something rich about me. From that place I shall no leading need.

EDGAR: Perhaps your nips will be healed by the cool but soothing breezes there. Give me thy arm. Poor Tommy shall lead thee.

Exeunt

IV.2   Enter Gonorrhea and Edmund

GONORRHEA: Welcome, my lord! We should better get to know one another.

EDMUND: I am at your service, Madam Gonorrhea.

GONORRHEA: Sounds goodly to me. I love the sound of my name in your mouth.

Enter Oswald

GONORRHEA: Now where's my mild husband?

OSWALD: Madam, within. He is much changed. I told him of the French army that was landed. He smiled. I told him that you were coming. He said, 'the worse'. And of Worchestershire's treachery and the loyal service of his son Edmund, then did he call me sot. I am no sot! Sot am I not!

GONORRHEA: Then shalt we go no further now. Back, Edmund, to my brother-in-law. Hasten his musters.

EDMUND: I will not only hasten his musters. I will pour hot mustard up his bung!

GONORRHEA: Well said. You're my kind of man! I'm so through with my girly husband! If you would like a strong woman, wear this. (*Gives him a favour.*)

EDMUND: What is it? It looks too fem.

GONORRHEA: Spare speech! Decline your head. Let this kiss stretch thy spirits up into the air. (*Kisses him on the top of the head.*) Are you stretched like a man?

EDMUND: O madam, I am mightily stretched!

GONORRHEA: What a man! But for now, farewell.

EDMUND: Yours in the ranks of death!

Exit Edmund

OSWALD: Madam, here comes your husband.

Enter Albany

GONORRHEA: I have been worth the whistling.

ALBANY: O wife, you are not worth the dust which the rude wind blows in your face.

GONORRHEA: Ha! Says he who farts in the cart when we go to the mart!

ALBANY: You are lower than a peasant's butt! You will wither and come to a terrible end.

GONORRHEA: No more! Your text is vile.

ALBANY: Wisdom and goodness to the vile seem vile. What have you done, been tigers, not daughters, your mother and the Earl treated most barbarously, like monsters of the deep.

GONORRHEA: Skim-milk-livered man! Thou bearest a cheek for blows! The King of France and my sister, what's her name? –

ALBANY: Cordelia.

GONORRHEA: Yay, Cordelia! Spread their war-like banners in our noiseless land, whilst thou, a moral fool, sits still and cries 'Alack, alack, why do they do so?"!

ALBANY: Fiend! Double-Fiend!

GONORRHEA: Say that again and I'll –

ALBANY: Triple-Fiend!

GONORRHEA: I'll rebuke your genitals to all and sundry!

ALBANY: You wouldn't dare!

GONORRHEA: I spit on your manhood! Mew!

Enter a Messenger

ALBANY: What news?

MESSENGER: O, my good lord, the Duke of Cornwall is dead, slain by his servant, while twisting the noble tits of the Earl of Worchestershire.

ALBANY: Not so! Not so!

MESSENGER: I am just the Messenger, good sir.

ALBANY: Poor Worchestershire! Has he at least one good tit left?

MESSENGER: I know not every detail, sir. (*to Gonorrhea*) This letter craves a speedy answer. 'Tis from your sister.

GONORRHEA: From Cordelia?

MESSENGER: No, from Reagan.

GONORRHEA: (*aside*) In one way, I like this well. Although who know how it will all turn out. (*Aloud*) I'll read and answer.

Exit

ALBANY: Where was his son Edmund when they did twist the noble Earl's noble nips?

MESSENGER: With your wife. Hint, hint.

ALBANY: What hint? He is not here.

MESSENGER: No, my good lord, not now.

ALBANY: Knows Edmund of this wickedness?

MESSENGER: Ay, my good lord. 'Twas he that informed against his father and quit the house on purpose that their nipple business have the freer course.

ALBANY: Dear Earl, I thank thee for the love thou showed the Queen and vow to avenge thy poor, blessed nips! (to Messenger) Come, friend, and tell me what more thou knowest.

Exeunt

IV.3   Enter Kent and a Gentleman

KENT: Do you have any idea why the King of France is no longer marching to save the day?

GENTLEMAN: The word on the street is that he left something imperfect back in France, something that required his personal return.

KENT: Have you by any chance delivered letters to the Queen of France, formerly known as Cordelia?

GENTLEMAN: I did, sir.

KENT: You look like someone who would deliver letters to the Queen of France!

GENTLEMAN: She took the letters, read them in my presence and now and then an ample tear trilled down her delicate cheek.

KENT: So Cordelia was moved?

GENTLEMAN: Unless she but had a speck of dust in her eye.

KENT: She is a good lady.

GENTLEMAN: She looked so lovely as she wept.

KENT: Of course she did. But did she make no verbal question?

GENTLEMAN: Once or twice, she heaved the name of mother, pantingly, forth, as if it pressed her heart with grief, cried 'Sisters shame, shame!' Then even more she shook water from her eyes.

KENT: Shook water?

GENTLEMAN: So to speak. Then she turned away to deal with her grief alone.

KENT: Did she mention me?

GENTLEMAN: I don't know, sir. Who are you?

KENT: Never mind. It does not matter. I am but a mere earthling under the vast stars. Have you spoke with her since?

GENTLEMAN: I have told you too much already, sir.

KENT: And I thank the gods that I happened to run into you.

GENTLEMAN: The stars above must have willed it to be.

KENT: It was predicted at my birth!

GENTLEMAN: And mine! But let me tell you more about Cordelia's tears.

KENT: Must you?

GENTLEMAN: Her tears parted her eyes like pearls from diamonds dropped.

KENT: I get the picture.

GENTLEMAN: Like tears from a mastodon when it sees its offspring trampled by a dinosaur.

KENT: A what?

GENTLEMAN: Like a giant lizard with a terrible toothache, cried she.

KENT: No more, I beg you! I cannot stand it. Have you spoke with her since?

GENTLEMAN: No.

KENT: Was this before or after Queen Lear went naked with her hair a mess in the storm?

GENTLEMAN: I'm not sure.

KENT: Something tells me Queen Lear would not wish to see Cordelia.

GENTLEMAN: Even for comfort?

KENT: Her three daughters are all confused in her storm-worn brain.

GENTLEMAN: Alack! Where is the Queen?

KENT: You do not mean her injury, I trust?!

GENTLEMAN: Merely do I bring letters.

KENT: One can have too many letters. Nevertheless, I will bring you to our mistress and leave you to attend on her. Meanwhile, I must wrap me up awhile. When I am known aright, you shalt not grieve.

GENTLEMAN: You somewhat resemble someone from court, named Kent.

KENT: Kent was banished. I am not he! O to be vanished but not banished! All this anarchy! Go along with me, sir.

Exeunt

IV.4   Enter, with drums and colours, Cordelia, Doctor, and soldiers

CORDELIA: Alas, my mother is as vexed as the sea, singing aloud, and off-tune, crowned with rank weeds, nettles, cuckoo-flowers, or so I hear. And her hair a mess. (*to soldier*) Search every acre and bring my mother to me.

Exeunt soldiers

CORDELIA: (*to Doctor*) Doctor, what wisdom dost thou have to restore her bereaved senses?

DOCTOR: First we try leeches! Then maggots.

CORDELIA: Really?!

DOCTOR: Or I can bleed her!

CORDELIA: She's anemic already!

DOCTOR: Are you the doctor or am I?!

CORDELIA: Well, I'm the Queen of France.

DOCTOR: Madam, I defer. There is a means, however, that will close the eyes of anguish.

CORDELIA: You mean kill her?

DOCTOR: I mean to soothe her with med'cines made of garish flowers.

Enter a Messenger

MESSENGER: I bring news, madam!

CORDELIA: I only want good news!

MESSENGER: The British powers are marching hitherward.

CORDELIA: Our preparations stand in expectation of them. O dear Mummy, it is thy business that I go about. It is not France and its ambitions here I do promote. I swear! But love, dear love, and my aged mother's right. Soon may I see her and in her eyes a shining light!

Exeunt

IV.5   Enter Reagan and Oswald

REAGAN: Stop here and talk. Are my brother-in-law's, also known as Albany's, powers set forth?

OSWALD: Ay, madam.

REAGAN: Himself in person there?

OSWALD: Do you mean is he there in person?

REAGAN: I do, blockhead!

OSWALD: Your speech is convoluted at times, madam.

REAGAN: Nay, you have a peasant's ear! Is my sister in charge?

OSWALD: Your sister is the better soldier.

REAGAN: Good! Why were the Romans great? Because they took what they wanted and gave nobody a casino afterwards! We shall emulate them.

OSWALD: Indeed, madam.

REAGAN: Have you seen Edmund around? Is he as handsome as ever?

OSWALD: I know not, madam.

REAGAN: Oh, you, you're such a lousy envoy.

OSWALD: I am sorry, madam.

REAGAN: Does he write to my sister Gonorrhea?

OSWALD: I can find out, if you like.

REAGAN: Tell Edmund I said hello.

OSWALD: Most assuredly, milady.

REAGAN: I should not have let the Earl of Worchestershire go after we tortured his nips. Wherever he moves, he moves hearts against us.

OSWALD: I dare say. The Earl is much discussed in the villages.

REAGAN: We'll get his ass yet, you watch! Our troops set forth tomorrow. Are you sure Edmund does not write to my sister? What's in that message you carry? Let me see it.

OSWALD: Madam, I had rather …

REAGAN: I know that your lady does not love her husband – I am sure of that – and who can miss the way her eyes follow him? Tell me! I know you are of her bosom?

OSWALD: Of her bosom, madam? Not I.

REAGAN: You are, I know it! Therefore, take this note. My lord is dead. Edmund and I u n d erstand each other. He wishes my hand more than your mistress's. You may redeem yourself by learning more. If you do find Edmund, give him this note. Tell him it's from his honey bunny. (*Hands him a note.*) So fare you well, even though you are a blockhead. And, if you run into the Earl, preferment falls on him who cuts short his complaints, if you catch my drift?

OSWALD: Should I meet him, madam, I should show what party I do follow.

REAGAN: Better and better, my good fellow.

Exeunt

IV.6   Enter the Earl of W. with Edgar, who is wearing peasant's clothes.

EDGAR: And still my father does not recognize me. Most fortunate! Even in these different clothes that I found! Who says disguises do not work!?

EARL of W: When shall I get to the top of the hill?

EDGAR: You do climb it now. Look how we labour.

EARL of W: I see nor feel no hill! The ground is even!

EDGAR: It is most horribly steep. Do you not hear the sea?

EARL of W: No, truly.

EDGAR: Your other senses grow imperfect when your nips hurt.

EARL of W: They do hurt. I have noticed that your voice is different, that thou speakest in better phrase and matter than you, or someone like you, didst before.

EDGAR: You are much deceived. In nothing am I changed but in my garments.

EARL of W: No, you are better spoken.

EDGAR: Come on, sir. Here's the place you asked for. Over there, beyond that bluff is the cliff's edge. Though why you want it escapes me quite. Unless it is to cool thy twisted nips in the ocean's breezes.

EARL: Oh, do not ask why I want the cliff. You have been kind to lead me where my pain can end.

EDGAR: Yay, the cool air up here will be a balm to your …

EARL of W: – Yes, to my migraine nipples. Do not enquire further! (*Aside*) This man does not realise I mean to jump!

EDGAR: If he jumps and survives, he will be so relieved he won't want to jump again! Sir, close your eyes and run but some short distance, where you will find your relief.

EARL of W: Are you certain there's a cliff there with fishermen below as small as mice?

EDGAR: Unless they be tiny, tiny fishermen in fact.

EARL of W: Clear the way. Stand off! And let me hear thy going.

EDGAR: Keep closed your orbs.

EARL of W: They are. Now I bid you farewell. Bid me farewell.

EDGAR: Farewell. I'm sure this is the best course of action for my only father!

EARL of W: If my son Edgar live, the gods bless him!

EDGAR: Run forward with thy eyes closed and bare thy nips to the salt-soothing air!

(The Earl of W shuts his eyes and runs forward, then stops and does a little hop as he leaps and falls down.)

EARL of W: (*opens his eyes*) I leapt from that cliff up there. (Points upward.)

EDGAR: (*in a different voice*) Ho, you, sir! Friend! Speak! Are you dead or alive?

EARL of W: Away and let me die! I just now did jump off a cliff.

EDGAR: Fall did you, sir, perpendicularly. I saw you with these my eyes. And yet you live!

EARL of W: Your voice sounds familiar. Didn't you just lead me to the cliff?

EDGAR: Your ears deceive you, sir. I just happened to pass by.

EARL of W: You also sound like my son Edgar before he went mad and into hiding.

EDGAR: It is my accent, sir. We all sound alike. Do not question those who do you good. Now that you have fallen from a cliff, you can but be ready to go on with life.

EARL of W: Would someone who cared for me risk me having a heart attack during such a fall?

EDGAR: 'Tis most wondrous, like much in life!

EARL of W: I hope that mad beggar up there is okay.

EDGAR: When he passed me, I directed him to a local shelter.

EARL of W: His state still troubles me.

EDGAR: There is only so much we can do. Give me your arm, sir.

(Edgar helps up the Earl.)

Enter Queen Lear dressed fantastically with wild flowers.

But who comes here? Surely not the Queen!

LEAR: It is the Queen Herself! (*Twirls.*)

EDGAR: O thou side-piercing sight!

LEAR: You're not so hot yourself! What's the password? Do you like my hair?

EDGAR: Sweet marjoram?

LEAR: Pass.

EARL of W: I know that voice. (*Falls to his knees before Lear.*) It is my Edgar!

EDGAR: No, that is not your Edgar!

EARL of W: It is my Edgar! I'd know him anywhere! (*calling*) Are you not my very Edgar?

LEAR: I am the Queen of all Britain! See how everyone quakes when I speak?! What is thy cause? Accused of adultery? Thou shalt not die! The wren goes to it! Peasants try! Let copulation thrive! The Earl's bastard son was kinder to his father than my licit daughters – Gonorrhea, Reagan and what's her name?!

EARL of W: Ophelia. Amelia?

LEAR: Cordelia! See, my mind grows clear. But I could use a sniff of civet. Here's money for you. (*Gives flowers.*)

EARL of W: O let me kiss that hand.

LEAR: Let me wipe it first. It smells of mortality. (*Wipes her hand on the Earl.*)

EARL of W: Dost thou know me?

LEAR: You did me a kindness once involving a hovel.

EARL of W: I did, Your Grace.

LEAR: And was for it was rudely stripped and tweaked.

EARL of W: Do you want to see what they did?

LEAR: No, thank you.

EARL of W: It still hurts.

LEAR: I said no, thank you!

EDGAR: I would not believe this from report, and yet I see it as it is!

LEAR: Are we not pitiful, the all of us?

EDGAR: I am the most pitiful, bereft of father, betrayed by brother, and these clothes do not fit.

EARL of W: No, I am the most pitiful. You should see my nips!

ALL: No, thank you!

    Enter the Fool.

FOOL: No, it is I the Fool, who is the most pitiful of all! Shrunken and mocked and barely tolerated even if my jokes are wonderful! Sickly, and almost dead, and yet here I am unwilling to fade away. My stool improves with each hour. Do you want proof? It's never looked better. You cannot trump a Fool's stool.

ALL: No, thank you!

LEAR: I am glad to have my Fool again. Take my coronet of weeds!
    (*Takes off her coronet of flowers, gives it to the Fool.*)

FOOL: O, mother, thou dost restore my heart! (*They kiss.*)

LEAR: A Queen and her Fool, it does not get better than this!

FOOL: You should see the Fool's stool.

LEAR: Jesus H. Christ, no stool!

FOOL: Okay, okay.

EARL of W: That I should come to this, with nips aflame and a Fool's stool my study!

LEAR: I know thee, sir. Thy name is hard to pronounce. Is it not?

EARL of W: No, it's Worchestershire. Or it was. My son Edmund has stolen my title.

LEAR: We both were not blessed in our children. Yet I shall give thee comfort.

EARL of W: Oh?

LEAR: As Queen of all Britain, I rename thee Earl of Dover!

EARL of W: Majesty, how can I ever thank thee enough?

LEAR: Do everything I ask henceforth and keep your mouth shut when you don't like something.

EARL of W: Of course, Your Majesty.

LEAR: Here is a minor coronet. (*Takes the coronet off the Fool's head, places it on the Earl's head.*)

FOOL: Hey! And not nonny, nonny!

LEAR: Fate is fickle, Fool.

> Enter a Gentleman and two Attendants. The Earl and Edgar draw back.

GENTLEMAN: Here the Queen is! Lay hands upon her!

LEAR: What, a prisoner? Fate is even fickler than I thought! Let me have surgeons! I am cut to the brains!

GENTLEMAN: You mistake us, madam.

LEAR: I will not die bravely. I will flee!

Exit Lear running with Attendants

GENTLEMAN: A sight most pitiful to see in the meanest wretch, past speaking in a queen. At least she has one daughter who redeems nature from the general curse that two others have brought her to.

EDGAR: (*coming forward*) Hail, gentle sir!

GENTLEMAN: Sir, speed you. What's your will?

EDGAR: I believe the Queen mistook your purpose. You are here to assist the Queen, yay?

GENTLEMAN: We root for the Queen!

EDGAR: Do you hear aught of a battle?

GENTLEMAN: Everybody knows that, that can distinguish sound.

EDGAR: But how goes the battle is my question?

GENTLEMAN: The main descry stands on the hourly thought.

EDGAR: What does that mean?

GENTLEMAN: That though the Queen herself be here, or hopefully somewhere near, her army is moved on.

EDGAR: I know not what to think, and yet I thank thee, sir.

GENTLEMAN: I must move on!

Exit Gentleman

EARL of W: (*coming forward*) Ye gods above, let not my worser spirit tempt me to end my life before you please!

EDGAR: (*using yet another dialect*) A most good prayer, father!

EARL of W: Who are you?

EDGAR: A poor, multilingual fellow down on his luck.

EARL of W: And I am the Earl of Dover. Or I may be. Who knows if the Queen signed the proper papers. She did not even tap me on the shoulder with a sword. I so want to be Dover instead of Worchestershire!

EDGAR: Give me your hand, sir. I will lead you to some resting place. (*Takes his hand.*)

EARL of W: Hearty thanks, sir!

Enter Oswald

OSWALD: Aha, a proclaimed prize! Most happy! Thou old, unhappy traitor with a traitor's tits! The sword is out that must destroy thee. (Brandishes sword)

EARL of W: Lo, these injured orbs upon my chest can beat your sword any day or night!

EDGAR: (*intervening*) Stop!

OSWALD: Wherefore, bold peasant, darest thou support a published poet?!

EDGAR: (*correcting*) Published traitor!

OSWALD: What did I say?

EDGAR: Published poet.

OSWALD: Let go, slave, or thou diest!

EDGAR: Good gentleman, go your way and let poor folk like us pass. Am I plain enough?

OSWALD: Out, dunghill!

EDGAR: I am no one's dunghill! (*They fight.*)

OSWALD: Slave, thou hast slain me! Slave, take my purse!

EDGAR: I don't carry a purse. I don't need a purse.

OSWALD: Bury my body and give the letters which thou dost find about me to Edmund.

EDGAR: Yet more letters!

OSWALD: Seek him out wher'er he be! (*Dies.*)

EDGAR: Don't pick a fight if you can't win it. I know thee well, a serviceable villain, as duteous to the vices of thy mistress as badness would desire.

EARL of W: What, is he dead?

EDGAR: Sit you down, father, and rest you. Meanwhile, I will search his pockets. The letters that he speaks of may be my friends. I know I should not read other people's letters, but I'll make an exception in his case. And he did ask me.

EARL of W: Your scruples, sir, commend you.

(*Edgar reads the letter.*)

Hi from Gonorrhea! Let our reciprocal vows be remembered, Edmund. From my husband's loathed bed save me. And help me to your bed. Hint, hint!

EARL of W: What does she mean?

EDGAR: Rest thy brain, father. (*Finishes the letter.*) *Your eager, would-be wife!*

EARL of W: Does she mean … ?

EDGAR: Yes, father, yes.

EARL of W: Why do you keep calling me 'father'?

EDGAR: Because you are old and reverent, nothing more. This ungracious letter shows nothing less than a plot upon her true husband's life! And with my brother, no less!

EARL of W: Really?

EDGAR: Rest! For God's sake, your brains are addled!

EARL of W: I cannot rest. The Queen is mad. Her hair is bad. My old orbs ache yet. Better I were distracted. So should my thoughts be severed from my griefs. (*Sound of a drum far off.*) Perchance that far-off drum will do the trick.

EDGAR: Perchance. Perchance it is too late. But give me your hand and I will bestow you with a friend.

Exeunt

IV.7   Enter Cordelia, Doctor, and Kent

CORDELIA: Wait, stop! I have a thought out here in the middle of the field!

KENT: Yes?

CORDELIA: Kent, are you not?

KENT: Yes.

CORDELIA: I'd know you anywhere. How should I live and work to match thy goodness?

KENT: To be recognized is quite enough, milady.

CORDELIA: Those clothes you wear are memories of the worser hours. Prithee take them off!

KENT: Off?

CORDELIA: Don't get your hopes up, boy. I merely meant change those clothes.

KENT: I have grown used to these, if I may, madam.

CORDELIA: They are a terrible disguise, Kent. But suit yourself. Pun intended!

KENT: I thank thee, madam.

CORDELIA: And I thank thee for all thy service. (*to Doctor*) How does the Queen?

DOCTOR: She sleeps well, a little dyspepsia.

CORDELIA: O you kind gods! Continue to watch after my benighted mother!

DOCTOR: So please Your Majesty, let us wake the Queen. She hath slept long.

CORDELIA: I think more leeches are in order, but according to your expertise.

DOCTOR: I dosed her with some peasant urine, and she seems to have benefited well. We also put on her some fresh garments. And I fixed her hair.

Enter Gentleman ushering Queen Lear in a chair, accompanied by servants. All fall to their knees.

GENTLEMAN: Be by, good madam, when we do awaken her. Your presence may temper her.

CORDELIA: Very well. What if she flies off the handle again?

GENTLEMAN: Let's hope, madam.

CORDELIA: (*kneeling by the chair and kissing the Queen's hand*) O my dear mother, let this kiss repair those violent harms that my two sisters have in thy reverence made.

KENT: She's a keeper!

CORDELIA: Was this a face to be opposed against the jarring winds? Nay! Mine enemy's dog, though he had riddled me with rabies, should have stood that night against my fire! Yay! Who'll give me a yay?

KENT: Yay!

CORDELIA: She wakes! Speak to her!

DOCTOR: Madam, do you so. It is fittest.

CORDELIA: How dost my royal lady? How fares Your Majesty?

LEAR: (*waking up more*) Not too bad. But you do wrong me to take me out of the grave. What's your name?

CORDELIA: Cordelia.

LEAR: Such a pretty name. I had a daughter named Ophelia or Amelia.

CORDELIA: Do you know me?

LEAR: You are a spirit. Where did you die? How did it feel?

DOCTOR: She's scarce awake. Let her alone awhile.

LEAR: Where have I been? I don't think it was Hawaii.

CORDELIA: No, it was not Hawaii.

LEAR: Would I were assured of my condition.

CORDELIA: Look upon me, madam. And hold your hand in benediction over me. (*Lear falls to her knees.*) No, madam, you must not kneel.

LEAR: Pray do not mock me. I am four score and upward and, to deal plainly, I fear I am not in my perfect mind. Methinks I should know you and this man, yet I am doubtful for I am ignorant what place this is, nor these garments, or where I did lodge last night. Do not laugh at me, for I think this lady to be my child Cordelia.

CORDELIA: And so I am, I am.

LEAR: Be your tears wet? Yet weep not! If you have poison for me, I will drink it. Your sisters have done, as I remember, done me wrong. You have some cause; they have not.

CORDELIA: No cause, no cause.

LEAR: Am I in France?

KENT: In your own queendom, madam.

LEAR: Do not abuse me.

DOCTOR: Be comforted, madam. The great rage, you see, is killed in her. Desire her to go in; trouble her no more till further settling.

CORDELIA: Will it please your highness walk?

LEAR: You must bear with me. Forget and forgive. I am old and foolish. But my hair looks great, I know not how!

CORDELIA: You are my special Queen.

Exeunt all but Kent and the Gentleman

GENTLEMAN Hold it true that the Duke of Cornwall was slain by his servant?

KENT: That's the word on the country road.

GENTLEMAN: Bad times! Who is in charge now of his people?

KENT: The bastard son of Worchestershire, who now, I think, goes by the name Duke of Dover,

GENTLEMAN: All this name-changing is not good! I heard that Edgar, his banished son, is with the Earl of Kent in Germany.

KENT: Don't believe everything you hear. Or see. Or think.

GENTLEMAN: If only there were something like an Internet to separate fact from fiction.

KENT: Indeed!

GENTLEMAN: I think the approaching battle will be bloody.

KENT: I think so too. Nice chatting with you.

GENTLEMAN: May we bump into each other like this again.

Exeunt

V.1   Enter, with drums and colours, Edmund, Reagan, gentlemen and soldiers

EDMUND: (*to a gentleman*) Do you know if the Duke of Albany has decided to change his mind again?

GENTLEMAN: He is full of alteration, true.

EDMUND: (*to Reagan*) What thinks the sweet and widowed lady here?

REAGAN: We'll have to kill that vacillating prick!

EDMUND: Spoken like a valiant lady, which one must love.

REAGAN: Now, sweet lord, do you not love my sister.

EDMUND: Yay, but only as a sister.

REAGAN: For one such as you, I doubt that matters in your lusts!

EDMUND: That thought abuses you.

REAGAN: I suspect you two have been bosom to bosom.

EDMUND: We have not touched bosoms! I swear it on my honour, madam.

REAGAN: Endure her not, will I. Be not familiar with her, bosom or no bosom!

EDMUND: Fear not. Here they come!

Enter, with drums and colours, Albany, Gonorrhea, and soldiers

GONORRHEA: Look at us! Our drums and colours are better than thine!

REAGAN: Ha! In your dreams, dear sister!

GONORRHEA: (*aside*) I had rather lose the battle than that my sister here should loosen me and Edmund.

REAGAN: (*to audience*) Did you hear that? She should keep her thoughts to herself.

ALBANY: Our loving sister, well met! I hear that some are gossiping about my so-called vacillation. I am deliberative, not vacillating.

GONORRHEA: (*aside*) Like a virgin on her wedding night!

ALBANY: I heard that!

GONORRHEA: I care not!

ALBANY: The Queen is come to her daughter Cordelia. It touches us as France thus invades our land.

EDMUND: You speak nobly, sir.

REAGAN: Why do you tell him that?

GONORRHEA: We need to stick together to defeat those troops. We can quarrel betwixt ourselves afterwards.

EDMUND: I am sure there will be only peace after. (*to Albany*) I shall attend you presently at your tent.

REAGAN: Sister, you'll go with us then?

GONORRHEA: No!

REAGAN: 'Tis most convenient. Pray go with us.

GONORRHEA: If only to keep an eye on you, sister mine.

EDMUND: Both sisters, will you not come, pray you both?

GONORRHEA: I like not this.

REAGAN: I like not this.

      Exeunt

      Edgar enters as Albany is going out.

EDGAR: Your Grace, if you would speak with man so poor as me, hear me, one word.

ALBANY: (*to his soldiers*) I'll overtake you!

EDGAR: Before you fight the battle, ope this letter.

ALBANY: Yet another letter to ope?!

EDGAR: If you have victory, let the trumpet sound for him that brought it. Wretched though I seem, I can produce a champion that will, through physical valour, prove what is avouched there.

ALBANY: Why should I listen to you? Nonetheless, stay till I have perused thy letter.

EDGAR: When time shall serve, let but a herald cry and I will appear again.

ALBANY: I understand. You need time to dress up like this champion you mentioned.

EDGAR: My lips are mum on that.

Enter Edmund.

EDMUND: The filthy French are in view! Draw up your powers. Here is the guess of their true strength and forces. (*Hands Albany a letter.*)

ALBANY: Another letter?! Jesus Christ! (*Crosses himself.*)

EDMUND: Haste is now urged upon you!

ALBANY: Be it so!

Exit Albany

EDMUND: (*to audience*) To both these sisters have I sworn my love. Each is jealous of the other. Which of them shall I take? (*Cackles.*) Ha! Ha! Ha! And I haven't even wooed Cordelia yet! One? Two? Or all three?! None can be enjoyed if all are left alive! And 'tis Albany here must surely perish. Oh, I am so bad! And yet so sexy! And as for Queen Lear herself, no pardon, none. No mercy! No Place for Mom!

Exit.

V.2   Alarm within. Enter, with drum and colours, Lear, Cordelia holding her hand, and soldiers, cross the stage.

LEAR: (*looking around*) Where are we going?

Exeunt

Enter Edgar and the Earl W.

EDGAR: Here, father, take the shadow of this tree to be your host. If I can get back, I'll bring you comfort. If I can't, have a good life.

EARL of W: Grace go with you, sir!

Exit Edgar.

Alarm and retreat within. Re-enter Edgar.

EARL of W: Back so soon? Have I met you before?

EDGAR: You must away, old man! Give me your hand! Away!

EARL: No further, sir. A man may rot and decay and decompose even here.

EDGAR: What, in ill thoughts again? Men must endure.

EARL of W: Who says?!

EDGAR: Their going hence as their coming hither.

EARL of W: What bullshit!

EDGAR: Father, no!

EARL of W: 'Tis bullshit, yet I will give it one more try.

    Exit both.

V.3   Enter in conquest Edmund. Lear and Cordelia are prisoners with their hands tied. Captain present.

EDMUND: Some officers take away these prisoners. We'll decide later what to do with them. (*Cackles.*) I'm so bad, so bad! I give myself goosebumps!

CORDELIA: We are not the first who with good meaning have incurred the worst. For thee, oppressed Queen, I am cast down.

LEAR: And for thee too, am I.

CORDELIA: But shall we not see Gonorrhea and Reagan bespattered with tears when they see our plight? They are kin!

LEAR: No, no, no, no! Come, let's away to prison. We two alone will sing like birds in a cage. Tweet, tweet! Tweet, tweet! And we'll chirp of court gossip, who loses and who wins. Whose reputation falls or rises on a whim!

EDMUND: Here's a whim for you. Take them away!

LEAR: Oh, do not whim on the mighty of spirit! (*to Cordelia*) Have I embraced you today? (*Embraces her.*) Wipe thine soggy eyes. In time, these villains shall be devoured by beasts!

CORDELIA: But what of mercy, Mother?

LEAR: They shall taste what starvation tastes like! Their frail flesh shall be simmered in a cauldron!

CORDELIA: Mother!

LEAR: What?! It's circa 500 A.D.! Let us go off and plan more revenges.

Exeunt Lear and Cordelia, guarded.

EDMUND: Come hither, Captain. You're here. You might as well say something.

CAPTAIN: I'll do it, my lord.

EDMUND: Take this note. And go follow them to prison. If thou dost as this instructs thee, thou shall make thy way to noble fortunes. Either say thou wilt do it or thrive by other means.

CAPTAIN: I do not follow.

EDMUND: Art thou a dullard? Or is it my princely, orotund lingo that baffles thee?!

CAPTAIN: Oh, you mean . . . ? (*Puts invisible knife to his throat.*)

EDMUND: Carry it so as I have set it down in this note. (*Hands him a note.*)

CAPTAIN: I cannot read, but I think I catch your drift.

EDMUND: Read my drift well, sir. Read it well.

Exit the Captain

Flourish. Enter Albany, Gonorrhea, Reagan, and officers.

ALBANY: Oh, here's Edmund! What luck! (*to Edmund*) Sir, you have shown today your valiant strain and Dame Fortune led you well.

EDMUND: I only did what any villainous bastard would do.

ALBANY: You are the best villainous bastard I have ever met.

EDMUND: I thank you, sir.

ALBANY: Now I do require those prisoners of you, so to use them as we shall find their forgotten merits and we can spend some forty minutes forgiving one another.

EDMUND: Sir, I thought it fit to send the old and miserable Queen to some retention and appointed guard. The question of Queen Lear and Cordelia requires a fitter place than this.

ALBANY: Sir, by your patience, I hold you but a minor participant in this war, not as a brother.

REAGAN: Methinks our pleasure might have been demanded ere you spoke so far. Edmund led our powers, bore the commission of my place and person, which may well stand up to call itself your brother.

GONORRHEA: Not so hot, hot sister! Edmund may 'stand up' in your 'place' and 'person.' But we need not hear of such things here in public!

REAGAN: He's the best.

ALBANY: Your husband is not even rotten yet!

REAGAN: At least my husband's dead! Sister, you are an adulteress!

GONORRHEA: Who ha, who ha! Look who's calling who names!

REAGAN: Lady, I am not well. Else I should answer from a full-flowing stomach.

GONORRHEA: Full-flowing with sperm, is it?

REAGAN: (*to Edmund*) Sir, witness the word that create thee here my lord and master.

GONORRHEA: No, he's my lord and master!

ALBANY: A bastard your lord and master!?

GONORRHEA: And twice the man you are! Or ever were!

ALBANY: Oh, so? Let us show our penises to the assembled as proof of what needs proof!

REAGAN: No, let the drum strike and prove my title Edmund's.

GONORRHEA: Foolish sister if ever there was one!

ALBANY: Edmund, I arrest thee on capital treason!

EDMUND: Like hell!

ALBANY: And in your ascendency you can have this gilded serpent, my wife! Reagan, you have been outfoxed. I know my wife! You have been poisoned!

REAGAN: You mean with poison?

ALBANY: No, I mean with indigestion! Of course with poison, several, most like.

REAGAN: But I poisoned her!

GONORRHEA: Or so you thought, bitch! I spat it out without one drop passing to my blood. Ha! Ha!

ALBANY: (*to Edmund*) Thou art armed. Let the trumpet sound. If none appear to prove upon thy person thy heinous treasons, then there is my pledge. (*Throws down his glove.*)

REAGAN: O I am sick, most sick!

EDMUND: Proclaim me, you worthless clod, will you?! (*Throws down his glove.*) There's my exchange!

ALBANY: Throw your glove, will you?! I throw my shoe! (*Throws a shoe.*)

EDMUND: Your shoe?! I spit upon your shoe! Here be my leotards! (*Attempts to throw them but can't get them off.*)

ALBANY: Well, I'm waiting.

EDMUND: All I really need is a sword! Or two! (*Takes two swords and waves them while stumbling around in his leotards, trying to pull them up.*)

ALBANY: You lack royal grace, sir!

EDMUND: What of it? Against any who step forth to challenge me, I am prepared now to maintain my honour and dignity by combat!

ALBANY: A herald, ho!

Enter a Herald.

Trust to thy single virtue, Edmund.

REAGAN: My sickness grows upon me.

ALBANY: She is not well. Convey her to my tent.

Exit Reagan, supported.

ALBANY: Come hither, herald. Let the trumpet sound and read out this. (*Hands out a note. A trumpet sounds.*)

HERALD: (*reading*) If any man of quality (or woman) or degree within the lists of the army maintain upon Edmund, supposed Earl, that he is a manifest traitor, let him (or her) appear by the third sound of the trumpet. He is most bold in his defence.

(*First trumpet*)

Again!

(*Second trumpet.*)

Again!

(*Third trumpet.*)

(*Trumpet answers within. Edgar enters armed, a trumpet before him.*)

ALBANY: Ask him (or her) his or her or their purpose here!

HERALD: What are you? Your name, your quality, and your answer to this summons. And of course your pronouns.

EDGAR: My name is lost, but I am as noble as the adversary. As for my pronouns, just guess! Who speaks for the Earl?

EDMUND: Me, me, and me! What sayest thou to me?!

EDGAR: Draw thy sword. Here is mine. Mine, mine, mine, mine! (*Draws his sword.*) Behold! By my pronouns, thou art a coward, false to the gods, to thy brother, and to thy father!

EDMUND: By my pronouns, am I none!

EDGAR: Thou liest, pronoun-boy!

EDMUND: Legally, I should ask thy name, but since thy outside looks so fair and warlike, I will not haggle. By rule of knighthood, I toss this charge of treason back into your face! Pronoun that! This sword of mine will show whose might is right. Trumpets, speak!

(*Alarms, a fight with swords, Edmund falls.*)

ALBANY: (*to Edgar, about to slay Edmund*) Spare him! Spare him!

GONORRHEA: Edmund, by law, you were not bound to answer an unknown opponent. You are not vanquished, but cheated!

ALBANY: Goddamn it, Dame! Stop! Or I will make you read another letter! Yours!

GONORRHEA: No, not that!

ALBANY: Thou worse than any name. Read here thine own evil. (*Shows her a letter.*) (*She grabs at it.*) No tearing, lady! Thy words betray thee!

GONORRHEA: I did not write it! I dictated it, maybe. That doesn't count.

ALBANY: Do not woman-splain to me! (*to Edmund*) Knowest thou this paper?

EDMUND: Ask me not what I know.

GONORRHEA: I am out of this space!

    Exit Gonorrhea

ALBANY: Go after her. She's desperate. Govern her.

    Exit an officer

    I hope she'll be all right!

    (*All the others turn their heads to look at Albany.*)

    I can't help it. I love a strong woman!

EDMUND: (*to Edgar*) What you have charged me with, that have I done. The time will reveal all. Yet that is past, and so am I. But what art thou that has bested me? If you're noble, I do forgive thee. If you're a peasant, I spit on your mother's pronouns!

EDGAR: Let's exchange charity.

EDMUND: No! Charity is for sissies.

EDGAR: I am no less in blood than thou art, Edmund. My name is Edgar and thy father's son.

EDMUND: Edgar, not!

EDGAR: Yes, that Edgar, of many faces and many voices. Even I don't know who I am at times.

EDMUND: I used to think you were something of a clown. Yet now I see that thou art a worthy prince.

EDGAR: I know it.

ALBANY: Where have you been hiding, Edgar? And do you know where your father is?

EDGAR: It is not a brief tale, but I will tell it all.

ALBANY: That's all right. We don't need every detail.

EDGAR: First there was a proclamation I had to escape. Naturally, I slipped into a madman's rags and screamed and carried on.

ALBANY: You can tell us more, over mulled wine, later.

EDGAR: Then I ran into my father with his tortured nips and became his guide, as would any son. Nay, I did not take him to a surgeon or an apothecary. That would be too simple. I never revealed myself as his son to him. That would be too simple. He asked me to lead him to the cliffs of Dover. I suspected that he wished to jump, and of course the strain of thinking he had jumped to his death – but survived – did him a world of good. At first! But then, despite my many ministrations, his heart burst smilingly, and I left him dead under a tree.

EDMUND: This speech of yours hath moved me. And I may live to do such good yet.

EDGAR: Thank you, brother. You're legit in my eyes!

EDMUND: But speak you on. You look as if you have more to say.

ALBANY: If there be more, hold it in, for I am almost ready to dissolve in tears, hearing all this.

EDGAR: A little more. I ran into a man I was sure was formerly known as Kent. I told him what happened to his employer, the beleaguered Queen. The tale unsettled him and he clamoured like a babe with an irritating diaper, and there I left him in a trance.

ALBANY: So you left your father dead under a tree and Kent in a trance?

EDGAR: O do not thank me, sir. It was what anyone would do.

Enter a Gentleman with a bloody knife

GENTLEMAN: Help, help! O help!

EDGAR: What kind of help?

ALBANY: Speak, man!

EDGAR: What means this bloody knife?

ALBANY: Don't tell me my wife is dead!

GENTLEMAN: No, sir. She sacrificed a chicken to the gods instead. She's resting now.

ALBANY: She's a bitch, but I love her.

GENTLEMAN: And, by the way, your wife confessed to poisoning the Duchess Reagan, but who also has survived because the poison was made in China and did not work.

EDMUND: I was engaged to them both! Never again!

EDGAR: Here comes Kent in disguise, as usual.

Enter Kent

KENT: I am come. No more disguise! (*Takes off his disguise.*) I am Kent and I have come to serve my Queen openly. Is she not here?

ALBANY: Ut oh! All may not turn out so well, I fear! Speak, Edmund! Before this recent conversion, did you do ill to the Queen and Ophelia – I mean Cordelia?

EDMUND: I may have. My mind is clouded. I'm a bastard.

Enter Gonorrhea and Reagan

Oh, no, old girlfriends!

ALBANY: A fitting threesome!

KENT: Did I miss something?

EDMUND: This Edmund was beloved. The one the other poisoned for my sake.

ALBANY: Brag not, you're still a bastard! There are loose ends here that must be tied. Let's see. I send my wife and her evil sister to be teachers of our youth!

REAGAN: No! Please never that!

GONORRHEA: I'd rather die!

ALBANY: You want a strong man, I'll show you a strong man! Take them away to a school and let them try to teach! Good luck with

that! (*Weeping loudly, Reagan and Gonorrhea are dragged off.*)
All right, are there any more loose ends? What about you, Kent?

KENT: I always shall make myself of use, sir.

ALBANY: I shall find some place, some role for thee! (*Kent bows.*)

EDMUND: I remember me now. I pant for life, but some good I mean to
do despite my own nature. Quickly send to the castle, for my writ
is on the life of the Queen and Cordelia. Pray send in time!

ALBANY: Run, run! O run!

SOLDIER: Run, run! O run!?

EDGAR: To whom, my lord? Who handles the paperwork? Send thy
token of reprieve!

EDMUND: Well thought on, Edgar, for once. Take my sword. Give it to
the captain.

EDGAR: (to soldier) Haste thee for thy life.

Exit soldier

EDMUND: The captain hath a commission from thy wife and me, to
hang Cordelia in the prison and lay the blame upon her own
despair,

ALBANY: The gods defend her. Bear this bastard hence awhile.

(*Edmund is borne off*)

Enter Lear with a comatose Cordelia in her arms, followed by
officers and others.

ALBANY: What's here?

LEAR: Howl! Howl! Howl! How many howls is that?

CORDELIA: (*waking up*) Three. (*Falls back into a coma.*)

LEAR: Are you all men of stone? Yes, she came out of her coma to count my howls, but who knows what will happen to my lovely Cordelia. This may be a tragedy yet.

KENT: Oh, nay! Not a tragedy!

EDGAR: Such horror!

LEAR: She is heavy! I will put her down. No, I will carry her and carry her and carry her!

KENT: O madam, I will help you tote your daughter. It is I, Kent!

LEAR: Prithee away! Kent never looks like Kent! It is a disguise!

EDGAR: It is indeed the noble Kent, your friend.

LEAR: Hold steady Cordelia while I breathe a moment. (*Hands Cordelia to Edgar and Kent, who hold her up although she keeps swooning.*) Cordelia, stay a little. No word for me? Her voice was ever soft. Don't let her fall. She might bounce.

EDGAR/KENT: No, Your Majesty.

LEAR: Mine eyes are not of the best. But are you not Kent?

KENT: The same – your faithful servant Kent.

LEAR: I should not have banished thee. Correct?

KENT: No, Majesty, perhaps you should not have.

LEAR: Well, you are welcome now. Don't let Cordelia fall!

KENT: Nor are your other daughters dead. They are punished more than that, with teaching school to the unwilling who trudge there.

LEAR: O happy day! If I know them, and I do, they will still claim that I gave them my lands.

KENT: You did, madam.

LEAR: Nay, read the small print! My eyes are not so bad they canst not deal with small print. I hereby reclaim my properties and lands according to what is there on the last page – the small print! I am still Queen!

KENT: It is a much happy day then!

LEAR: What's a much-happy day? And, no, I'm not now giving you, Kent, or you, Edgar, any lands of mine! I have learned my lesson from my teacher-daughters!

Enter Edmund

EDMUND: I did not perish from my wound! The leeches helped. I may have a little limp, but some ladies find that attractive. I shall beget a litter of bastards yet!

Enter the Earl of W.

EDGAR: Father, is that you? I thought I left you under a tree.

EARL of W: You did, you loveable imbecile. But I managed to find my way here anyway. As for my abused nips, the Lord is my comfort. (*Makes the sign of the cross.*) In the name of the Father, of the Son, and of the Holy Ghost. (*Makes another sign of the cross.*) In the name of the Father, of the Son, and of the Holy Ghost (*Makes a third sign of the cross.*) In the name of the Father, of the Son, and of the Holy Ghost! See, all better!

EDMUND: Father? Can you ever forgive me for taking your title?

EARL of W: Give it back.

EDMUND: Okay.

EARL of W: Henceforth I am the Earl of Dover!

(*They embrace. Edgar joins them in the embrace.*)

ALBANY: Well done! It is good to see the family thrive.

LEAR: I think, despite all this gladness, that I am going to croak. (*Grabs at her throat, has a coughing spell.*) No, I think it was just a hairball. Don't ask!

ALBANY: Are we all settled then, as God and comedy would have it. Remember, a comedy is the comfort food of life!

KENT: Sir, I hate to remind you, but what is my fate to be?

ALBANY: You aren't married, I believe. Why don't you marry Cordelia?

KENT: Okay.

ALBANY: It's done then! Wake her up.

CORDELIA: (*waking up*) I'm already married. To the King of France.

LEAR: But that was an arranged marriage. And French! I hereby declare it null and void, by the wave of my hand. It is good to be an autocrat! But do you and Kent feel anything at all for one another? We do not want to exchange one arranged marriage for another.

KENT: I do feel a special hard-on for Cordelia. I never let on before.

CORDELIA: I like a man who likes disguises! It makes me tingle!

LEAR: Well matched! I declare thee wife and husband.

(*Kent and Cordelia embrace.*)

KENT: However, I do have one question. As Cordelia was married before, I must ask if that marriage was consummated.

CORDELIA: No, I am still a vegan!

KENT: Close enough. My bride! (*They embrace again.*)

ALBANY: So then, can we wrap this up at last?!

(Offstage voice of the Fool.)

FOOL: Wait but a minute more! Guess who's been left outside this door.

LEAR: Who's that? It can't be …

Enter the Fool

FOOL: O it can be – in a comedy! *As You Like It, What You Will, All's Swell That Ends Swell*! Need I go on? Old Will Shakespeare knew how to end a play! With a laugh, a laugh a laugh to keep dark grief away! (*Turns toward Queen Lear*) There she is! O Mummy! Mummy! (*The Fool runs toward Lear and jumps into her arms.*)

LEAR: (*cradling the Fool*) O my boy! My boy! You are indeed my boy! I acknowledge thee at last. My special, special, special, non-binary boy!

(All applaud.)

BLACKOUT

ROME DIDN'T FALL.
IT WAS PUSHED

CHARACTERS: (7)

IGNORAMUS, male, any age, smarter than he is given credit for

PIUS ANXIUS, male, any age, a killjoy

TITUS GASEOUS OBNOXIUS, male, over forty, an oafish Roman

OTHERS, 4 other actors to play all the other parts, best at 2 males, 2 females

SCENE 1

SETTING: On the road in ancient Rome, A.D. IV.

> (There is a donkey cart with barely enough room for two riders. We cannot see the donkey, but perhaps some scenery can change now and then to show progression, with the help of stage characters to move it)
>
> (At times, characters directly address the audience, or make asides.)
>
> (IGNORAMUS drags his donkey cart from the back of the stage up to the front.)

IGNORAMUS: (to audience) Greetings! I hope you are well. I am. They call me Ignoramus. That is not my real name. But that is what people call me. I am on my way to stop the fall of the Roman Empire. I have heard that it is in trouble, and I wish to help. I'm not exactly sure how far it is to Rome, but my trusty donkey cart will get me there, I hope. (Points.) That is my donkey. (There is no donkey.) His name is Invisible. He doesn't want to go to Rome. I hope to persuade Invisible to transport me there anyway.

(The cart creaks as he rolls it back and forth.)

Oh, if only there were some other means of transportation! I told my cousin that, but he just scoffed and that's how I got my nickname of Ignoramus. I intend to pick up travelers to help me drive or at least provide company. I have been told by many to be wary of highwaymen and brigands, but I think most people are good-hearted if you just treat them well. No?

TITUS: (offstage) Hey, pal! You got a ride? (Appears in a toga, nicer than a tunic.)

IGNORAMUS: I don't know, sir. From your toga, it would seem you might have your own mode of transportation, a chariot perhaps. Yes?

TITUS: Oh, I have many chariots and steeds and even camels, but I'm traveling light these days. I can help you drive your cart. What say you?

IGNORAMUS: That sounds most promising, sir.

TITUS: Where is your ass?

IGNORAMUS: I beg your pardon?

TITUS: Surely you have an ass!

IGNORAMUS: I have a donkey. He's right here. He's Invisible.

TITUS: I can see that. But can he pull the two of us?

IGNORAMUS: I'm not sure. Invisible is his name.

TITUS: I wouldn't want to have to push you out of your own cart, would I? (Laughs.)

IGNORAMUS: Perhaps you should wait for another cart.

TITUS: Not at all. Not At all. (He jumps into the cart.) (He does a Roman salute.) I am Titus Gaseous Obnoxius! (IGNORAMUS is reluctant to salute back, but finally does.) I am of the Patrician class. Which class are you?

IGNORAMUS: Oh, I don't pay attention to class.

TITUS: (loudly) What?! How can you not pay attention to class?!

IGNORAMUS: Just call me Ignoramus, I guess.

TITUS: You're not a runaway slave, are you?

IGNORAMUS: No, sir.

TITUS: Are you sure? You look like one. Let me see your forehead.

IGNORAMUS: I beg your pardon?

TITUS: To see if you have a tattoo there. Come, come, show me!

IGNORAMUS: (reluctantly shows his forehead) Are you satisfied?

TITUS: Push up on your hair. Come, come.

IGNORAMUS: (pushing his hair higher) There!

TITUS: You can't be too careful these days. Slaves running away left and right! I actually saw one who had tried to remove the tattoo on his forehead. All that remained was the word "runaway." I settled his hash, let me tell you. I called the authorities, but they let him off with just a slight crucifixion! Can you imagine!?

IGNORAMUS: Perhaps one day there will be no slavery.

TITUS: What?! Are you mad? How do you think the economy would function without slavery?! As a matter of fact, the main reason I want to get to Rome, besides a vacation, is to see about opening a slave trading office there. Start out small, then expand to other places. I hear very good things about up-and-coming Lithuania. Very good workers. And easy on the eye. I can let you in on some real bargains if we keep in touch. What do you say?

IGNORAMUS: I'll keep you in mind, sir.

TITUS: And why are you going to Rome?

IGNORAMUS: I want to save it from falling.

TITUS: Really?

IGNORAMUS: I don't know if I can. After all, I'm just one person.

TITUS: Well, let me tell you, when they get rid of the slaves, that's when Rome will fall, you can bet your ass on that!

IGNORAMUS: Let's agree to disagree.

TITUS: What nonsense! Just be glad I don't report you to the state for sedition.

IGNORAMUS: That's very kind of you, sir. Maybe I won't go today, after all. I'm feeling a little weak in the …

TITUS: It's probably your bile. It's very important to maintain balance in the bile.

IGNORAMUS: You think so?

TITUS: I have no patience with all this use of clean water, I'll tell you that! Bunch of molly coddles! Why did the gods give us dirt if they didn't want us to use it?!

IGNORAMUS: I'm sure I don't know, Titus.

TITUS: Call me Gaseous.

IGNORAMUS: If you insist.

TITUS: I do. By the way, what is that odor I detect near this cart?

IGNORAMUS: Odor?

TITUS: Yes. Very pungent. (Sniffs.) I think it's coming from your ass. (Sniffs again.)

IGNORAMUS: You mean my donkey?

TITUS: Most likely. Don't you smell it?

IGNORAMUS: (Sniffs.) I do smell something, yes sir.

TITUS: Well, don't look at me! Just because my name is Gaseous! It's coming out of your donkey.

IGNORAMUS: Well, I don't know what to do about it.

TITUS: Well, beat it! Make it stop!

IGNORAMUS: I am not going to beat my donkey!

TITUS: What?! He who won't beat his ass is not favored by the gods. Everybody knows that!

IGNORAMUS: I do not know that. I never heard it before.

TITUS: My great grandfather used to say it all the time. He said it was what kept Rome great.

IGNORAMUS: That we beat our asses?

TITUS: You sound doubtful. We certainly didn't conquer Carthage by not beating our asses! If memory serves, we even beat their asses! (about the cart) By the way, this cart if far too cramped for more than one person.

IGNORAMUS: Oh, sorry. Perhaps you should wait for another ride. (Offers to help him out of the cart.)

TITUS: No, Ill rough it. What are we Romans made of if not times just like this!

IGNORAMUS: Are you sure?

TITUS: Onward!

(IGNORAMUS sighs, but gets into the cart, takes the reins.)

IGNORAMUS: (to the donkey) Giddyup.

TITUS: Don't be so soft-spoken. (yells) Move that ass, ass!

IGNORAMUS: I don't think yelling is a good idea.

TITUS: Yelling is an excellent idea most of the time, except when your barber is shaving your neck. (Laughs.)

IGNORAMUS: I've never had a barber shave my neck.

TITUS: Thracians make the best barbers. Get yourself a Thracian every time.

IGNORAMUS: I don't see myself owning a Thracian anytime soon.

TITUS: Whatever you do, don't get a barbarian. They'll cut your throat in a second and a half!

IGNORAMUS: I'll try to remember that.

TITUS: I have a little trick to help: "When it comes to slaves/ Thracians for shaves / Never barbarians. They're knaves."

LIGHTS DOWN.

LIGHTS UP.

SCENE 2

    (The cart has moved a little.)

TITUS: (squirming) Are we there yet?

IGNORAMUS: I don't think so. It's slower with two. (points.) Oh, look! Another hitchhiker.

    (PIUS comes into view, thumbing a ride.)

PIUS: Ride! Ride!

TITUS: Don't pick them up. It's too crowded already.

IGNORAMUS: One more won't hurt.

TITUS: Oh, God! I mean, gods!

IGNORAMUS: Come join us, fellow.

PIUS: (groveling) Oh, thank you, thank you, kind sir. I am most grateful.

    (They make room for PIUS in the cart.)

IGNORAMUS: Everybody comfy?

TITUS: Hardly.

IGNORAMUS: You can always get out here, sir.

TITUS: No! Onward!

PIUS: Allow me to introduce myself. I am called Pius Anxius.

IGNORAMUS: Glad to have you aboard, Pius Anxius.

TITUS: (grumbles) Whatever happened to Samaritans? One of them could give you a ride.

PIUS: Actually, I turned down a ride from a Samaritan about an hour ago.

TITUS: Oh?

PIUS: He had twenty people in his car, just about the size of this one.

TITUS: They say we Romans like orgies. But you have to draw the line somewhere!

PIUS: Heavens, nobody was doing anything untoward in the cart. I wouldn't have liked that.

IGNORAMUS: I've never tried an orgy.

TITUS: They're over-rated, if you ask me. I did one once. One orgy is informative. More than one orgy is a *lifestyle*!

IGNORAMUS: (to PIUS) You wouldn't have a map by any chance? I forgot mine.

PIUS: As a matter of fact, I do. (Pulls out map.) I presume we're headed toward Rome, so we don't really need a map, do we? And why is that? (Conducts the other two.)

TITUS/IGNORAMUS: (tired, sing-song) Because all roads lead to Rome.

PIUS: Exactly!

IGNORAMUS: What if you're not going to Rome?

TITUS: Everybody's going to Rome!

IGNORAMUS: (to PIUS) And why are you going to Rome, if I may ask?

PIUS: I'm going there to become a eunuch.

(The other two are startled.)

TITUS: My God. … Gods!

IGNORAMUS: Really?

PIUS: Oh, yes. I have long yearned to become a eunuch.

IGNORAMUS: Are you sure you know what that means?

PIUS: Lots and lots of study. They don't just let anybody become a
eunuch.

TITUS: Some of my best friends are eunuchs.

IGNORAMUS: I've never met a eunuch, to the best of my knowledge.

PIUS: Believe me, it doesn't just happen overnight.

IGNORAMUS: No?

PIUS: You have to study and study and study. Rome wasn't built in a
day. Nor is your certified eunuch.

IGNORAMUS: Excuse me, but isn't it rather difficult to be a eunuch
aside from all that studying?

PIUS: It depends on whether you want to be a castrato or one of the less
committed ones, such as Thlibae or Thladiae. Pardon my poor
Latin.

IGNORAMUS: I don't think I want to know the difference.

TITUS: One group is just bruised. The other is crushed.

IGNORAMUS: Please!

TITUS: Oh, grow up! Of course, the castrati go the Full Monty.

PIUS: I haven't yet decided which type I will choose. I vary from day to
day.

IGNORAMUS: Well, think long and hard about it. I don't think you can
go back. But I'm no expert on eunuchs.

TITUS: Sometimes I wish I were a eunuch. They have such an easy life!

PIUS: If you're really good at it, you might get to hang out with the Vestal Virgins.

IGNORAMUS: The keepers of the Sacred Flame?

PIUS: That's the word on the street.

TITUS: I hear the Vestal Virgins are not much fun.

PIUS: I heard they are when you really get to know them. I hear that if the right strings get pulled, you might even become a Vestal Virgin.

TITUS: My second cousin on my father's side used to be a Vestal Virgin.

PIUS: (impressed) Really?! I'm impressed. Naturally, though, I would never do anything unlawful to get ahead. Such as pull strings.

TITUS: Oh, me neither.

IGNORAMUS: (shading his eyes) Who's that up ahead?

PIUS: (shading his eyes) It looks like a pack of women. I mean a group of women.

TITUS: (shading his eyes) They look like virgins!

IGNORAMUS: How can you tell?

TITUS: Even at my age, I have XX/XX eyesight. (pronounces it Ex Ex Ex Ex)

IGNORAMUS: That's amazing.

PIUS: Stop the cart! Let's meet and greet these ladies.

IGNORAMUS: All right. (Pulls on the reins, stops the cart.)

    (PIUS and TITUS get out of the cart.)

(Enter VESTAL VIRGINS, played by the Others, including men.)

PIUS: Hoy there, virgin ladies! We greet you with great reverence.

VESTAL #1: Name thyselves, ruffians. We know thee not.

PIUS: Fear not! I am Pius Anxius.

TITUS: And I am Titus.

IGNORAMUS: They call me Ignoramus.

VESTAL #2: We are the famous Vestal Virgins. No doubt thou hast heard of us.

PIUS: We were just talking about you. And I can only speak for myself, but I'm such a fan.

VESTAL #3: (a male) Why, thank you.

TITUS: Me too. Getting much?

VESTAL #3: I beg thy pardon?

TITUS: I've got a big one. (He leers at the Vestal Virgins.)

VESTAL #2: That's quite the pickup line!

TITUS: You bet! Thou beteth? Whatever. Once in a while it actually works. Not the line, my organ.

VESTAL #2: (doubtful) I beteth.

TITUS: What brings you ladies our way today?

VESTAL #2: Bad luck?

VESTAL #1: We're just out for a walk.

TITUS: Would you like a lift in our cart?

IGNORAMUS: I don't want to be rude, but I don't believe there is room.

VESTAL #3: That's fine with us. Cooped up in the temple all the time, we just wanted some fresh air.

TITUS: I loves me some fresh air. (Stretches his arms over his head, breathing.)

VESTAL #2: What's that sudden smell? (to TITUS) Did you let one?

TITUS: One what? No, it was the donkey.

VESTAL #2: What donkey?

TITUS: (pointing to empty space) That donkey!

VESTAL #3: I see no donkey.

TITUS: That's because you haven't seen me! (Flips his toga up.)

VESTAL #3: Oh, god. Gods.

IGNORAMUS: Would you know how far from Rome we might be?

VESTAL #1: Fifty-two, point eight miles.

IGNORAMUS: How do you know that?

VESTAL #1: We Vestals go walking and running when we can. One gets a sense of distance.

PIUS: You have walked fifty-two miles?

VESTAL #2: (with male voice) And will have to walk back, apparently.

VESTAL #1: Keeps you out of mischief, Androgyny.

VESTAL #2: Oh, pish off!

PIUS: (shocked) My goodness! Such language!

VESTAL #1: It's not easy keeping these ladies under control.

VESTAL #2: (aside to PIUS) Don't ever become a Vestal Virgin!

VESTAL #1 I heard that!

VESTAL # 2: Good!

VESTAL #1: All right, ladies, it's time to practice! This is as good a
place as any.

(A general grumbling from the Vestals.)

VESTAL #1: Don't be like that. Nobody likes a grumpy Virgin. Get out
your new cheer.

(Reluctantly, the Vestals take out pieces of parchment.) (They
do some warmup stretches.)

TITUS: Hey, this sounds hot. Let's wait and watch.

IGNORAMUS: It's going to be dark soon.

PIUS: Oh, please, just one cheer!

IGNORAMUS: Okay, just one.

VESTAL #3: Oh, we'll have an audience.

VESTAL #1: Are we ready, ladies? ... Hit it!

VESTALS: (with cheerleader moves)

> HAIL, HAIL, VIRGIN VESTA!
> THOU ARE THE VERY BESTA!
> PATRONESS OF HOME AND HEARTH!
> WE PRAISE THEE TILL WE ALMOST BARTH! ZIP! ZIP! ZIP
> HOORAY!
> NEVER NAUGHTY, WE JUST PRAY!
> ZIP! ZIP! ZIP HOORAY!
> NEVER NAUGHTY, WE JUST PRAY!

(add more choreography, if possible on shoulders)

WHY VIRGINS ARE PICKED TO PROTECT THE HOME
ONLY THE GODS KNOW – BECAUSE IT'S ROME?
WHY VIRGINS ARE PICKED TO PROTECT THE HOME
ONLY THE GODS KNOW – BECAUSE IT'S ROME!!!

(The Vestals strike a big cheerleader pose to end with a
flourish.)

(The three watchers applaud, with TITUS the loudest.)

TITUS: (whistling, if he can, with his fingers) Ladies! You had me at
"hail, hail."

VESTAL #1: Not bad, ladies. But we'll work on it

TITUS: (to PIUS) Good stuff, huh?

PIUS: I think they should rewrite that cheer. I don't think Vestal Virgins
would cheer like that.

TITUS: Oh, come on.

PIUS: I'm serious. I found it anti-religious and offensive. I blame the
writer of this piece. It may even border on blasphemy.

(The Vestals are upset by this criticism.)

VESTAL #1: I'm sorry if we may have given offense.

PIUS: As keepers of the Sacred Flame, you ought to be more
circumspect.

TITUS: I thought it was great.

PIUS: Not.

TITUS: Was.

PIUS: Not!

TITUS: Was!

(The two are close to fighting.)

IGNORAMUS: (to quell the situation) Excuse me, ladies. Can you answer another question perhaps?

VESTAL #1: What might that be?

IGNORAMUS: I hear that Rome is about to fall. Do you know this to be a fact, or is it just a rumor?

VESTAL #3: It's just a rumor.

VESTAL #4: It's a fact.

VESTAL #3: Rumor.

VESTAL #4: Fact!

(They are about to fight.)

IGNORAMUS: (trying to soothe them) I'm sorry I asked. I just want to save a trip if I don't need to go.

VESTAL #1: We're just fine in Rome. We have bread and Netflix.

PIUS: Do you know if they have any openings for eunuchs? I'm going to need a job.

VESTAL #2: They're oversaturated with eunuchs is what I hear.

PIUS: Oh, dear.

VESTAL #3: There are some openings for gladiators.

(There is agreement among the Vestals about the gladiators.)

PIUS: Well, that's good to know. To tell the truth, I've flirted with ide of becoming a gladiator.

TITUS: Are there any gladiators who are eunuchs?

VESTAL #1: I really can't say. Girls?

(The Vestals agree that they don't know.)

PIUS: Maybe I could be the first gladiator eunuch!

IGNORAMUS: Don't you have to know somebody?!

TITUS: Not in Rome! You earn your position!

IGNORAMUS: Unless you inherit it.

TITUS: Only the right people inherit their positions.

IGNORAMUS: Well, let's not argue about politics. It's hard enough with
the cart being so small.

TITUS: Inheriting your position is not politics!

IGNORAMUS: Well, goodbye, ladies! So long! Enjoy your exercise!
(Takes the reins.)

TITUS: Hey, you almost left me behind!

IGNORAMUS: (insincerely) Oh, sorry.

(TITUS gets into the cart, as does PIUS.)

IGNORAMUS: And we're off! (The scenery moves.)

PIUS: (immediately) Are we there yet?

IGNORAMUS: Not quite.

PIUS: Let's play some cart games, to pass the time.

TITUS: I don't like games. Unless there's bloodshed. Roman games!

PIUS: I know a very good game we can play. It's called See a Leper.

IGNORAMUS: What?

PIUS: We ride along and whoever sees a leper first gets to punch the
other person's arm, as hard as they like.

TITUS: Sounds sort of fun.

PIUS: It can be, if your eyesight is good.

TITUS: On the other hand, how many lepers can there be on the road?

PIUS: You'd be surprised.

TITUS: A friend of my friend's sister was a leper.

IGNORAMUS: Leave me out. I've got to concentrate on driving this thing.

PIUS: Of course. You're our designated driver. Now, no sipping wine while driving!

TITUS: I haven't seen a single leper yet. (Joking) Or a married one, either! (Laughs.)

PIUS: Keep your eyes peeled. Sometimes they sort of blend in with the terrain.

(LEPER #1 appears, dressed in bandages from head to toe.)

PIUS: Oh, there's one! My point!

(LEPER #1 waves. An arm falls off.)

TITUS: I saw him first!

PIUS: I saw him first! I get to punch you.

TITUS: Okay, punch away. I'm a Roman!

(PIUS punches TITUS on the upper arm.)

TITUS: Ouch!

PIUS: That's one!

TITUS: (rubbing his arm,) You just wait.

(LEPER #2 appears, also in bandages.)

PIUS: (seeing the Leper) Leper! (He punches TITUS in the same spot.) Gotcha!

TITUS: Not fair! I wasn't looking.

PIUS: That's two for me, none for you!

TITUS: You're cheating!

PIUS: Maybe I wouldn't make such a poor gladiator after all.

(LEPER #2 staggers in front of the donkey cart)

IGNORAMUS: (to donkey) Whoa! Whoa, there! Watch the leper!

TITUS: Look out! They're contagious!

PIUS: Watch out!

(The leper is hit by the cart, falls, and is run over.)

IGNORAMUS: (upset) Oh, my god! … Gods!

TITUS: Don't you dare get out of this cart to check on him!

IGNORAMUS: What? He's –

TITUS: He's in a better place now.

PIUS: I agree. Everything happens for a reason. Roll on, driver!

(They roll on. After a few moments, LEPER #2 gets up and staggers off.)

PIUS: You know those lepers looked amazingly like the Vestals. Did you notice?

TITUS: If they didn't want to get run over, they shouldn't have gotten leprosy in the first place!

PIUS: Only the gods know how they got it, and I, for one, don't want to know.

TITUS: Exactly! But once a leper, always a leper, if you ask me!

PIUS: Of course, some of my best friends are lepers. I just don't like them in the roads.

(LEPER #3 appears.)

TITUS: There's another one! (Punches PIUS on the upper arm.) Gotcha!

PIUS: Ouch!

IGNORAMUS: Do you know any other cart games?

PIUS: (petulantly) No!

IGNORAMUS: (looking back) I hope we weren't a hit and run.

TITUS: Whatever does that mean? You're not one of those fucking Christians are you?

IGNORAMUS: No.

TITUS: Good! God, they're awful! So pushy!

PIUS: I hear they're even worse when you get to know them.

IGNORAMUS: How about some lunch?

TITUS: Lunch? I'm game.

IGNORAMUS: Did you bring any food with you?

TITUS: I didn't. I never do. I like to catch mine on the hoof or the wing. Nothing like fresh food.

PIUS: I'm afraid I eat very little.

TITUS: I eat the very little too! (Laughs loudly at his own joke.)

PIUS: I usually give most of my food away.

TITUS: (sarcastic) You are so good, my friend!

PIUS: I can only try to be. (Reaches into his clothing for a bottle.) I did bring something to drink. You can't rely on those roadside watering holes. (Holds up the bottle for them to see.)

TITUS: What is it?

PIUS: Urine.

TITUS: Eww.

PIUS: Mine!

TITUS: Double eww! (Makes a face.) You drink your own urine?!

PIUS: It's cleaner than most, and utterly refreshing. Do you want a swig?

TITUS: Good god, no! … Gods.

PIUS: More for me! (Takes a swig.)

TITUS: I had to eat cockroaches and elephant when I was in the army. And I did it without complaining. I had to eat flies and peanut butter one summer when there was plague. But you'll never get me to drink my own piss!

PIUS: Suit yourself. (Takes another swig from the bottle) Ahh!

IGNORAMUS: You two! What would I do without you for companionship!?

TITUS: Exactly!

IGNORAMUS: Well, I can share what I brought with the two of you, I suppose.

PIUS: (pitifully) Or we could just watch you eat.

IGNORAMUS: Let me see what I have. (Gets a basket from the cart. Opens it.) How about some cheese?

PIUS: What kind?

IGNORAMUS: Goat cheese.

TITUS: I hope it's made from real goat. And I don't mean the milk!

IGNORAMUS: Or I have some olives and figs?

PIUS: Are they low calorie?

IGNORAMUS: I don't know.

PIUS: No thank you then.

TITUS: I don't give a fig for figs! (Laughs at his own joke again.)

IGNORAMUS: How about some wine? I have red, white and green.

PIUS: Green wine?

IGNORAMUS: It's pretty potent, so I dilute it with asparagus juice.

PIUS: Sounds healthy.

TITUS: Sounds sissy to me! (Makes spitting noises.) Did I ever tell you about the orgy I attended back in B.C.?

PIUS: I'm sure you are about to.

TITUS: First of all, I wasn't invited, so I had to sneak in.

IGNORAMUS: Of course.

TITUS: So ones of their lackeys comes up to me crouching in a corner and says, Where's your invite, buster? So I says, Here's my invite, pal" and I show him my horse dick and, what'd you know, they invited me to stay!

PIUS: But naturally you declined.

TITUS: Yeah, I declined on one of them eatin' couches and declined all
night! (Dirty laugh)

IGNORAMUS: Are you part of the Fall of Rome?

TITUS: What are you talking about?! I didn't even throw up.

PIUS: Could we change the subject please?

TITUS: When I have fourteen more orgy stories to tell?!

PIUS: Let's save them for the road.

IGNORAMUS: (finding something in the food basket) Anyone care for
some dormouse? I forgot I put it where it wouldn't go bad.

PIUS: You can't be too careful with spoiled dormouse.

TITUS: I had some spoiled dormouse one time, back in B.C. I thought I
was gonna die. Big chunks of –

PIUS: Please! Enough! I don't want to hear about chunks of dormouse.

IGNORAMUS: (to TITUS) I think he's right.

TITUS: Pardon me for trying to pass the time with some marvelous
stories!

PIUS: I think we can all just keep quiet for a while. To center ourselves.

(Immediately, a gladiator with a trident and a net runs on,
chasing LEPER #4.)

GLADIATOR: Come back here, you!

LEPER #4: Try and make me! (The leper has just a tiny shield for
defense.)

GLADIATOR: (to the three in the cart) Stop that leper! He's a runaway!

LEPER #4: It's all a misunderstanding! My owner freed me when I developed leprosy!

GLADIATOR: Yeah, right. Where's your document of proof?

LEPER: (searching through his rags) It's here somewhere, if I can just find it. (Can't find it.)

GLADIATOR: That's what she said! (Laughs at his joke.) Okay, enough of this playing around! "I have my document!" "I have my papers!" That's what all these lepers say! But I say, "Never trust a leper!" (Taking gladiatorial posture with trident and net.) Here, fishy, fishy! Come on, fishy, fishy."

(The GLADIATOR and LEPER #4 face off, trident and net versus little shield.)

IGNORAMUS: Gentlemen, please, don't do this!

TITUS: What are you talking about? The games brought right to my cart! It doesn't get any better than this! (Arranges himself to watch the fight.)

PIUS: I'm not watching unless we offer a sacrifice to the gods first.

IGNORAMUS: There will come a time when nobody feels the need to sacrifice to the gods or fight to the death.

TITUS: Oh, shut up! You're nuts!

PIUS: I can see why you are called Ignoramus.

IGNORAMUS: You mark my words. No fights to the death. Maybe a little Mixed Martial Arts.

PIUS: I don't want to watch, but let's get this fight over. We've got to get to Rome, So that I can become a certified eunuch.

TITUS: I think you're already halfway there.

PIUS: Who wouldn't drink the pee pee?

IGNORAMUS: Let's go before Rome falls.

LEPER #4: (to the three in the cart) Are you gonna watch us or not?

TITUS: Go!

(The GLADIATOR and LEPER #4 circle one another.)

LEPER #4: Come on, hot stuff! You think you're better than a leper, don't you? Well, you're not. (Waves the tiny shield. Limps a bit.)

GLADIATOR: When I get finished with you, you'll be nothing but—

LEPER #4: What? A pile of rags?!

GLADIATOR: If that! I bet your leg isn't the only thing about you that's limp!

LEPER #4: (to the three watching) He thinks he's so high and mighty! But's he's just a Centurian turned gladiator! Shame on him!

GLADIATOR: You wish you were a gladiator, rag boy!

TITUS: Now there's some trash talk!

LEPER #4: I'm proud of my origins. I come from a long, glorious line of lepers!

GLADIATOR: I'm just working as a gladiator on a temporary basis. My legion ran out of funds and had to lay me off.

LEPER #4: You must be pretty bad then. Is there anything more pitiful than a laid-off gladiator!?

GLADIATOR: How about a limping leper with a tiny shield?!

TITUS: (clapping encouragement) More! More fighting!

PIUS: I'm betting on the leper. But I won't watch! (Hides his eyes.)

TITUS: You're on, Pius Delicius!

PIUS: Pius Anxius!

TITUS: Five drachmas say the gladiator makes the leper cry!

PIUS: Two to one on the leper! (They bump fists.)

IGNORAMUS: I think we should be moving on. Really.

TITUS: Not right in the middle of the fight!

IGNORAMUS: It's the start, not the middle.

> (The GLADIATOR and LEPER #4 parry back and forth for a
> minute or so.)

> (Eventually, the GLADIATOR gets LEPER #4 on the ground
> and holds the trident over his neck.)

GLADIATOR: Whatcha gonna do now, rag boy?!

TITUS/PIUS: Yeah! Yeah! Give it to him!

> (The GLADIATOR looks to the three watchers for their
> decision.)

GLADIATOR: What's it to be, fellas – life or death? (Holds the trident
closer to LEPER #4.)

> (TITUS and PIUS confer together quietly, then stand up.)

TITUS: (a thumb down) Death!

PIUS: It's thumbs *up* for death!

TITUS: Since when?

PIUS: (to IGNORAMUS) Which is it?

IGNORAMUS: I don't know.

(TITUS and PIUS shrug.)

TITUS/PIUS: (as one) Death!

(Their fingers are all over the place.)

GLADIATOR: You heard 'em, rag boy. Good fight! (He kills LEPER #4.)

TITUS/PIUS: Yay! Yay!

(GLADIATOR takes a bow, several.)

(TITUS and PIUS clap. IGNORAMUS shakes his head in disgust.)

PIUS: That was terrific!

(Suddenly, LEPER #4 jumps up and gets a chokehold on GLADIATOR. They move around with various grunts and near-escapes. But finally GLADIATOR dies. LEPER #4 lets go of the body.)

LEPER #4: I got him! I got him! … But, alas, my wound is likewise fatal! (to GLADIATOR) Splendid fight, brave gladiator! (He collapses.)

TITUS: Oh, my god. They're both dead!

PIUS: (correcting him) Gods. But you're correct. It was thrilling!

IGNORAMUS: Can we go now?

TITUS: Even you have to admit it was exciting.

IGNORAMUS: Okay, a little.

PIUS: We got two deaths for the price of one. And no animals were hurt in the show.

TITUS: And now, off we go!

IGNORAMUS: Shouldn't we bury the bodies?

TITUS: Why? They served their purpose. Fuck 'em!

PIUS: On to Rome!

(The scenery moves, or parts thereof, indicating progress.)

LIGHTS OUT.

LIGHTS UP.

SCENE 3

(The same.)

TITUS: My butt hurts.

PIUS: I need to pee.

IGNORAMUS: All right, a pit stop. I need to feed and water Invisible.
(The cart stops. They get out.)

TITUS: Can't you get another donkey?

IGNORAMUS: No, I can't!

TITUS: Well, don't bite my head off because you can't afford a new
donkey.

IGNORAMUS: Listen, this isn't working out.

PIUS: What do you mean by that?

IGNORAMUS: He travels fastest who travels alone.

PIUS: But we're company!

TITUS: Yeah, that's bullshit!

IGNORAMUS: I'm not that desperate.

PIUS: But what about us? You can't just leave us here in the wilderness.

TITUS: He's absolutely right! There are wild animals out here. (The sound of a wild creature, unclear which one.) You hear that?

IGNORAMUS: (lying) No.

TITUS: Listen more closely.

(All three listen closely, ears cupped.)

(There is another animal sound, a different one, also unknown.)

PIUS: It's a pigmy wild boar.

TITUS: Are you sure? I thought it was a zebra in heat.

PIUS: It could be a horse-dicked jackass.

TITUS: Or maybe a eunuch being made! And not too soon!

PIUS: Or a macho hippo with with bad breath!

TITUS: How about a prima donna who drinks its own piss?! Talk about bad breath!

IGNORAMUS: Gentlemen, please!

(A wild animal of uncertain species runs past them.)

PIUS: What was that?

TITUS: I don't know. It didn't look good.

PIUS: No, it didn't.

TITUS: Maybe it's the Undead.

PIUS: (suddenly hysterical) Not the *Undead!* Please, please, not the *Undead!*

TITUS: Is it because we didn't bury the Gladiator and Leper #4?

IGNORAMUS: We could go back and bury them.

PIUS: Yes! … Wait. Maybe it's gone.

> (They all listen again, but with a different ear this time.) (A different strange wild animal runs across the stage.)

TITUS: Did you see that?

PIUS: No.

IGNORAMUS: I did. I think we should leave.

TITUS: No! I'm going after it.

IGNORAMUS: (weary) No, don't go after it.

PIUS: It's the *Undead!* (Goes hysterical again.)

IGNORAMUS: It's pretty lively for the Undead.

TITUS: I need a weapon of some kind.

IGNORAMUS: I don't have one. Let's leave.

PIUS: I don't have a knife or a sword or a spear or a mace. But I do have this! (Shows the bottle of urine.)

IGNORAMUS: Your urine?

PIUS: (to TITUS) Take it. Throw it on the wild creature.

TITUS: Yes, this ought to work! (Takes the bottle of urine.)

> (The wild animal runs in and grabs the bottle of urine and runs off with it.)

IGNORAMUS: (to PIUS) What else have you got?

PIUS: If all three of us go, we can wrangle it, then strangle it.

TITUS: Wrangle and strangle?

IGNORAMUS: (teasing) Wrangle and strangle?

PIUS: You're not taking this seriously enough!

IGNORAMUS: We could have been a mile away if we had just left.

TITUS: No wild animal is going to tell me where I can go and when!

> (Another wild animal runs on, stops, then slaps TITUS across
> the face, then runs off.)

PIUS: Well, they were here before we were.

TITUS: You don't know that! Maybe they just moved in!

PIUS: Wild animals have rights too, even if they're not Roman.

TITUS: Not when they're eating us!

IGNORAMUS: Yeah, I draw the line there myself.

PIUS: Some of my best friends are wild animals.

TITUS: Do you think Rome got to be what it is because it was
sentimental about wild animals?!

PIUS: When not in Rome, as we are not, don't do as the Romans do.

TITUS: Who said that?

PIUS: I did.

IGNORAMUS: I don't think it's going to catch on.

PIUS: I do.

TITUS: I'm off to catch that beast. Who's going with me?

PIUS/IGNORAMUS: Not me.

TITUS: Then I go alone! (Holds up the urine bottle, stalks off.)

PIUS: I have to give it to him. He's brave.

IGNORAMUS: (calling) Goodbye, Titus!

> (The wild creature comes on carrying TITUS in his arms like a
> child, puts him down, and leaves.)

IGNORAMUS: Good job, Titus.

TITUS: (shaking fist at the departed beast) He's nothing but an n-word!

PIUS: (to audience) Don't worry. It will be cut.

IGNORAMUS: If you guys are coming, then come. If not, then stay!
(Starts to leave.)

TITUS: Can't we have a long, aesthetic discussion about the use of the
n-word in art?

IGNORAMUS: No!

PIUS: How about lots of word play and dated puns, like in Shakespeare?

IGNORAMUS: Shakespeare hasn't even been heard of yet!

PIUS: That's modern education for you!

> (Suddenly all the beasts rush in as a group and begin to stalk
> the three human beings.)

IGNORAMUS: I think we're being stalked.

PIUS: Are you sure? We probably shouldn't be on their land.

TITUS: Oh, my god! … Gods.

> (They run to the cart and scramble aboard.)

PIUS: I'll drive! (Takes the reins.)

TITUS: Hurry! They're gaining on us.

IGNORAMUS: Maybe I should drive.

PIUS: There's no time! I'll do it!

(The cart moves or the scenery at least does.)

TITUS: Onward!

(The cart moves offstage.)

(The beasts stop stalking.)

BEAST #1: (about the cart) *We* should get one of those drivey things.

BEAST #2: Too dangerous.

(One of the beasts notices the bottle of urine that PIUS has dropped.)

BEAST #3: What's this? (Picks up the bottle.)

BEAST #4: One of them dropped it.

BEAST #3: (pulls out the stopper) Let's try it.

BEAST #4: I'm not so sure.

BEAST #3: On, come on. Nothing ventured, nothing gained.

BEAST #1: That is so true. That's how we learned not to eat Brussels sprouts. Remember?

BEAST #2: And quinoa!

BEAST #3: Here goes nothing! (Drinks the urine.)

(The others await his decision.)

BEAST #3: It has a robustness about it, with a touch of Sparta. I like it. It tastes terrible.

BEAST #4: Must be a fine wine then.

BEAST #3: I think you're right, Sommelier. The finest! (Holds up the bottle.) Lucky us!

LIGHTS DOWN.

LIGHTS UP.

SCENE 4

(The same.)

(The donkey cart makes its way back across the stage, the same way it left.)

IGNORAMUS: I've lost track of where we are. (He stops the cart.)

PIUS: You mean we're lost?

IGNORAMUS: Apparently so. I have a terrible sense of direction.

TITUS Then why do you drive?!

IGNORAMUS: I don't see you driving. Didn't you offer to, once upon a time?

TITUS: They took away my chariot license.

IGNORAMUS: Oh?

TITUS: I was driving under the influence.

IGNORAMUS: Of what?

TITUS: Watered-down wine.

IGNORAMUS: Everybody drinks that.

TITUS: I know. I guess I cheated on the water.

PIUS: He who …

TITUS: Oh, shut up on your he-who's. I don't see you driving.

PIUS: I'm not old enough to drive.

TITUS: Bullshit.

PIUS: Well, if there's another reason, I'm not telling you!

IGNORAMUS: Enough! We've got to find the right road. And don't say
they all lead to Rome. They obviously don't.

PIUS: Don't bite my head off. I'm not the one who got us lost.

IGNORAMUS: Oh, god. … Gods.

TITUS: Speaking of the gods, why don't we pray for directions?

PIUS: Excellent idea!

IGNORAMUS: Okay, you two pray. I don't pray.

PIUS: (shocked) You don't pray?!

TITUS: You don't pray!? No wonder we got lost.

PIUS: I'm sure we got lost for a reason.

IGNORAMUS: I don't think it's going to do any good, but pray away.

PIUS: Dear gods up on Mt. Olympus, we beseech you in our plight for
assistance!

TITUS: Good start.

PIUS: We three poor, miserable scum of the earth ask you to guide our
way to Rome.

IGNORAMUS: Scum of the earth?

TITUS: The gods like that.

PIUS: Yes, you have to lay it on thick.

TITUS: (taking over the prayer) We kiss your godly feet in humble supplication to solicit – (looks to PIUS for help)

PIUS: – to solicit the true course to central Rome, avoiding all accidents and false tributaries along the way, until we can reach one of your glorious temples and worship you as you, and only you, deserve.

TITUS: And we'll throw in a sacrifice! A big one! Maybe a bull. (Looks at the invisible donkey.) Even a donkey!

IGNORAMUS: Hey! You're not sacrificing my donkey! Jesus Christ!

TITUS: Who?

IGNORAMUS: Your prayer doesn't seem to be working.

PIUS: Give it time. The gods are busy.

TITUS: That's right. Sometimes it takes years to get an answer.

IGNORAMUS: We haven't got years.

TITUS: I remember back when I was a just a toddler, I prayed for a new bicycle, but I didn't get one.

PIUS: (to IGNORAMUS) What's a bicycle?

TITUS: I still haven't received that bicycle. But in my heart I know that one day there will be a bicycle and the gods will give it to me.

PIUS: You're on the lam, aren't you?

TITUS: No!

PIUS: Money-laundering drachmas! Or something like that.

TITUS: Shut up and keep praying.

IGNORAMUS: Maybe if we backtrack that way … (Points off.)

TITUS: Titus does not backtrack!

IGNORAMUS: Maybe we ask somebody for directions, who's not a wild beast or a leper.

TITUS: A real man never asks for directions.

PIUS: He just wanders around and around until he stumbles on where he wants to go!

TITUS: He took the words right out of my mouth.

IGNORAMUS: Well, I confess I haven't a clue where we are. (Stops the cart.) Let's give Invisible a rest. (calling) Good donkey!

PIUS: Yes, that way the vultures can get better look at what's coming.

TITUS: I heard that if you skip to your left three paces and whistle the Roman National Anthem vultures won't eat you.

PIUS: Really?

IGNORAMUS: We don't have a Roman National Anthem. We're an Empire.

TITUS: Well, I think we should at least try the skipping part. Nothing ventured, nothing gained.

PIUS: What have we got to lose?

IGNORAMUS: Our dignity, as we die?

TITUS: Here I go! (He skips sideways four times.) Da Dum!

PIUS: (skips sideways also, ends by singing) I left my heart in the Roman Empire. For birds to eat. But they did not!

TITUS: (joining him in song) When I come home to you, Roman Empire, your vultures will not wait for me!

TITUS/PIUS: (harmonizing) For me!

IGNORAMUS: (sarcastic) That should keep the vultures away. And everything else.

TITUS: I'm not afraid to die.

PIUS: Nor am I.

IGNORAMUS: I am!

TITUS: I've had a good life.

PIUS: (to the audience) Why don't you tell us about it?

TITUS: I think I will.

(They sit on the ground.)

TITUS: I was born to a rich family in western Italy.

PIUS: What's Italy?

IGNORAMUS: We're in it. Or we will be.

PIUS: What?

IGNORAMUS: It's complicated. Continue, Titus.

TITUS: I married young. Twice. But I was unlucky in love. Both my wives died of the plague. Separate plagues.

PIUS: Oh, I'm sorry.

TITUS: Thank you. They were ungrateful bitches, but what can you do?! Then my two sons, one from each wife, were eaten in a pie that my nasty cousin, Vicius, made for me.

PIUS: No! That's terrible.

TITUS: Thank you.

PIUS: (after a hesitation) How was the pie?

TITUS: Once I learned what was in it, I could barely finish it.

IGNORAMUS: Good for you. A true Roman!

PIUS: I could go for some pie right about now. (Smacks his lips.)

TITUS: Anyway, I have never remarried or sired any other children. So I am going to Rome to die in a gutter near the Forum.

PIUS: Do you really want that?

TITUS: Yes, I already have the gutter picked out and engraved. (Writes in the air) TITUS GASEOUS OBNOXIUS!

IGNORAMUS: You'll be remembered for all eternity.

TITUS: One can only hope. Earthquakes come, the earth opens up, and there goes your urn!

(The three mourn for the loss.)

TITUS: So, Pius, tell us your story. We've become friends, sort of. Tell us, please.

PIUS: I was always a nervous child. In fact, my parents told me they almost named me Nervus. But then decided on Pius. I have always tried to live up to my name.

IGNORAMUS: It's very you.

PIUS: I got my first job when I was eleven. A good job. I was a swabber in the baths in my home town.

TITUS: Remind me. What's a swabber?

PIUS: I had a bucket and a rag and I used to swab the behinds after my betters did their business.

TITUS: By 'business' you don't mean … ?

PIUS: I do. I do. They liked to conduct business, meaning business business while doing that other business. Two birds with one stone, so to speak.

TITUS: I'm sure that it made you the man you are today. And Rome great!

PIUS: I daresay it did. Everything happens for a reason.

TITUS: But you didn't continue swabbing? Was there a recession?

PIUS: Yes, the Great Recession of two A.D. I wandered around after that. Odd jobs. I pre- slaughtered fowl for sacrifices for the squeamish. But that grew old fast. I sold the works of Pliny the Younger on stone tablets hovel to hovel, but few would buy. I was even on the dole for a while and lived hand to mouth on leftover bread from my local colosseum. Always stale!

TITUS: You poor boy.

PIUS: But then I decided to pull myself up by my sandal straps and go to Rome to become a certified eunuch.

TITUS: Good for you! I must say, Pius, that I find your story very touching.

PIUS: Thank you, Titus.

TITUS: Call me Gaseous. Like my friends. My former friends! You were correct, Pius. I am on the lam for financial irregularities at the bank of Gaul. But they'll never catch me now!

IGNORAMUS: Very interesting, both of you. But perhaps we ought to try to become un-lost now.

TITUS: Oh, no, you don't. You're not getting off the hook so easy, not after the other two of us have spilled our guts out.

IGNORAMUS: I'm a very uninteresting character. The less said about me, the better.

TITUS: Come, come!

IGNORAMUS: Go, go! I'm a very private person.

TITUS: Do we have to torture it out of you?

IGNORAMUS: I wouldn't advise that you try. (Stares them down.) Come along, Invisible, let's make Rome before it falls!

(All of a sudden there is the sound of thunder and lightning.)

PIUS: (hysterical) Oh, heavens, it's the *Undead!*

IGNORAMUS: No, I think it's a storm coming.

TITUS: A storm? How can you tell?

(Another clap of thunder and lightning.)

IGNORAMUS: I asked a fortune teller before I left. She said to beware the Ides of October.

PIUS: She's good! It's October.

(Wind blows over them.)

TITUS: The gods are angry at us!

PIUS: Yes, it feels like Jove's breath!

(More wind blows.)

TITUS: Bad breath. Like mine!

(Lightning flashes.)

IGNORAMUS: Maybe we need to shelter in place a little longer. Maybe it'll pass.

PIUS: And maybe it won't! I think the gods smelled a bit of doubt in the air!

IGNORAMUS: What doubt in the air?

PIUS: Let's not name names, but it was you, Ignoramus, with your oh-so-subtle jibes at piety and faith!

IGNORAMUS: I don't know what you're talking about. (to donkey) Invisible, stay still! He's spooked by the weather.

TITUS: (reaching up) I feel wetness in the air.

IGNORAMUS: It's just rain.

PIUS: What's rain? If this is Italy, there is no rain here.

IGNORAMUS: It's not Italy yet, and it is rain!

PIUS: You are well named, Ignoramus! You should be famous, Ignoramus!

IGNORAMUS: The storm will pass.

PIUS: You don't know that.

IGNORAMUS: It's my best guess, from past experience.

PIUS: If we have to rely on experience, we're all lost! Let's cast some runes.

IGNORAMUS: Runes?

TITUS: To see the weather to come! Runes always tell the truth!

PIUS: Naturally! I just happen to carry a set of runes with me. (Takes out the runes.) Here they are! Even better! If it were here, I could wash my chariot. Every time I wash my chariot, water falls out of the sky. Like that! (Snaps his fingers)

IGNORAMUS: If we just wait, the rain will pass.

PIUS: So will life!

TITUS: (to PIUS) That's good. Very good.

PIUS: Thank you. I'm here all week!

IGNORAMUS: We could hide under the cart.

TITUS: Good idea! Come on!

(The three men hide under the donkey cart.)

PIUS: This is much better.

IGNORAMUS: Let's get the donkey under here too.

TITUS: No way!

IGNORAMUS: He needs shelter just like we do!

TITUS: A donkey does? Come on!

IGNORAMUS: Trust me, he does. (He brings the invisible donkey under the cart.)

PIUS: There isn't enough room!

TITUS: Pius is right!

(They finally get settled under the cart. A pause.)

IGNORAMUS: At last!

PIUS: (after a sniff) Titus?

IGNORAMUS: Gaseous?

TITUS: It was the donkey! I told you not to put him under here!

PIUS: (to audience) How many fart jokes can you have in one play?

TITUS: You can never have too many fart jokes or too few lepers!

(A wind blows hard. The three of them are thrown about.)

IGNORAMUS: Calm down. Calm down.

PIUS: I'm calm.

TITUS: I'm calm!

IGNORAMUS: Steel yourselves. I think that last gust blew away our
donkey.

PIUS: No!

TITUS: How can you tell?

IGNORAMUS: A minor god told me. Plus, I don't see him.

PIUS: We can't get very far without our donkey.

TITUS: What's that in that tree over there? (Points.)

PIUS: Good eye, Titus!

TITUS: I've still got it!

IGNORAMUS: I think you're right. Invisible is over in that tree.
(calling) Invisible? Are you all right? (Sound of a donkey: Hee
haw!) Stay there, boy! I'm coming to get you. (Gets out from
underneath the cart.)

(IGNORAMUS goes off, then comes back carrying the
invisible donkey, with difficulty.)

IGNORAMUS: Whoa! Whoa there, donkey! Whoa!

TITUS: Kill it! That'll calm it down!

IGNORAMUS: No!

PIUS: (to audience) No animals were harmed in the making of this play.

IGNORAMUS: (to TITUS) We need the donkey!

TITUS: You got to teach 'em a lesson! You want donkeys running wild in the streets?!

IGNORAMUS: You want to pull the cart, Gaseous?!

PIUS: No! No! Don't let him pull the cart. We'll never survive!

IGNORAMUS: Someday there will be other kinds of power. Right now, we need donkey power.

(IGNORAMUS arranges the donkey at the head of the cart.)

TITUS: That's not right! Put the cart before the donkey!

IGNORAMUS: Not a good idea.

TITUS: It is too! The donkey can push the cart with its nose!

IGNORAMUS: Shut up, Gaseous.

TITUS: Nobody talks to me like that and lives!

IGNORAMUS: (looking beyond TITUS) What's that coming?

TITUS: Oh, no you don't! I'm not falling for that old trick. Let's settle this like men! (Puts his dukes up.)

PIUS: No, he's telling the truth. There is something coming this way! (to audience) But still offstage.

IGNORAMUS: It's lava!

TITUS: The soap?

IGNORAMUS: Not that old! It's new lava flowing down from that volcano that just erupted.

TITUS: I didn't hear a thing.

IGNORAMUS: You should try a hearing aide.

TITUS: What's that?! Some new-fangled device? That's what slaves are for!

IGNORAMUS: It's coming!

PIUS: (to the audience) That's what she said?

IGNORAMUS: This is no time for old jokes! That lava's going to roll over us and entomb us forever!

TITUS: Let it catch me fighting to the death! (Turns toward the lava with his fists up.)

PIUS: Let me turn too. (Points to his left cheek.) This is my best side.

IGNORAMUS: While you two are posing, the lava is flowing!

PIUS: That needs a little work. It doesn't quite rhyme.

IGNORAMUS: Well, pardon my broken Latin!

TITUS: I think the lava is stopping!

PIUS: Are you sure?

TITUS: I think so. (Points.) Right beyond us!

PIUS: Well, that wasn't very dangerous after all.

IGNORAMUS: Look out! There's a little more coming.

PIUS: (to audience, counting out the beats one by one) That's … what … she … said!

IGNORAMUS: The lava is going to stop, I think. Just a tiny bit more. If we could just stop those she-said jokes! They're so old!

PIUS: You've got to keep a sense of humor during a tragedy.

IGNORAMUS: Who said that? Seneca?

PIUS: The Greek philosopher – Aristotle Onassis.

IGNORAMUS: Was he before or after B.C.?

PIUS: Before P.C.

TITUS: Now those were the days! Thank the gods the lava seems to be cooling.

IGNORAMUS: Just over there, just a few meters away.

PIUS: We're safe!

IGNORAMUS: I don't know why we are having so much bad weather: fierce winds, volcanic eruptions! Who knows what's next.

TITUS: I blame it on anal sex!

IGNORAMUS: You don't say.

PIUS: Don't look at me!

IGNORAMUS: What anal sex?

TITUS: It's all around us.

IGNORAMUS: Somehow, I doubt it.

TITUS: Trust me, it's everywhere these days.

PIUS: Well, I certainly don't approve of it!

TITUS: Okay, okay, I admit I tried a bit of it in my teens. But nowadays it's gotten completely out of hand. No wonder our weather is so terrible!

PIUS: It's something the gods reserve for themselves, and we have no right to anal sex if we're mere mortals. And we are!

(Suddenly four PIRATES in head scarves with short swords rush onto the stage.)

PIRATE #1: Hold there, stupid travelers!

TITUS: I beg your pardon! Who are you?

PIRATE #2: We're pirates, that's who!

PIUS: We're done for! The winds and the lava didn't get us. But the naked pirates will!

PIRATE #3: We're not naked!

PIRATE #4: We're not savages. Just pirates!

TITUS: We have nothing of value on us. Nothing!

PIRATE #1: Oh? What's that you're riding in?!

PIUS: You wouldn't take our cart, would you?

PIRATE #1: Wouldn't we?! (Laughs evilly.) This is a *cart*-jacking and there will be no survivors! We are pirates and we are ruthless! (All four PIRATES laugh evilly, in different ways.)

BLACKOUT

END OF ACT I

ACT II

SCENE 1

SETTING: The same, then a street in ancient Rome.

> (All are standing frozen in the same places as at the end of Act
> I.)

PIUS: But how can you be pirates?! We're not at sea.

PIRATE #2: We're land pirates! We banded together because all of us get seasick if we get on a boat.

PIRATE #1: But we're equally ruthless!

IGNORAMUS: (under his breath) And toothless?

PIRATE #3: I heard that!

PIRATE #4: What did he say?

PIRATE #3: You heard him. He's right there.

PIRATE #4: I'm getting a little deaf, asshole.

PIRATE #1: Enough quarreling amongst us! We have to decide how to kill them.

PIUS: It's bad luck to kill a eunuch.

PIRATE #1: Oh? Who says?!

PIUS: It's well known in the best circles.

PIRATE #1: Are you a eunuch?

PIUS: I'm an aspiring one.

PIRATE #1: So far as I know, aspiring doesn't count.

TITUS: I can vouch for him. He's almost a eunuch. I'm sure he'll make an excellent one.

PIRATE #1: We can help you get there! A cut here. A cut there!

PIUS: That's very nice of you, but –

PIRATE #4: Let's just flay them!

(The three hostages cringe.)

PIRATE #2: Oh, but that's so messy. Let's just skewer them and get it over with.

PIRATE #1: We've got to toy with them first.

IGNORAMUS: No, you don't.

PIRATE #2: Let's make them walk the gangplank!

IGNORAMUS: What gangplank? We're not on a boat.

TITUS: (to IGNORAMUS, under his breath) Don't be a show-off.

PIRATE #4: I heard that!

TITUS: (to PIRATE #4) Don't pay any attention to him. He thinks he knows everything.

PIRATE #4: (meaning Pirate #1) Yeah, I know some people like that myself.

PIRATE #1: I heard that!

PIRATE #4: So flay me!

PIRATE #1: Don't tempt me!

PIRATE #4: You know what, Number One, I'm tired of your shit! Boss! Boss! Boss! Just who the hell do you think you are?!

PIRATE #1: You've got it absolutely right, Pirate #4. I'm the boss boss boss of this pirate crew!

PIRATE #4: We've been talking about you behind your back for years. Did you know that?

PIRATE #1: So what?! When you lead, you get snivelers and whiners complaining about this, that, and the other thing. But what do they do about it!? Nothing!

PIRATE #4: Who are you calling a sniveler?! I've never sniveled once in my life!

PIRATE #1: Put up or shut up, snivel-nose. (Raises his sword.)

PIRATE #4: Which of you men are with me!? (#2 and #3 raise their hands) Good!

PIRATE #1: You can't do this. It's a mutiny! You'll all hang!

PIRATE #4: We're on land. So it can't be a mutiny!

PIRATE #1: Don't think you can get off on a technicality.

PIRATE #4: (to #2 and #3) Take him, my mutineers! Take him down a peg. And give it to him as a leg!

(PIRATE #1 begins a sword fight with the other three pirates.)

PIRATE #1: We'll see who has a peg leg to stand on when we're finished here!

(They fight some more, fighting around and even over the three hostages.)

TITUS: My money's on Number 1.

PIUS: My money's on the second one. But it would be rude to call him Number 2.

IGNORAMUS: I think we should try to make our escape while they're fighting, not betting.

PIUS: Oh, you are such a killjoy! Jeez!

(The four PIRATES exit fighting.)

IGNORAMUS: Okay, okay, let's go now. (Goes to the cart.)

TITUS: (looking back at the offstage Pirates) I wish I had an AK-47 automatic assault rifle!

IGNORAMUS: Just wait. You will.

PIUS: (to IGNORAMUS) I don't think they allow donkeys in central Rome. You may have to sell your ass.

IGNORAMUS: I'm not selling my ass in Rome!

TITUS: I think you can buy a temporary license.

PIUS: Are you sure?

TITUS: Or try a bribe.

IGNORAMUS: I'm not giving a bribe for my ass – my donkey – either.

PIUS: Aren't you the proud one!

IGNORAMUS: How much do you think I can get for it?

PIUS: Your ass?

IGNORAMUS: Invisible.

PIUS: How much for your invisible ass? I'm no expert, but –

IGNORAMUS: Who's going with me and who's staying behind?

TITUS: I don't like your behind. I'm going with you!

PIUS: I guess I am too. He travels best who travels with others.

IGNORAMUS: Wrong quote. But let's go!

(They start to hop into the donkey cart.)

(Suddenly, PIRATE #3 runs back.)

PIRATE #3: Wait! … I forgot to give you something.

(Uses a different weapon on each traveler: a short sword, a knife, a mace, all rubber.)

(The three fall to the ground.)

PIRATE #3: (as he runs off with the cart whipping Invisible ahead of him) Never underestimate a pirate, even seasick, and on land! (Exits.)

(The three on the ground moan.)

TITUS: This time I think we're really goners.

PIUS: I think you're right, Gaseus.

TITUS: I know we didn't always get along, but actually it was very nice getting to know you.

PIUS: Thank you, Gaseus. I feel the same.

IGNORAMUS: Too bad it's under these circumstances!

PIUS: Do you think we'll just lie here and bleed to death?

TITUS: (proudly) Like in a true Roman tragedy!

PIUS: Life is like a play, with its entrances and exits. Its comic actors. Its tragic ones.

TITUS: Like us. Tragic!

PIUS: The best is when the characters go out in a monologue while dying
—

IGNORAMUS: But not too long.

PIUS: A monologue about truth in art, about the place of
underrepresented minorities in society, about –

IGNORAMUS: Maybe we can manage to stagger to an oasis somewhere.

PIUS: (continuing his monologue) About more and better roles for
women in the arts. About whether Greek lives matter. About –

(Enter CHRISTIAN #1.)

CHRISTIAN #1: I hate to cut you off, but do you three perchance need
help?

IGNORAMUS: Yes! Yes!

TITUS: Yes! Please!

PIUS: I haven't finished my monologue yet!

IGNORAMUS: Save it for the theater!

CHRISTIAN #1: (calling to offstage characters) Come, my fellow
Christians. These poor folk have need of our help.

(Three more CHRISTIANS enter, one of them still partly
dressed as a PIRATE.)

CHRISTIAN #2: In the name of the Christ, what has happened here?
Come, let us minister to these afflicted.

(The CHRISTIANS go over and attend to the wounds.)

PIUS: Oh, thank you. Thank you. Who are you again?

CHRISTIAN #1: We are Christians. We go out in the mornings and find
those who need our help.

CHRISTIAN #2: We're known as the Early Christians. I'm sorry we're a
little late today.

CHRISTIAN #3: (looking) That wound looks pretty bad. Let us minister.

CHRISTIAN #4: Indeed it does. Of course not as bad as the wounds on Jesus as he hung on the cross for us.

CHRISTIAN #3: Of course. (pointing at TITUS) And that one's going to need an ICU. (to TITUS) Do you have health insurance?

TITUS: What?

CHRISTIAN #3: Or perchance Medicaid?

TITUS: I don't know what you're talking about.

IGNORAMUS: We were attacked by pirates. They even cart-jacked us.

CHRISTIAN #3: Cart-jacked! The villains!

CHRISTIAN #1: Let us pray that these poor gentlemen get better.

(The four CHRISTIANS gather together, hands folded in prayer.)

CHRISTIAN #1: Let us pray!

IGNORAMUS: Do you mind treating our wounds first, if you can?

CHRISTIAN #4: Without a prayer?!

IGNORAMUS: I do believe we might be without a prayer if we don't get some medical treatment soon.

CHRISTIAN #2: None of you is practicing birth control, I hope? We can't treat you if you are.

(The three wounded swear they are not practicing birth control.)

CHRISTIAN #1: Are you Christians or pagans?

THE THREE: Pagans!

CHRISTIAN #1: Do you wish to become Christians?

THE THREE: Not really.

CHRISTIAN #1: Are you sure?

IGNORAMUS: I suppose we can get treatment in Rome, if we can survive that long.

PIUS: And if we can even get there!

CHRISTIAN #3: I have some leeches we can use. (Shows box.)

PIUS: (hysterical) No *leeches!* I hate *leeches!*

CHRISTIAN #3: All right, all right. No leeches! (Puts away the box.)

CHRISTIAN #4: (examining TITUS) This one looks like he's got a broken tibia. I may have to fracture it again to set it right.

TITUS: I don't need a tibia. Leave it be. (to PIUS) What's a tibia?

PIUS: I don't know. I don't know Latin terms.

TITUS: I thought we were speaking Latin.

IGNORAMUS: It's your shinbone. Which is connected to the fibula.

TITUS: Which is connected to my labia?

IGNORAMUS: I don't think so.

LIGHTS DOWN

LIGHTS UP.

SCENE 2

> (The three wounded men are now treated, in splints and bandages.)

PIUS: I hope these aren't the same bandages used by the lepers. (Sniffs them.)

CHRISTIAN #1: Is that all the thanks we get?!

PIUS: (ungrateful) Thank you.

TITUS: Yes, many thanks for the second fracture.

IGNORAMUS: How can we ever thank you enough?

CHRISTIAN: I doubt that you can. But of course, we four will be rewarded up above one day. (Points to Heaven.)

IGNORAMUS: So you had an ulterior motive in helping us?

CHRISTIAN #1: A touch perchance. We are sinners and need all the help we can get.

IGNORAMUS: I don't begrudge. Just trying to understand.

CHRISTIAN #1: There is one other little thing you could do for us.

IGNORAMUS: What's that?

CHRISTIAN #1: Baptism.

TITUS: What's that?

CHRISTIAN #2: We just want to dunk you in that pool of water over there. (Points off.)

PIUS: Why?!

CHRISTIAN #2: Oh, just as a favor on your part for what we did for you.

TITUS: You want us to get dunked in some water?

CHRISTIAN #3: We could bring the water over here!

CHRISTIAN #1: Is that allowed? The unbaptized should come to the water.

CHRISTIAN #3: Not in an emergency. And if this isn't one, I don't know what is.

CHRISTIAN #1: I'm not sure it'll work on total pagans if we don't dunk them completely.

CHRISTIAN #3: I happen to have a dipper with me. I'll use that! (Gets the dipper somewhere.) I found one!

CHRISTIAN #1: We may have to run this by Rome. I wish there were a Pope or somebody to decide.

CHRISTIAN #3: It's not a heresy. No need to fret. It's still water poured on their heads. It'll work!

PIUS: You're going to pour water on our heads?!

CHRISTIAN #1: Remember, we did fix your wounds.

CHRISTIAN #3: I'm going for water! (Runs offstage.)

(Pause.)

IGNORAMUS: (after a beat) How about a drink of water?

TITUS: I think they're just joshing with us. They won't waste water out here in the desert.

CHRISTIAN #3: (offstage.) Here I come! (Runs back on, the dipper full of water.)

IGNORAMUS: (warning) You won't!

PIUS: (to audience) Will he? Won't he?

CHRISTIAN #3: (to audience) Will I? Won't I?

(Everybody on stage and in the audience is wondering if real water will be used.)

(If at all possible, a dipperful of real water is spilled on TITUS.)

(A second dipperful appears and PIUS gets doused.)

(They don't like the water and protest.)

IGNORAMUS: Not me! Not me!

CHRISTIAN #4: (to #3) I have a spare dipper of water. (Gets it somewhere. Hands it to #3.)

IGNORAMUS: Pardon me, but I don't think the water is going to –

CHRISTIAN #3: (throwing the water on him) You're baptized!

IGNORAMUS: Oh, God ... Gods.

CHRISTIAN #3: No, just one – God. And you have pleased Him.

IGNORAMUS: If you're going to do that, at least get some into my mouth.

CHRISTIAN #3: Now your souls are saved!

IGNORAMUS: Somehow I doubt it.

CHRISTIAN #3: Oh, do not doubt! You can never be unbaptized now.

CHRISTIAN #1: You can enter Heaven!

IGNORAMUS: I just want to get to Rome.

CHRISTIAN #1: Oh, Rome is very wicked! Don't go there!

IGNORAMUS: So I hear. But can I trust everything I hear?

CHRISTIAN #4: We must leave now, my brethren. It is getting late and we have many other acts of charity to perform.

(The CHRISTIANS gather and say a quick prayer, all mumbles.)

TITUS: Goodbye, Early Christians!

PIUS: Lovely meeting you!

IGNORAMUS: I guess we'll have to walk the rest of the way. (to CHRISTIANS) Can you at least point us in the right direction to Rome?

FOUR CHRISTIANS: (all pointing in different directions) That way! That way! This is the path! Down that way and turn to the right!

(The CHRISTIANS leave as one, still pointing in different directions.)

IGNORAMUS: Well, at least they treated our wounds. Do you two think you're well enough to travel without the cart?

TITUS: I am! I don't feel a day over eighty!

PIUS: I'll manage.

IGNORAMUS: Does either of you, or both, have a better sense of direction than I do? Or those Early Christians do?

(Enter SOOTHSAYER wearing a funny hat.)

SOOTHSAYER: I do! Listen to me!

IGNORAMUS: Who are you?

SOOTHSAYER: I am a soothsayer. I know the sooth!

PIUS: What's the sooth?

TITUS: I think it's something like the truth, only more of a vague guess.

SOOTHSAYER: My sooth is guaranteed! One hundred and ten percent!

IGNORAMUS: How much does it cost?

SOOTHSAYER: For you, my friends, a discount.

TITUS: We'll pay the full amount.

PIUS: That's correct. No discount sooth for us.

SOOTHSAYER: All I require is half of what all three of you have on you.

IGNORAMUS: Just for directions?

SOOTHSAYER: Where do you want to go?

IGNORAMUS: Shouldn't you know that already?

SOOTHSAYER: Smart guy, huh? Okay, let's see how you do on your own. (Starts to leave.)

IGNORAMUS: Wait!

SOOTHSAYER: Say you're sorry.

IGNORAMUS: I'm sorry.

SOOTHSAYER: Say "I'm sorry, soothsayer."

IGNORAMUS: I'm sorry, soothsayer.

SOOTHSAYER: Now say it three times, real fast!

IGNORAMUS: (stumbling over the words) I'm sorry, soothsayer. I'm sorry, soothsayer. I'm sorry, soothsayer.

SOOTHSAYER: And also: "Soothsayer, I'm sorry."

IGNORAMUS: (resigned, but carefully) Soothsayer, I'm sorry.

SOOTHSAYER: I guess that will have to do. But something tells me you're not truly sorry.

IGNORAMUS: And the road to Rome would be … ?

SOOTHSAYER: Let me prognosticate!

PIUS: That's sounds dirty.

SOOTHSAYER: (goes through gyrations, hands on his head, eyes
rolling)

TITUS: Is it working?

SOOTHSAYER: I'm almost there! (Does some more gyrations) That did
it! Whew!

PIUS: (to TITUS) I think we're being scammed.

SOOTHSAYER: One more thing before I give you the directions.

IGNORAMUS: What's that?

SOOTHSAYER: Payment for my services. Half of what you three have.
Whatever that is.

IGNORAMUS: Shouldn't you know how much that is?

SOOTHSAYER: Even a soothsayer has gaps! You're getting on my
nerves, whatever your name is!

IGNORAMUS: Shouldn't you – (Cuts himself off before saying "know
that.")

SOOTHSAYER: I know your names!

TITUS: You do?!

SOOTHSAYER: I can tell by examining small clues about you.

TITUS: Okay, you're on. What's my name!

SOOTHSAYER: (hand on forehead) Let me think. Let me think! Your
name is Obnoxius!

PIUS: Very good!

TITUS: What are my other two names?

SOOTHSAYER: Coitus Interruptus!

TITUS: Wrong!

SOOTHSAYER: Well, I got one name right!

PIUS: And what is my name?

SOOTHSAYER: Self-rightius Virtuus!

TITUS: Not bad!

IGNORAMUS: I won't ask mine. Just the directions.

SOOTHSAYER: You, sir, are called Ignoramus. But actually you are
    smart and well-informed, just not given the credit you deserve,
    because it's four A.D. That's IV A.D.

IGNORAMUS: I'm impressed. Did you cheat?

SOOTHSAYER: Maybe. Maybe not. You tell me!

TITUS: Let's settle up and get on the road! (Takes coins from his
    clothes.) Here's half of mine.

PIUS: And mine. (Gives coins.)

IGNORAMUS: And mine! (Gives some coins.)

SOOTHSAYER: (looking through the coins) Somebody's trying to
    shortchange me.

TITUS: It's me. (Hands another coin over.)

SOOTHSAYER: More!

PIUS: Remember, soothsayer, although we are wounded, there still are
    three of us to your one. If I were you …

SOOTHSAYER: All right, all right. Don't get all Roman with me. Or I might give you the wrong directions!

IGNORAMUS: Give us what you have. But you were very good on my name, Ignoramus.

SOOTHSAYER: A little flattery never hurts. You take this road here. (Points.) And you go (in Roman numerals) XV miles straight ahead. But when you get to a big red barn you curve a little to the left and go XXX meters until you come to a big brown barn, which has the name FLAVIA'S PLACE on the side of it. Stop there and have a cocktail and a concubine, if you're so inclined. Then you –

PIUS: Are we almost there?

SOOTHSAYER: Then you pass three old crucifixes and –

TITUS: We're there?

SOOTHSAYER: Almost. You'll see a yellow barn on your right and just beyond that will be –

IGNORAMUS: Rome?

SOOTHSAYER: Not quite. I'm only half-finished.

IGNORAMUS: I think we should get on the road and ask again when we get to the red barn.

TITUS/PIUS: I agree.

SOOTHSAYER: Suit yourselves! Goodbye!

OTHERS: Bye! Goodbye! So long!

 (The three travelers trudge on in the direction the
 SOOTHSAYER first pointed to.)

 (They exit.)

SOOTHSAYER: (to audience) I lied. There's no red barn.

LIGHTS OUT.

LIGHTS UP

SCENE 3

(The three enter in single file.)

PIUS: I'm thirsty.

TITUS: I need to go to the privy.

IGNORAMUS: I need to fornicate. But I think we're all out of luck. It can't be too much farther.

PIUX: Are you sure?

IGNORAMUS: I have no idea, actually. Let's stop and sort out our options.

(They stop.)

TITUS: We could split up and each take his chances.

PIUS: You could both carry me.

IGNORAMUS: Maybe there's a chariot service that we could pay to come and transport us to Rome.

TITUS/PIUS: Don't be ridiculous!

IGNORAMUS: Sorry, just a thought.

(Enter two women with a few pieces of luggage. WITCH is dressed like a man.)

TITUS: Now who's this?

PIUS: They appear to be two women, possibly from Rome.

IGNORAMUS: They look like two women, one dressed like a man.

TITUS: How can you tell?

IGNORAMUS: Because she looks like a woman dressed like a man. That one. (Nods toward WITCH.)

WITCH: Stand off, fellows! We are fierce and terrible!

IGNORAMUS: But badly disguised.

WITCH: I am called Prostate the Large! Be wary of me!

BITCH: And I am a Harpy from Harpy Valley!

(They show their gnashing teeth.)

IGNORAMUS: We mean you no harm.

BITCH: You'd better not or we'll rip you a new one!

PIUS: A new one what?

IGNORAMUS: Let's move on. (Starts to move on.)

TITUS: Can you tell us one thing. Are we on the right road to Rome?

BITCH: As a matter of fact, yes, we can. We're on the road that leads away from Rome.

PIUS: Going on vacation?

WITCH: No, we have been banished by the authorities and forced to leave.

TITUS: What did you do?

WITCH: I practiced witchcraft. Or so they said.

TITUS/PIUS: (frightened) Not that! No witchcraft! (Their hands go up in defense.)

WITCH: It was homeopathic witchcraft.

PIUS/TITUS: Not that! (Again their hands go up in defense.)

IGNORAMUS: I don't know what that means.

WITCH: Only natural ingredients: eye of newt, tongue of frog, Tylenol.

IGNORAMUS: And you got banished just for that?

WITCH: Well, I did do a little spell or two on the side. Nothing heavy-duty.

BITCH: You changed a Senator into a pig!

WITCH: He was already a pig! I just curled his tail. And his penis.

BITCH: They accused *me* of bitchcraft!

WITCH: Well, you were guilty!

BITCH: Shut up! (to the men) They always banished me because I refused to wear a mask during the last pandemic.

PIUS: Why wouldn't you?

BITCH: Does the emperor wear a stupid mask?! Of course not! So I'm not putting that thing on my face.

IGNORAMUS: Do you have the plague?

BITCH: Do I look like I have the plague/!

IGNORAMUS: Sort of.

PIUS: You wouldn't have any just plain water with you, would you?

BITCH: Don't give him our water!

WITCH: I do have some water with me. Special water.

TITUS: Don't drink it.

PIUS: You can't judge these poor women just because of their clothing and their behavior.

TITUS: Are you both witches?

BITCH: No!

TITUS: Which is the witch?

BITCH: She's the witch. I'm the bitch!

IGNORAMUS: And Rome banished you because you're a bitch?

BITCH: Yes! But if a man did or said what I did, they would never call him a bitch!

IGNORAMUS: Uh, I think they might.

BITCH: (angrily) Like hell they would! You men all stick together!

IGNORAMUS: Been here, done this.

BITCH: You want to hear some more? Huh?

IGNORAMUS: Yeah, woman-splain it to me. On the other hand, don't. I've got to get to Rome.

BITCH: So you don't want to hear what's wrong with you men, huh?

IGNORAMUS: Oh, God! Not now!

PIUS: (correcting him) Gods. Plural. (Points to Heaven.)

WITCH: For a small price, I could fix you fellas a nice, refreshing concoction to take on the road with you.

IGNORAMUS: I'm not that thirsty. (to TITUS and PIUS) If you're going with me, let's go.

PIUS: Do you have any dates? Pitted?

BITCH: No dates! And no dates with us either!

PIUS: I want *dates*, not a date!

WITCH: How about that refreshing concoction?

PIUS: What's in it?

WITCH: That's my little secret.

BITCH: Nuts! Are you allergic to nuts?

PIUS: I don't believe so.

WITCH: Nuts in mimosa!

BITCH: Eunuch nuts.

PIUS: (almost throwing up) Oh, please!

BITCH: Salted.

PIUS: Stop!

IGNORAMUS: I thought you wanted to be a eunuch.

PIUS: I think I'm changing my mind.

WITCH: I also have some tiger tit.

PIUS: What's that good for?

WITCH: (laughing) Well, it's not good for the tiger, I'll tell you that!

TITUS: Does it go well with eunuch nuts?

WITCH: It's a meal you'll never forget.

BITCH: Are you going to buy some or not?

IGNORAMUS: No, we're not.

BITCH: Then get out of our face! (to WITCH) Come on, let's move on!

    (The two start to move along.)

PIUS: Very nice to meet you. Sorry about your banishment.

BITCH: We'll live!

WITCH: She's always right. I don't know what I'd do without her.

TITUS: Goodbye! I'm also very sorry about your banishment.

WITCH: You sure you don't want to try a brew I made before I left. Bull's pizzle and chickory plus a secret ingredient. Delicious! I can put a little umbrella in it. Gluten-free.

IGNORAMUS: No.

WITCH: Makes the male member stand up like Caligula's stallion! (Makes her arm like a horse dick.)

(All three men come back, interested.)

TITUS: Really?

PIUS: Sounds fabulous.

IGNORAMUS: Well, why didn't you say so before? (Stops himself.) No! No, no! I'm off!

(IGNORAMUS heads off. TITUS and PIUS reluctantly leave too.)

TITUS: Well, we could at least try it!

LIGHTS DOWN.

LIGHTS UP.

SCENE 4

(A beggar appears.)

BEGGAR: (to audience) Alms? Alms for a poor beggar? Alms? (When he gets no alms.) Alms for the homeless! (No response.) Fuck you!

(TITUS, PIUS, and IGNORAMUS come into view, still on the road to Rome.)

TITUS: I pissed back there. (Points off.)

IGNORAMUS: I'm pooped. (Sits down.) I hope Invisible is okay.

TITUS: I wouldn't count on it.

IGNORAMUS: I'm not.

PIUS: I'm constipated.

TITUS: We don't care.

(The BEGGAR approaches them.)

BEGGAR: Pardon me, do you have a drachma or two to spare?

IGNORAMUS: No.

PIUS: We're tired.

BEGGAR: But not too tired to pull our one little drachma.

TITUS: Get a job!

BEGGAR: There are no jobs out here.

TITUS: Then move.

BEGGAR: If I had but one drachma, I could survive. (Holds out a hand.)

PIUS: I'll pay you if you carry me to Rome.

BEGGAR: How much?

PIUS: One drachma.

BEGGAR: Not enough.

IGNORAMUS: How much are you willing to take to give us that
information? And don't say one drachma.

BEGGAR: One drachma.

IGNORAMUS: Never mind. I have a feeling it's about thirty miles.

BEGGAR: But you're not sure, are you?

PIUS: How about a blow job?

BEGGAR: What?!

PIUS: To carry me to Rome. Plus one drachma.

BEGGAR: I don't lean in that direction.

PIUS: I don't either. But I'm tired.

IGNORAMUS: Can you at least lean in the direction of Rome?

BEGGAR: One drachma!

IGNORAMUS: By the way, a drachma is Greek!

BEGGAR: It is? Okay, one denarius. Euros?

TITUS: Why don't you move along, pal?

BEGGAR: That'll cost you!

IGNORAMUS: One drachma?

BEGGAR: Plus one denarius. All right, I'm giving you one chance.
(Pulls out a tin cup. Shows it to the others. He picks up a stone
from the ground and places it very deliberately in the cup.)

PIUS: Is that supposed to scare us?

BEGGAR: (rattling the stone in the tin cup) It could be a gun. It could be a gun.

TITUS: What's a gun?

IGNORAMUS: We don't have guns yet.

BEGGAR: (reconsidering, then shakes the tin can again) It could be a *k*-nife. It could be a *k*-nifc. (mispronouncing it with a "k" sound: -*k*-nife)

TITUS: What's a *k*-nife?

IGNORAMUS: The "k" is silent.

BEGGAR: It is? Since when?

IGNORAMUS: Drop the "k" and drop the *k*-nife. … knife.

BEGGAR: (shaking the tin can again) It could be a short s*w*ord. (Says the "w," not "sord")

IGNORAMUS: You drop the "w" in "sword."

BEGGAR: This Latin is hard! It's not my first language. Why have those letters if you don't pronounce them?!

IGNORAMUS: I don't know! God, you're annoying!

BEGGAR: (correcting) You're not so smart! It's "Gods, you're annoying!" Plural!

PIUS: (to IGNORAMUS) And don't take the names of the gods in vain.

IGNORAMUS: Let's hit the road. (Starts to leave.) (He stops bends down and hits the road with his hand.) I hit the road!

BEGGAR: Lest anyone here or nearby think for one moment that the plight of the homeless is any less important because it is mentioned here in ancient times, when people didn't have feelings, didn't feel pain and hunger, couldn't afford to feed their pets, died young and then lay forgotten, entombed in their own grief and loneliness! I am but one such person. They are not amusing! Especially not me! Feel! Don't laugh! Feel! Feel! Feel!

(After a moment, the other three applaud.)

BEGGAR: Thank you. One drachma.

IGNORAMUS: We can't help everyone we meet up with in this life. But here is one drachma. (Hands a coin to BEGGAR.)

BEGGAR: Oh, thank you, kind sir. Thank you. Thank you. (Pulls out a magazine from his clothing.) Can I interest you in some porn? (Tantalizes the three with the porn.) Hot stuff! All new positions. Things you haven't seen before, ever. Guaranteed!

IGNORAMUS: Really?

(The three travelers come over to BEGGAR, interested in the porn.)

TITUS: Oh, look at that!

PIUS: (looking) Disgusting! (But then he looks closer.)

IGNORAMUS: I've seen worse.

(They continue to examine the porn magazine, mulling over it.)

BEGGAR: (to audience) One drachma?

LIGHTS DOWN.

LIGHTS UP.

SCENE 5

(The three wayfarers enter, exhausted from their trek.)

PIUS: I feel spent.

TITUS: I feel pretty … exhausted.

IGNORAMUS: It looks like Rome is going to fall.

(Enter four BARBARIANS, dressed as such.)

PIUS: Shall we try to hide?

TITUS: Romans don't hide! They come, they see, they conquer!

PIUS: These persons look like savages.

TITUS: Are we Romans or are we not?! We fight to win, and when we
see a country we like, we take it.

PIUS: Yay us!

BARBARIAN #1: What have we here? Romans?

PIUS: I'm from Lithuania.

TITUS: Me too.

BARBARIAN #1: Well, Lithuanians, if you want to live, you will tell us
how we sack and pillage our way to Rome.

IGNORAMUS: Who are you?

BARBARIAN #2: We're barbarians!

IGNORAMUS: I should have guessed.

BARBARIAN #3: We are intent on bringing about the fall of Rome!

IGNORAMUS: Come back in 476 A.D., more or less. I know it's not consistent with my character, but I just can't let the actual date be misrepresented here!

BARBARIAN #1: We heard that Rome is falling now.

IGNORAMUS: Come back in 2000 years. You'll do a lot better then than now.

BARBARIAN #1: We thank you, Lithuanian, for this information. We will go back home and practice our sacking and pillaging. (to other BARBARIANS) Company, attention! (The BARBARIANS come to attention.) Company, march!

(The BARBARIANS march off in unison.)

TITUS: They're very disciplined, especially for barbarians.

IGNORAMUS: Yes. I think they may conquer the world. They're just smart enough.

PIUS: Well, there is only one thing left we can do to save ourselves.

TITUS: What's that?

PIUS: Pray. Pray like we've never prayed before!

IGNORAMUS: To which god? Who's the god of travel?

TITUS: I'm not sure.

IGNORAMUS: Is it Mercury?

PIUS: Let's do generic.

TITUS: I think the gods –

PIUS: – and goddesses!

TITUS: – like to be addressed personally. I've heard they won't answer generic prayers.

PIUS: I hear that they answer every single prayer.

IGNORAMUS: Only not always the way you want.

PIUS: You are too cynical by half!

IGNORAMUS: I guess that leaves a half to go.

PIUS: (praying) Dear gods and goddesses, high above us up on Mt. Olympus or wherever you dwell, or may be at present, please take pity on the plight of we three lowly, unworthy travelers lost here only you know where!

IGNORAMUS: (chiming in, sort of) Yeah, nowhere!

PIUS: Please tell us how to proceed!

TITUS: Is it that way? Or this? (Points in different directions.)

PIUS: By all that is holy and propitious we beg you to give us a sign!

TITUS: A sign to help us find our faltering, stupid way to the Eternal City!

IGNORAMUS: In the name of the Emperor do we pray!

(GODDESS # 1 appears, all dressed up.)

GODDESS #1: You called?

PIUS: Goddess! You've come! (The three men kneel.)

GODDESS: I liked your prayer, even if it was a bit generic. What do you want this time?

PIUS: The path in life! The proper road!

IGNORAMUS: Or at least the right directions to Rome.

PIUS: Excuse me, lovely Goddess, I do not know which one you are. You are the first one ever to actually appear to me.

GODDESS #1: I am Minerva.

PIUS: And you do … ?

GODDESS #1: Wisdom, medicine, and handicrafts. Which do you require?

TITUS: Don't you expect a sacrifice first?

GODDESS #1: For you, since it's your first time, no sacrifice needed.

PIUS: Oh, thank you, kind Goddess!

GODDESS #1: Let's just say that I am making the sacrifice for you! That's a little goddess joke of mine. Get it?

TITUS/PIUS: (laughing too hard) That's hilarious! Such wit!

GODDESS #1: Calm down, boys. Don't overdo it. Not that you can!

IGNORAMUS: Can we please get the directions to Rome?

GODDESS #1: (about IGNORAMUS) I don't like this one. He doesn't grovel right!

PIUS: Ignore him, please. He's an ignoramous.

GODDESS #1: This time I'll *ignore* the ignoramous. (Waits.) That's another little divine joke!

IGNORAMUS: (reluctantly) Very good, very good.

GODDESS #1: Well, since you asked, each according to your way, I'd say that the best route to Rome is … (She is not sure.) that way! North! (Points.)

GOD #1: (entering) That's not north. That's east.

GODDESS #1: It's north.

GOD #1: East!

GODDESS #2: (entering) It's west!

IGNORAMUS: Oh, God! I know, I know – *gods!*

GOD #2: (entering) South!

IGNORAMUS: Oh, shit!

PIUS: Do not use vulgar language in front of the gods!

IGNORAMUS: They have a worse sense of direction than I do!

PIUS: So they're a trifle weak on directions. But let me ask about other things.

GOD #2: Ask away. I like this guy.

PIUS: If I get to Rome, what is the best career choice for me there? Should I become a eunuch or try something else?

GODDESS #1: I think you'd make a perfect eunuch!

PIUS: Really?

GOD #1: I don't know about that. He seems to me more like an ass swabber in the baths.

PIUS: I've already done that! I'm looking for something else. Something more fulfilling.

GODDESS #2: How about an attendant to the Emperor?

PIUS: Now that's more like it. Do you know him?

GODDESS #2: You can say Goddess #2 recommended you.

PIUS: How wonderful! Thank you! Remind me what you are goddess of again.

GODDESS #2: I am Juno, goddess of love, marriage, and fertility.

PIUS: Of course! … And how does that apply to me?

GODDESS #2: Occasionally I dabble in imperial appointments.

PIUS: Tremendous!

GODDESS #2: Naturally, if I were to get you one of those, a sacrifice
would be nice.

PIUS: But of course.

GODDESS #2: A big sacrifice. A daughter or something.

GOD #2: I think he might make a first-rate fluffer in a bordello.

TITUS: What do you see for me?

GODDESS #1: Dead by fifty.

GODDESS #2: Forty-one.

GOD #1: Arrested in Rome for financial crimes. Tortured to death
slowly.

GOD #2: Becomes a Christian is thrown to the big cats. Big ratings!

GODDESS #1: No, small cats! They sit on his face.

GODDESS #2: No, he gets to Rome, goes free on all charges. But
becomes a eunuch out of belated guilt.

TITUS: I'm not becoming a eunuch no matter what you gods say! Get
your act together! Who can we trust if not you gods?!

(The four divinities are incensed.)

IGNORAMUS: Well, here's a breakthrough!

GOD #1: We're leaving! If we're not treated better than this, we're out of
here! (All the divinities agree. And begin to leave.)

GODDESS #1: And don't expect us to return to you ingrates ever again,
except in Portugal, where they know what respect is.

(They exit, angry.)

IGNORAMUS: When troubles come, they come not single spies ... but always in groups of four. Why is that?

PIUS: (to audience) Budget.

LIGHTS OUT.

LIGHTS UP.

SCENE 6

(The three travelers trudge on.)

IGNORAMUS: Something tells me we're near the end. Just not the desired end.

TITUS: In Rome?

IGNORAMUS: No, dead on the road to Rome, our bones picked clean by vultures.

PIUS: Oh, not a tragedy! Please! American audiences don't like tragedies!

TITUS: He's right. I have never told anyone this before, but when I was a young man I appeared in a tragedy in a traveling theater company. We bombed. And I never acted again. Out of necessity, I became a man of business. Eventually, I became a crook. Let me spare you the details, but I was not a good person. All I can hope now is that my poor bones out here, just short of Rome, picked over by vultures will go some way to making amends for my many, many sins. Thank you for listening.

PIUS: If I die here, I will leave behind the few scribblings I have managed to write on this trip, unseen by any but myself. (Shows some parchments inside his clothing.) At least the world, or some of it, will see that I was a sensitive soul just looking for love on the road of life. But, alas, I did not, could not, find it. Thank you.

IGNORAMUS: I guess that leaves me, to tell my story, finally.

TITUS: You don't have to bother.

PIUS: So true.

IGNORAMUS: No, I want to. I did not set out on this journey to save Rome from falling. That was just a cover story I made up.

PIUS: Oh?

TITUS: I don't think I'm going to like this.

IGNORAMUS: I was born in a small village that my father passed through on one of his conquests. I am the illegitimate son of our unbeloved Emperor.

TITUS: Of Pompus Vainglorius?

IGNORAMUS: The same. I met him just one time, when I was seventeen. He happened to be out conquering near the village where he had conceived me, my mother now deceased. He was not a good father. Indeed, I'd say he was a bad father. But he did recognize me as his biological son. We have the same widow's peak. He recently summoned me to Rome to honor him in his upcoming proclamation as Emperor Forever. Perhaps you have heard of this proclamation. My father, the Emperor, had at first agreed that he would be Temporary Emperor for a short time after the untimely passing of the previous emperor.

PIUS: Maximus Dickus.

IGNORAMUS: Precisely. But now my father has violated his solemn oath and soon will become Emperor Forever. He even has his physicians infusing his body with glands and special fluids to prolong his life. I am on my way, or I was, to stop my father from taking the throne forever. I have heard often of his monstrous shortcomings, his madness, his neglect of his people during the recent pestilence, his venality, and his poor Latin. He must be removed from power. If I had not sickened and soon expired on this road, I surely, as the gods are my witnesses, for whatever that's worth, made certain that my terrible father would resign by my hand. I had come to prevent the fall of Rome, indeed, but only by stopping the monster, the Emperor, my father.

TITUS: A sad tale. But I would have joined you in your task! I swear it!

PIUS: And I too, moved by your eloquence and just generic pity.

IGNORAMUS: Thank you, thank you both. But it is not to be. (Chokes.)

(The scenery changes quickly to a street.)

TITUS: Good grief, I think we have made it to Rome after all! How time flies!

(Enter the Emperor with four GUARDS.)

EMPEROR: What have we here before us?!

GUARD #1: It looks like your son, my Emperor!

EMPEROR: It does, even though he's not seventeen anymore. That's for sure.

GUARD #2: Who are these ruffians with him?

EMPEROR: I haven't the faintest idea.

IGNORAMUS: Father? Where are we?

EMPEROR: We're only a quarter mile from the imperial palace.

IGNORAMUS: I'm all turned around.

EMPEOROR: I came out to a rally with my base, on the event of my elevation to – (Signals to the GUARDS.)

GUARDS: (as one) Emperor Forever!

EMPEROR: You got to give it to my Praetorian Guard! Stand back and stand by, fellas!

(He applauds his GUARDS.)

GUARDS: (together) Emperor Forever!

EMPEROR: Aren't they great?! Who's gonna keep me on the golden throne? They are, that's who!

IGNORAMUS: Father, can I whisper something to you?

EMPEROR: What?! His mother was a whisperer. A one-night stand in some crummy little hut, but whatcha gonna do?!

IGNORAMUS: Can I, Father?

EMPEROR: Oh, no you don't! I've heard the rumors about you.

IGNORAMUS: What rumors?

EMPEROR: That you are in cahoots with some to overthrow and replace me as Emperor, even though you are a bastard. It's a good thing I met up with you before you got to the palace and carried out your nefarious plot! You thought you would topple me, but it is I who will kill you!

IGNORAMUS: Father, I –

EMPEROR: Don't try to explain! Don't offer me excuses. I know all because I am a genius and have many ears!

IGNORAMUS: Many ears?

EMPEROR: In the court. My loyal ass-kissers. Like those four ass-kissers over there! (Points at the GUARDS.)

GUARDS: (as one) That's us!

EMPEROR: I should be home in the palace selling off Bassynia or something. Building a wall! Finishing another Pompus Vainglorius hotel! But I have to show my followers how much I think of them. (Takes out a book. Holds it up, upside down.)

IGNORAMUS: Is it the Christian Bible?

EMPEROR: It's called *The Art of the Deal.* Want to buy a copy before you die?

IGNORAMUS: Not really.

EMPEROR: I bet you haven't even read it!

IGNORAMUS: I heard you didn't even write it.

EMPEROR: I wrote every word! (Lowers the book.) Okay, that's enough entertainment for the masses for today. (Starts to leave.) Oh, I almost forgot. (to GUARDS) Kill my son!

GUARD #2: Kill your son?

EMPEROR: He's illegitimate.

IGNORAMUS: I guess it was not in the plans of the gods that I should overthrow the Emperor. Let me at least die with honor! (Bares his throat.) Cut quickly. And cut well.

(The GUARDS hesitate.)

EMPEROR: You heard him. Only cut slowly and make it hurt! (He makes the thumbs-down sign.)

(The GUARDS move as one unit toward IGNORAMUS, their shields held out.)

GUARD #4: (Claps hands overhead twice.)

OTHER THREE GUARDS: The sign!

(They turn as a unit and advance on the EMPEROR.)

EMPEROR: What's this? What are you doing? I said kill my son!

FOUR GUARDS: No!

EMPEROR: Do you want me to throw a tantrum?! I'll give you a goddamned tantrum! (Throws himself about, screaming and yelling for several very fierce seconds.)

GUARD #3: (forgetting himself) Hail, Caesar!

GUARD #1: Oh, no you don't! We are agreed!

GUARD #3: Sorry. Habit.

(The GUARDS advance as a unit toward the EMPEROR.)

EMPEROR: Stop!

TITUS/PIUS: Don't stop!

IGNORAMUS: Father, it's not too late to repent and change your ways!

EMPEROR: Kill him! I doubt that he's even my real son!

(The GUARDS advance on the EMPEROR and cover him with their shields, forcing him to the ground.)

GUARD #1: Smother him! Death to tyranny!

(They all push their shields on top of the EMPEROR.)

(Suddenly, he pushes a shield aside, puts his head out.)

EMPEROR: You're not getting rid of me that easy! You buggers! I know you're all buggering one another in the barracks! Buggering, buggering buggers!

(They manage to push the EMPEROR back underneath the shields.)

GUARD #1: Press!

(They press. The shields are pressed upward from below by the
EMPEROR, then slowly stop moving.)

GUARD #1: I think he's finally dead. Whew!

(There is a moment of silence. The EMPEROR comes up one
more time, tries to speak, but the final shield comes down and
silences him.)

IGNORAMUS: *Requiescat in pace.* So to speak. (to GUARDS) Would
you mind carrying my father's body off for a later proper burial?

(They carry the body off.)

(We hear them dump it.)

(They hurry right back.)

IGNORAMUS: Thank you.

GUARD #1: Hail to the next Caesar!

IGNORAMUS: Me? No!

GUARDS: You!

IGNORAMUS: But I was born illegitimate.

GUARD #1: We'll make a sacrifice to the gods. All of them! Then
everything should be fine. We've been plotting this for a long
time. Don't screw it up.

IGNORAMUS: Couldn't you have at least mentioned it to me?!

GUARDS: Hail, Caesar!

(They salute, then march off.)

TITUS: (to IGNORAMUS) Congrats.

PIUS: Yes, I second that.

IGNORAMUS: Thank you. May I call us all friends now?

TITUS/PIUS: Of course. Get in here! (They hug, all three of them.)

TITUS: But I guess we'll be going our separate ways now. Me to face criminal charges and possible crucifixion.

PIUS: Me to try to get into eunuch school. And I hear they've upped the qualifications.

TITUS: I happen to think you'd make a terrific eunuch. If you ever need a reference, don't hesitate to ask.

IGNORAMUS: I have an idea. Why don't you two come and work for me, with me, in the palace? New starts for each of you. All of us.

PIUS: Really?

IGNORAMUS: Titus, I can always use a good numbers man, especially when it comes to Roman numerals. My math is as bad as my sense of direction. We'll get your financial problems sorted out.

PIUS: But what would *I* do in the palace?

IGNORAMUS: You always know what's correct, Pius. Or what's considered correct at any given moment. Would you consider being head courtier? Of course, I wish to be completely transparent. I will listen to what you both tell me, but I will probably reject it most of the time. Do you understand and accept?

TITUS/PIUS: I accept. … Yes.

(They shake hands.)

(Enter CITIZEN, with the donkey cart, leading the invisible donkey.)

CITIZEN: Donkey for sale! Donkey for sale!

IGNORAMUS: Oh, my god, it's my donkey!

TITUS: How can you tell?

IGNORAMUS: I'd know him anywhere.

CITIZEN: Cart for sale! Cart for sale!

IGNORAMUS: And my cart that was cart-jacked! (to CITIZEN) Those belong to me, sir!

CITIZEN: Hey, hey, hey, I bought them from this guy who swore they were his!

IGNORAMUS: It's all right, Citizen. You will be paid. I am the new Emperor.

CITIZEN: Yeah, right.

IGNORAMUS: It's true.

TITUS/PIUS: It's true.

IGNORAMUS: We won't ask too many questions. I am just so pleased to have my donkey back again. (Goes over to the unseen donkey.) Invisible, it's so good to see you again! So good! (Hugs the donkey.)

PIUS: Don't make him a senator!

IGNORAMUS: Why not?

TITUS: Please don't!

IGNORAMUS: I'm joking. I won't! (to audience) And so ends our story, a comedy, perhaps? Or more?

BLACKOUT

DUEL

CHARACTERS (3):

VAXED, male, any age, duelist who has been vaccinated against Covid-19.

VAXLESS, male, any age, duelist who is opposed to vaccination for Covid-19

A SECOND, a male who attends both duelists

SETTING: A place suitable for a duel, pretty empty

TIME: The Present, modern dress

> (Enter VAXLESS with the SECOND, who carries two fencing foils.)

VAXLESS: Here I come. Look out, motherfucker!

SECOND: Please! Some dignity at least.

VAXLESS: I know, I know you don't want to be here, but since you have agreed to be my second, please indulge me a curse word or two.

SECOND: I'm not taking a position in this duel. Is that clear?"

VAXLESS: I know you say that, but secretly I believe you side with me. Vaccines are evil.

> (Enter VAXED.)

VAXED: They are not evil! They are good! I am good! I am Vaxed!

VAXLESS: They contain microchips that will control our brains.

VAXED: You are not only vaxless, you are clueless.

VAXLESS: And you are a blind puppet who takes orders from Biden.

VAXED: Because you won't get a little jab in your arm, you endanger the rest of the world.

VAXLESS: Because you got vaccinated, you are a wimp.

SECOND: We can still call it off and call the whole thing a tie.

VAXLESS: Never!

VAXED: Hand me my weapon.

SECOND: All right, here it is. (Hands the foil to VAX.)

VAXED: Thank you.

VAXLESS: And mine?

> (SECOND hands a foil to VAXLESS.)

VAXLESS: Thank you.

SECOND: Is it clear that I am not taking a side?

VAXLESS: Certainly. Bu secretly you agree with me.

VAXED: He agrees with me!

SECOND: No, I just happen to be friends with both of you.

VAXLESS: *En garde!* (Waves the foil around.)

VAXED: Right back at ya, bucko! (Waves the foil around.)

SECOND: Are the rules of this duel crystal clear? The one who stabs the other first wins!

VAXED: (to VAXLESS) And I will have vaccinated you!

VAXLESS: And if I stab you first I will infect you with the virus that is on the tip of the weapon.

VAX: No chance of that happening. I am vaccinated! Twice!

VAXLESS: Ah, but there is a new variant out now, and it's right there on my foil! (Shows it.)

SECOND: Maybe if I leave, there will be no duel. I'm sort of an enabler.

VAXED: We can fight without you.

VAXLESS: We most certainly can.

SECOND: I'm running out of patience. Is it a go or a no?

VAXLESS: (assuming a dueling position) Go!

VAXED: (assuming a dueling position) Go!

SECOND: One, two … On the count of three.

VAXLESS: (suddenly) Three! (Jabs at VAXED.)

VAXED: Hey! That's not fair!

VAXLESS: I don't care, you're infected now.

VAXED: (suddenly jabbing at VAXLESS) Take that!

VAXLESS: Oh, my God, I'm vaccinated!

VAXED: (laughs evilly) You're going to live because of me!

VAXLESS: Take it back! Take it back!

VAXED: Take it back?!

VAXLESS: (jabbing VAXED) Here's yours!

VAXED: I can already feel the new variant virus coursing through my veins.

VAXLESS: (laughing evilly) That's what you getting for trusting in science!

SECOND: I told you that a duel was not the answer!

VAXED: It is the answer! I just saved his life.

VAXLESS: I can already hear the voice in my brain telling me to obey. Yes, President Biden, I hear you!

VAXED: With this new variant in me I hear Marjorie Taylor Greene giving me my marching orders.

SECOND: I don't know who these people are. I told you I'm not taking sides.

VAXLESS: Hey! You're the cause of all this!

SECOND: No, I'm not!

VAXED: Yes, you are. No Second, no first.

SECOND: I knew I shouldn't have gotten involved.

(VAXED and VAXLESS unite as one and advance on SECOND.)

SECOND: Now, now.

VAXED: You should have stopped us!

VAXLESS: Exactly!

SECOND: Don't be ridiculous! Stop!

VAXED: You knew this was an outdated ritual, but you did nothing to stop it in its tracks.

VAXLESS: And that's why we're in the situation we're in.

(VAXLESS and VAXED stab SECOND.)

VAXED/VAXLESS: Take that!

SECOND: I can't believe this. OMG!

VAXED: Believe it. LOL!

SECOND: A plague on both your houses!

    (He dies.)

BLACKOUT

FERAL BOYFRIEND

—a one-act

CHARACTERS: (4)

MEGAN, a besotted woman in her teens or early twenties

BOYFRIEND, male, any age up to forty, appalling

MOM, female, in her late forties

DAD, male, in his late forties

SETTING: A restaurant represented by a table and four chairs

PRESENT TIME

At rise, MEGAN and BOYFRIEND are seated at the table.

MEGAN: They'll be here at any moment.

BOYFRIEND: Yeah, sure.

MEGAN: I can't wait for them to meet you.

BOYFRIEND: Yeah, sure.

MEGAN: They're going to love you like I do.

BOYFRIEND: Yeah, sure. (Yells at the unseen server.) No! We're not
ready! (Waves the server off.)

(Her parents hurry in.)

MOM: Oh, we're so sorry we're late!

DAD: Parking.

MOM: Please forgive us.

DAD: We don't want to make a bad first impression.

MEGAN: Oh, it's only ten minutes.

BOYFRIEND: More like twelve.

DAD: It's not like us.

BOYFRIEND: Why the fuck didn't you leave sooner?!

DAD: What?

BOYFRIEND: Apparently, you don't give a shit about us.

MEGAN: Now, Hiram, we talked about this.

BOYFRIEND: Shut up. Who asked you?

MEGAN: Nobody asked me, but –

BOYFRIEND: Then shut the hell up.

DAD: Hey!

BOYFRIEND: And don't any of you give me no goddamned lectures on how to behave.

MOM: We didn't mean to hurt your feelings.

BOYFRIEND: Let me be the judge of that. I'm post-feminist. Got it?

MOM: (trying to change the subject) Now where was that that you two met?

MEGAN /BOYFRIEND: Online.

MOM: How lovely. Was it a chat line, as they say?

MEGAN: Yes, it's called Fix Your Grammar. Every posting has to have at least one error in it. And people help you fix it.

BOYFRIEND: I thought it was called Fuck Your Granma.

MEGAN: It wasn't!

BOYFRIEND: I forget. I'm on so many chat lines. (Laughs)

MOM: I've never been on a chat line. You might say I'm not exactly a techie. If that's what it's called.

BOYFRIEND: A techie is not the only thing you're not.

MOM: I think that must be a compliment.

BOYFRIEND: My daughter by my first bitch is making my life hell. She's eleven.

MOM: How unfortunate. Do you want to tell us why?

BOYFRIEND: No, it's none of your business.

DAD: We're sorry!

BOYFRIEND: Oh, baby, let's leave this place. I'm bored.

MEGAN: Just a few more minutes, honey, and then we can go.

BOYFRIEND: And you'll suck it this time?

MEGAN: We'll have to see.

BOYFRIEND: You're sucking it, and that's all there is to it.

MOM: Please!

BOYFRIEND: Stop butting in. This is private between me and your daughter.

DAD: It doesn't sound very private to me.

BOYFRIEND: (to MEGAN) I told you I shouldn't meet them!

MEGAN: I think it's going very well.

BOYFRIEND: Am I middle-class yet?

DAD: We don't have class in America.

BOYFRIEND: Like shit we don't! I keep getting turned down for a promotion where I work. It's nothing but fucking class discrimination!

MOM: Do you mind if I ask where it is you work?

BOYFRIEND: I work in a mortuary.

DAD: Really? How interesting.

BOYFRIEND: I clean up the cum after men die. A lot of them ejaculate on themselves in their death throes.

MOM: I did not know that.

BOYFRIEND: Gotcha! Just tweaking your titties.

DAD: I beg your pardon!

BOYFRIEND: Oh, hold your horses. Can't you take a joke?

MEGAN: Isn't Hiram a breath of fresh air, Mom and Dad?

DAD: Well, let's tell Hiram a little about us, what do you say?

MOM: Yes, let's! I am a homemaker and I collect Lawrence Welk memorabilia.

BOYFRIEND: Amazing. So do I.

MOM: You do?

BOYFRIEND: It was a joke. (to MEGAN) I'm going to leave. (Almost gets up.)

MOM: Excuse me. I've got to go to the powder room.

MEGAN: I'll come with you, Mom. (Gets up.)

MOM: We won't be long.

DAD: I'll entertain Hiram while you're gone.

> (The two women go offstage.)

> (BOYFRIEND and DAD remain silent, look down.)

BOYFRIEND: (after a while) Your daughter has a nice pussy.

DAD: I didn't hear that.

BOYRIEND: Your daughter has a nice pussy.

DAD: Are you deliberately trying to provoke me or … ?

BOYFRIEND: I don't care enough about you to provoke you.

DAD: You will never marry my daughter.

BOYFRIEND: You want to bet?

DAD: I'm not a betting man.

BOYFRIEND: She already has begged me to marry her. I said no.

DAD: Our daughter has always had discretion problems. You won't be another one of them.

BOYFRIEND: She finds my charms irresistible.

DAD: You need to work on your public demeanor.

BOYFRIEND: I'd have the same thoughts anyway.

> (The two women return.)

MOM: I just needed to splash some cold water on my face.

MEGAN: I can tell that you two are getting along famously.

BOYFRIEND: That's us. I got to piss. (Gets up and leaves.)

DAD: (under his breath) Don't hurry back.

MEGAN: Dad!

DAD: He's awful! What's wrong with you?!

MEGAN: You two are just too uptight. That's the problem.

MOM: I know you don't want us to tell you what to do – about anything – but, honey, this man is not for you!

MEGAN: You're just jealous!

MOM: Jealous? That's the last thing I am!

MEGAN: Because I have found the perfect guy for me.

DAD: He's not the perfect guy for anybody.

MEGAN: And I'm going to marry him, if it's the last thing I do!

MOM: I think he's dangerous.

DAD: Yes! And incredibly rude.

MEGAN: You just don't understand how things are nowadays.

MOM: We will not let you ruin your life!

MEGAN: I don't want to live your life. That's for sure!

MOM: Here he comes!

> (BOYFRIEND re-enters with one hand covering something on one arm.)

BOYFRIEND: I couldn't piss. Sometimes I'm pee-shy.

MOM: Thanks for sharing.

BOYFRIEND: You're welcome. Are you pee-shy?

DAD: What's that on your arm?

BOYFRIEND: Nothing.

MEGAN: It is too! What is it, Hiram?

BOYFRIEND: You don't want to see it, trust me.

MEGAN: I don't want to see it. No, I do want to see it.

BOYFRIEND: Make up your mind.

MOM: She doesn't want to see it!

DAD: None of us want to see it, whatever it is!

BOYFRIEND: It's a cyst.

MEGAN: You have a cyst? I've never seen a cyst on you.

BOYFRIEND: I keep it hidden, believe it or not. I must have scraped it somehow in the restroom.

MOM: Can't you attend to it somewhere besides our table!

BOYFRIEND: I think it might be infectious.

DAD: An infectious cyst?

MEGAN: Maybe we should go to an Emergency Room.

BOYFRIEND: Take a look at it, Megan. (He pats the spot but doesn't reveal anything.)

MEGAN: I don't want to see it!

BOYFRIEND: My cyst is gonna get ya! (He lifts his hand, revealing what looks like a burst cyst.)

MEGAN: Oh, gross!

BOYFRIEND: It looks like mashed potatoes with some blood on them.

MEGAN: Cover it up! Cover it up!

BOYFRIEND: You want to taste it?

DAD: No, she doesn't want to taste it!

BOYFRIEND: You're not the boss of her. She can taste it if she wants to.

MEGAN: Exactly!

MOM: Is that a real cyst?

BOYFRIEND: Do you want to taste it to see?

MOM: I think that's a fake cyst!

BOYFRIEND: You got it, lady. Boo! (Shakes the arm with the cyst on it.)

DAD: If you think this is a funny prank of some kind …

BOYFRIEND: (laughing hard) It's hilarious! Hilarious!

MEGAN: Isn't he amazing?! How did you do that, honey?

BOYFRIEND: I carry a bottle of fake cyst juice with me. (He pulls a small bottle from a pocket and shows them.)

DAD: You carry around a bottle of fake cyst juice?

BOYFRIEND: It's the funniest thing ever! You should have seen the looks on your faces!

MOM: I do not appreciate your so-called sense of humor, young man.

BOYFRIEND: It could have been genuine cyst juice. How'd you appreciate that?

MOM: Well, this luncheon has been wonderful, but we do have to be going. (Gets up.)

BOYFRIEND: Sit down. We haven't even ordered yet. Who's hungry?

MEGAN: I'm the opposite of hungry.

BOYFRIEND: I'll get rid of this stuff on my arm and even the bottle. How's that?

DAD: It's too late.

BOYFRIEND: (getting up) I'll be right back. (He leaves with the bottle.)

MOM: (to MEGAN) Honey, let's escape right now, while we can.

DAD: Yes, I agree.

MEGAN: I think Hiram is special. I'm not going anywhere.

MOM: He's crazy!

MEGAN: He's different. He makes me tingle.

DAD: Megan, we've let you make most of your decisions according to your own desires, but –

MEGAN: Oh, poo! Poo, poo, poo on that. You don't seem to realize how happy Hiram makes me.

MOM: You don't need that kind of excitement. You need somebody like your father.

MEGAN: You mean boring?

MOM: Yes, boring.

DAD: Hey!

MOM: Somebody who will make you feel safe and protected.

MEGAN: I've had that all my life. Now I want somebody exciting, unpredictable.

BOYFRIEND: (entering) Somebody like me?

MEGAN: (rushing into his arms) Oh, Hiram! Hiram!

BOYFRIEND: Oh, Megan! Megan! Is that your name, Megan?

MEGAN: See, he doesn't even know my name for sure! He's my kind of man!

BOYFRIEND: Let's all sit down at our table and take stock of where we are.

(All four sit at the table.)

Okay then, I have an announcement to make.

DAD: What can you possible announce?

MOM: Indeed!

BOYFRIEND: I want to ask Megan to marry me.

DAD: No.

MOM: No!

MEGAN: Yes!

DAD: You're asking her here in front of us?

BOYFRIEND: Why not?

DAD: We don't give our blessing.

MOM: We don't even give our consent.

BOYFRIEND: I'm not asking for your blessing or your consent. I'm telling you.

MEGAN: You tell 'em, Hiram.

BOYFRIEND: She says yes. I say yes. I say it's settled.

MEGAN: Oh, I'm so happy!

BOYFRIEND: Do I know how to plan a wedding or what?

MEGAN: What do you say, Mom and Dad? Are you on board or not?

MOM: (to DAD) Maybe he'll settle down after they're married?

DAD: (to MOM) Maybe she'll get a divorce after a week?

BOYFRIEND: I have it all planned out. First we go to Vegas and have one of them ceremonies at the Little Chapel of Commitment, or whatever it's called. Then we drive to this tiny cabin I own, in Idaho.

MEGAN: Oh, Mom, he owns a cabin! How romantic! (to BOYFRIEND) You never told me you have a cabin.

BOYFRIEND: Then we stay in the cabin for the rest of our lives. I have it stocked with canned goods and a ten-inch TV.

MEGAN: How quaint!

BOYFRIEND: There won't be any need to go out for dinner for years.

MEGAN: We'll make love day and night!

BOYFRIEND: That's right, little darlin'. No telephone, no Internet, just peace and quiet. And fucking.

MEGAN: A few friends in now and again.

BOYFRIEND: No neighbors, no friends.

MEGAN: No friends, no neighbors. Just us. It'll be Heaven.

BOYFRIEND: No need to be polite and all fancy-like.

MEGAN: Just love and more love!

BOYFRIEND: I'll teach you the real meaning of love.

DAD: All this is not going to happen.

MOM: Over our dead bodies.

BOYFRIEND: …That can be arranged.

MEGAN: Wait a minute now. These are my parents. I don't like them,
but I don't want them killed.

BOYFRIEND: They're holding you back.

MEGAN: I know that. Oh, I'm so torn I don't know what to do.

DAD: You're torn about whether to kill your parents or not?

MEGAN: You always told me to be my real self. My real self is torn.

DAD: What if I kill your boyfriend instead?

MOM: I'll help.

BOYFRIEND: I don't think that's a good idea.

MEGAN: Why is everything in life so hard?! All I want is to live with
Hiram in a tiny cabin in Idaho forever and ever.

BOYFRIEND: I've changed my mind. I'm not marrying anybody!
Goodbye and good riddance! (He hurries out.)

MEGAN: That's it? It all ends like this?!

MOM: It's called a happy ending, sweetheart.

DAD: It's all for the best. Nobody's hurt.

MEGAN: But what about my happy ending?!

MOM: You'll find somebody else.

DAD: We don't always get what we want in this world.

MEGAN: Oh, now you tell me!

(The lights begin to fade.)

MEGAN: No! It's not going to end like this!

(The lights fade out.)

MEGAN: (in the dark) No! No! I want a happy ending!

(Lights Up.)

(The BOYFRIEND re-enters.)

BOYFRIEND: What about this? I still want to get married.

MEGAN: Thank God!

BOYFRIEND: But not to you, Megan. How about you, Mom?

MOM: Okay. I mean, no way.

BOYFRIEND: How about you, Dad? Want to marry me?

DAD: Not really.

BOYFRIEND: So I guess I have to marry Megan after all.

MEGAN: I am pregnant.

BOYFRIEND: Is the baby mine?

MEGAN: Of course it's yours, jerk!

BOYFRIEND: Unfortunately, I won't be around to see my baby.

MEGAN: Why not?

BOYFRIEND: Because I have developed a serious case of Monkeypox and I haven't much time left.

MEGAN: You mean M-pox?

BOYFRIEND: Yes, the rarest form. Terminal M-pox.

MEGAN: Is this my happy ending?

BOYFRIEND: It'll have to do. You'll be married. You'll have a baby.

MEGAN: A healthy baby!

BOYFRIEND: A healthy baby. And the horrible father will be dead.in
    no time.

DAD/MOM/MEGAN: Amen!

BOYFRIEND: You'll have your romantic comedy, God bless you. And
    my genes will live on!

    (Laughs maniacally.)

BLACKOUT

DON'T GET OLD

–a one-act

CHARACTERS: (4)

OLD MAN, over sixty

YOUNG MAN, a younger version of the OLD MAN

OLD WOMAN, on her own phone

ANOTHER MAN, any age, with his own phone

SETTING: A table, two chairs

PRESENT TIME

LIGHTS UP on OLD MAN sitting at the table

OLD MAN: I'm not here to complain. I hate when old people complain. I'm here to explain. I'm waiting for a return call from my favorite spa. I have left messages six times, but nobody has called me back. I need to go to the spa to get the so-called Earth Treatment. I've never had that one before. They say it's good for arthritis. The brochure says that they'll wrap me completely in strips of Mother Nature's healing earth. I can't wait! I think it's different from being buried alive in a casket. I sure hope so. If they put me in a grave, I swear I'm not going to tip! Certainly not twenty percent. That's how much the spa adds to the bill, whether you like the treatment you get or not. I think I need a visual aid to help clarify what I'm worried about. (to offstage YOUNG MAN) How about you?

(The YOUNG MAN enters dressed in just a spa robe.)

That's me, a few years ago. I think since this involves a spa robe, you'd rather see him in it than me. What happened to me?! I was twenty-two about twenty minutes ago. Now I'm twenty-four. Don't laugh. Indulge me. I don't feel a day over ____ (Fills in the actor's age)

I am fearful that I have been banned from the spa. The last time I was there, two months ago, there was a little incident with my robe. I asked for an extra large, but the one in my locker was a small. I was a small when I was ten, but not anymore. So I put on the robe I was assigned and it didn't fit well. (Points to the YOUNG MAN, having trouble closing his robe, etc) I still had my underwear on, thank god, but I saw this woman glance at me as I stepped out of the men's locker room. There was a two-inch gap. Nothing was really showing, but I think she reported me. One of the staff even came to the waiting room, where I was – guess what – waiting for my Earth Treatment. The staff member asked me to change my robe. So there I sat struggling to get out of the small robe into the larger one. People looked at me like I was some kind of pervert. And now they won't accept my credit card or return my calls.

(The phone rings.)

Oh, maybe this is them. (Answers his phone.) Hello.

OLD WOMAN: (on the other side of the stage, with a loud, screechy voice) Robby? Is that you? It's Irene O'Roarke, from Detroit!

OLD MAN: Who?

OLD WOMAN: Is that you, Robby? It's Irene! I am the sister of Pat, your best friend through high school. We were never friends, but I've been thinking about you. How the hell are you?

OLD MAN: I remember you. You played the Proud Princess in one of the shows I put on in my backyard. (cupping his hand over the mouthpiece or holding the phone away from his mouth) She wasn't very good.

OLD WOMAN: I was pretty good, wasn't I? That was the last show I ever did. How old were we then, about twelve, wasn't it?

OLD MAN: You were great, Irene!

OLD WOMAN: I was, wasn't I? I was pretty back then.

OLD MAN: I left Detroit years and years ago.

OLD WOMAN: Why don't you come for a visit?

OLD MAN: All my relatives are dead.

OLD WOMAN: Yeah, I lost my husband a year ago. You remember Boris.

OLD MAN: (not honest) Oh, yes. Boris

OLD WOMAN: He read one of your stories.

OLD MAN: Oh, did he?

OLD WOMAN: He said he didn't understand it.

OLD MAN: Well, that's a shame.

OLD WOMAN: I'm a writer now myself. Self-published. Don't tell anybody.

OLD MAN: I promise.

OLD WOMAN: I'll send you a copy. What's your address?

OLD MAN: Maybe I can get it on Amazon.

OLD WOMAN: Naw, give me your address. What is it?

OLD MAN: 623 …

OLD WOMAN: Let me get a pen. (Looks around, finds a pen.) I got it! 632 …

OLD MAN: 623

OLD WOMAN: 623.

OLD MAN: Parkway.

OLD WOMAN: How do you spell that?

OLD MAN: Parkway. P—

OLD WOMAN: T –

OLD MAN: No, P, as in Parkway.

OLD WOMAN: P.

OLD MAN: Then A, as in –

OLD WOMAN: Ass?

OLD MAN: Yes, A, as in ass.

OLD WOMAN: I've got to get this right ear fixed. I can't hear nothin'.

OLD MAN: We're getting there.

OLD WOMAN: I want you to read my book.

OLD MAN: I can't wait.

OLD WOMAN: It's all about this restaurant owner who says he loves me. He's Albanian. Do you know what that means?

OLD MAN: He's from Albania?

OLD WOMAN: He's a whole lot younger than me. His wife died when she slipped on some eggplant he spilled on the floor. He still feels very guilty about it. She was Albanian too.

OLD MAN: It sounds like it must have been very sad.

OLD WOMAN: It was very sad. She was a nice lady. But now he says he loves me. We haven't been intimate yet?

OLD MAN: Why not?

OLD WOMAN: I'm still Irish Catholic. He's of another faith.

OLD MAN: Don't wait too long.

OLD WOMAN: That's what I tell him! When I dine there with my friend Marlene, the Albanian always steps out of the kitchen and mouths the words "I love you" towards me. It's very romantic. I put it in my book.

OLD MAN: Well, it was wonderful to hear from you, Irene.

OLD WOMAN: Wait! Don't hang up yet. I don't have all your address.

OLD MAN: Why don't I call you back after I finish with this call I'm waiting on?

OLD WOMAN: I'll get your address right. We've got to keep in touch.

OLD MAN: Sure thing, Irene. I'll call you back.

OLD WOMAN: You don't have to if you don't want to.

OLD MAN: Goodbye for now.

OLD WOMAN: Okay, Robby. Great talking to you. Lots of hugs!

(They both hang up. The YOUNG MAN sits down.)

OLD MAN: (to audience) I need that spa treatment! (Uses his phone to call.) (after a bit) Hello! Yes, is this Spa Elite? (…) Yes, good to get somebody live on the line. You are live, right? That's a joke!

This is Robby – I mean Robert Winslow. I'm trying to make a reservation for an Earth Treatment. (…) Yes, I tried booking online, but my credit card was rejected. There isn't anything wrong, is there? There's plenty of credit on my card. I can use a different card. I really love your spa. It's the best spa I've ever been to. (…) You're welcome. I've left several messages. (…) Oh, no, no, I'm not complaining! I'm just trying to clarify and finalize my appointment. I'm not banished or anything like that, am I? (…) What would I be banished for? Oh, nothing. I misspoke. (Laughs too hard.) I'm just a senior who wants a spa treatment!

(The caller hangs up.)

Hello? Are you still there? Hello? (He hangs up.)

(The phone rings.)

Yes?

(Across the stage we see ANOTHER MAN with his own phone.)

ANOTHER MAN: Is this Mr. Winslow?

OLD MAN: Yes! Is this the spa?

ANOTHER MAN: This is Mr. Smith of the Internal Revenue Service.

OLD MAN: Who?

ANOTHER MAN: My badge number is 2277. I'm calling you about the money you owe the IRS.

OLD MAN: I don't owe the IRS anything.

ANOTHER MAN: According to our records, you failed to pay your entire tax bill.

OLD MAN: I am very careful with all my payments.

ANOTHER MAN: You owe seven thousand two hundred and two cents. If you do not pay us today, we will be sending a police office to your house.

OLD MAN: What?!

ANOTHER MAN: How do you want to pay? We accept credit cards.

OLD MAN: How about pelts? Do you accept pelts?

ANOTHER MAN: We do not accept pelts. Mr. Winslow you do not appear to be taking this seriously. The policeman is on his way right now to your house. But I can stop him if you pay seven thousand two hundred and two cents.

OLD MAN: I only have seven thousand two hundred and one cent. Can you still stop the policeman?

ANOTHER MAN: He is coming. He is coming. You'd better pay up!

OLD MAN: I'm a penny short!

ANOTHER MAN: In this case, I can make an exception. We will give you a discount of one cent, if you pay today.

OLD MAN: Oh, thank you, thank you. Who are you again?

ANOTHER MAN: I am Mr. Smith of the IRS. Badge 2277.

OLD MAN: How do I know you're who you say you are?

ANOTHER MAN: Don't fool with me, Mr. Winslow. The policeman is almost there!

OLD MAN: Let him come. My bodyguard will kick his butt.(Gestures at the YOUNG MAN to get up and make fists.)

YOUNG MAN: (gestures at his own chest as if to say Who me?)

ANOTHER MAN: Are you still there, Mr. Winslow?

OLD MAN: You bet your ass I am! Oh, there's the policeman at my
    door. (He is pretending.) My bodyguard has him by the throat.
    (Gestures to YOUNG MAN to grab the invisible policeman.)
    He's strangling the policeman!

    (Gestures to YOUNG MAN to strangle.)

YOUNG MAN: (as the strangled policeman) Help! Help! My throat! My
    throat!

ANOTHER MAN: If your bodyguard strangles our policeman, we won't
    be able to give you the discount!

OLD MAN: (to YOUNG MAN) Kill the policeman! Kill him! (Gestures
    at YOUNG MAN.)

YOUNG MAN: (as the strangled policeman) You're killing me! You're
    killing me! (Makes strangling noises.) Klunk! … I'm dead.

OLD MAN: (to phone) Your fucking policeman is dead, Mr. Smith.

ANOTHER MAN: You can't fool me, Mr. Winslow.

OLD MAN: And we're coming after you next!

ANOTHER MAN: No, you're not! You don't know where I am! Ha ha!
    Fuck you!

OLD MAN: We're tracing your phone call as we speak!

    (ANOTHER MAN hangs up his phone and runs off.)

OLD MAN: Try to scam me, will ya?! (Hangs up his phone.) (to
    YOUNG MAN) Take a rest, my friend.

    (Panting, the YOUNG MAN sits down to rest.)

    (The lights go down and then come up again.)

OLD MAN: (to audience) Should I phone the spa again? Or is that just
    making things worse?

(The phone rings.)

(answering) Hello?

(Appearing on the other side of the stage is OLD WOMAN on her phone.)

OLD WOMAN: Robby? Are you there? It's me, Irene O'Roarke.

OLD MAN: Irene?

OLD WOMAN: I didn't get your full address, Robby. So I can't send you my book. What is it again?

OLD MAN: I forget.

OLD WOMAN: You forget your own address?

OLD MAN: I'm getting up there in age, Irene.

OLD WOMAN: That's okay, Robby. I understand. Some days I can't remember my own name. Did I tell you about my Albanian?

OLD MAN: You did, Irene. You did.

OLD WOMAN: Did I tell you he ran off with my friend Marlene?

OLD MAN: He did?

OLD WOMAN: He was a womanizer! The bastard! And we weren't even intimate yet.

OLD MAN: I'm sorry to hear it.

OLD WOMAN: That he ran off or that we weren't intimate?

OLD MAN: I'm sorry about everything.

OLD WOMAN: When are you coming out to visit me?

OLD MAN: I don't think I can make it out there, Irene.

OLD WOMAN: We don't have to be intimate.

OLD MAN: That's good to know.

OLD WOMAN: We can just talk.

OLD MAN: We're talking now. Does that help?

OLD WOMAN: My cat died. She was nineteen. And blind.

OLD MAN: Can you get a new cat?

OLD WOMAN: They just die on you.

OLD MAN: Well, it's been great chatting with you, Irene.

OLD WOMAN: It has? That's nice to know. I don't want you to be
lonely out there.

OLD MAN: We'll talk soon.

OLD WOMAN: You promise?

OLD MAN: … I promise.

OLD WOMAN: I don't want you to be lonely.

(She hangs up.)

OLD MAN: (looking at his phone) Goodbye. (to audience) Where's that
damn spa?

(The phone rings.)

OLD MAN: (answering) Yes? (…) Yes, this is Robert Winslow. (…)
You what?! (…) You got my email? (…) When would I like to
come in for my Earth Treatment? (…) Yes, yes, the 27th at noon!
(…) Oh, thank you, thank you, thank you. I was worried when
you didn't get back to me. Not that I'm complaining! (…) You
were having trouble with your phones? No calls were getting
through? So I'm not banned from the spa? (…) You're glad I'm
coming back? Oh, thank you, thank you, thank you! I love your
spa!

(to the audience) Don't get old. Don't get old!

BLACKOUT

www.ingramcontent.com/pod-product-compliance
Lightning Source LLC
Chambersburg PA
CBHW061136120626
46546CB00005B/1814

* 9 7 8 1 9 5 9 2 5 7 0 0 4 *